D1045549

Tokyo

selection of restaurants and hotels 2008

A letter *from our Chairman*

I am thrilled to launch our first Michelin Guide for Asia, the Michelin Guide Tokyo 2008.

Our company's two founders, Édouard and André Michelin, published, in France, the first Michelin Guide in 1900 to provide motorists with practical information about where they could service and repair their cars and find quality accommodation or a good meal.

The star rating system for outstanding restaurants was introduced in 1926. These awards have become over the years, the benchmark of reliability and excellence in over twenty European countries and since 2005 in the United States.

For our first step in Japan, our teams have made every effort to understand the culinary tradition of Japan and to produce a selection that does full justice to the richness and diversity of the Tokyo restaurant and hotel scene.

As part of our meticulous and highly confidential evaluation process, Michelin inspectors – Japanese and European- conducted anonymous visits to Tokyo restaurants and hotels. The Michelin inspectors are the eyes and the ears of the customers, and thus their anonymity is key to ensure that they receive the same treatment as any other guest.

to our readers

The decision to award a Michelin star is a collective one, based on the consensus of all the inspectors who have visited a particular establishment. When giving one, two or three Michelin stars, there are a number of facts that we consider, including the quality of the ingredients, the technical skills and flair that goes into their preparation, the blend and clarity of flavours and the balance of the menu. Just as important is the ability to produce excellent cooking time and again. We make as many visits as we need to be sure of quality and consistency.

Édouard Michelin and François Busson, CEO Nihon Michelin had a dream; to see the launch of this first edition of the Michelin Guide Tokyo. Today, their dream has come true.

I sincerely hope that the Michelin Guide Tokyo 2008 will become your favourite guide to the restaurants and hotels in Tokyo. On behalf of all our Michelin employees, let me wish you the very best enjoyment in your Tokyo hotel and dining experience.

Bon appétit.

Michel Rollier
Chief Executive Officer
Michelin

"This volume was created at the turn of the century and will last at least as long".

The Michelin Guide's *Commitments*

This foreword to the very first edition of the MICHELIN Guide, written in 1900, has become famous over the years and the Guide has lived up to the prediction. It is read across the world and the key to its popularity is the consistency of its commitment to its readers, which is based on the following promises.

Anonymous inspections :

our inspectors make regular and anonymous visits to restaurants and hotels to gauge the quality of products and services offered to an ordinary customer. They settle their own bill and may then introduce themselves and ask for more information about the establishment. Our readers' comments are also a valuable source of information, which we can then follow up with another visit of our own.

Independence:

Our choice of establishments is a completely independent one, made for the benefit of our readers alone. The decisions to be taken are discussed around the table by the inspectors and the editor. Inclusion in the Guide is completely free of charge.

Selection and choice:

The Guide offers a selection of the best restaurants and hotels. This is only possible because all the inspectors rigorously apply the same methods.

Annual updates:

All the practical information, the classifications and awards are revised and updated every single year to give the most reliable information possible. Consistency: The criteria for the classifications are the same in every country covered by the Michelin Guide.

...And our aim :

to do everything possible to make travel, holidays and eating out a pleasure, as part of Michelin's ongoing commitment to improving travel and mobility.

Contents

The Michelin Guide over *The Years*

Today the Michelin Guide with its famous red cover is known around the world. But who really knows the story behind this "travellers' bible" that has served people in so many countries for such a long time?
After winning over Europe and the United States, Bibendum – "The Michelin Man" – is now in Japan, and will continue the fantastic adventure that started in France, a long time ago…

The first steps

Everything began one fine day in 1900, when André and Édouard Michelin published a guide to be offered free of charge to motorists. It included information to help these pioneers (barely 3,500 automobiles were on the road) to travel around France: location of garages, town plans, sights to see, lodgings and restaurants, and so forth. The guide was an instant success and became the indispensable companion to all drivers and travellers.
On the strength of this success and driven on by the development of the motor car, the *Manufacture française* extended the scope of "the little book with the red cover" to other European countries, beginning in 1904. A few years later (1908) the Guide France was published in English.

A star is born

As of 1920, the guide was no longer free, but marketed for sale. Little by little, the practical information gave way to a wider selection of hotels and restaurants. The mysterious, daunting "Michelin inspector" was, however, not in the picture at first. It was touring clubs and readers who contributed to the selection of establishments.

In 1926 the *Étoile de Bonne Table* – the first Michelin star – was awarded to places where "one dines well" and was later followed by two and three-star establishments (1931 for the provinces and 1933 for Paris). The focus was now on gastronomy and the quest for good restaurants became its real driving force.

A European journey

The guide flourished until the outbreak of war in 1939, when all guide activity was suspended. But it was revived in 1945 and, from 1950, a new generation of guides appeared – from Spain in 1952 to Switzerland in 1994. In 1982 Michelin's European credentials were confirmed with the publication of the Main Cities of Europe guide.

100 years young...

2000 was a winning year for Michelin: the Guide celebrated its 100th anniversary and Bibendum was voted best corporate logo of the century!

More dynamic than ever, the "little red guide" took on new challenges and set off for the United States. The guide *New York* not only lived up to expectations, but also the first edition was crowned "Best Restaurant Guide in the World". Next off the presses: San Francisco in 2007, Los Angeles and Las Vegas in 2008.

The newest challenge? Discovering the best restaurants in Asia. We begin with Tokyo, Japan, which was an obvious choice as one of the world's great capitals of fine cuisine. With this first edition, Asia joins the collection with a dazzling start: the restaurants in the 2008 edition are all starred!

Twenty countries covered in Europe, four guides to US cities and one guide to Japan: as the third millennium begins, the Michelin Guide confirms its truly international standing. Just a gleam in the eyes of the founders more than a century ago, Bibendum is now an international star to be proud of, carrying the Michelin tradition into the 21st century.

How to use this guide

1 ***Restaurants classification according to comfort***
(more pleasant if in red)

- X Quite comfortable
- XX Comfortable
- XXX Very comfortable
- XXXX Top class comfort
- XXXXX Luxury

2 ***Address and information about the restaurant***

3 ***Star for good food***
✿ to ✿✿✿

4 ***Type of cuisine***

5 ***Map references***

6 ***Prices***

7 ***Restaurant symbols***

- Cash only
- Wheelchair access
- Terrace dinning
- No smoking area
- Completely no smoking restaurant
- Interesting view
- Valet parking
- Car park
- 25 private room with maximum capacity
- Counter restaurant
- Reservation required
- Interesting wine list

8 ***Annual and weekly closing***

9 ***Opening hours, last order***

Locating the establishment: location on the town plan, with principal sights (p390.)

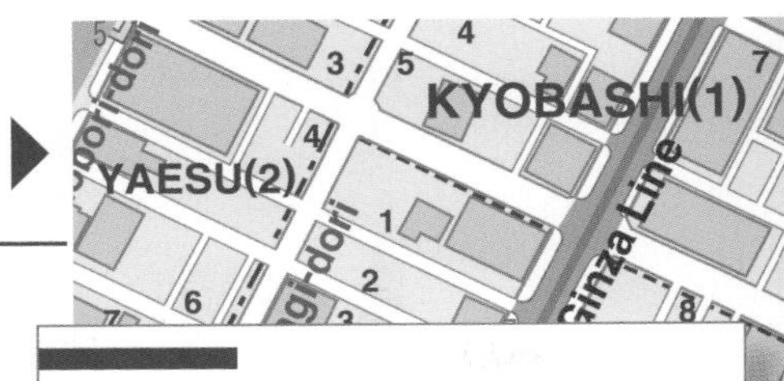

1 Hotel classification according to comfort
(more pleasant if in red)

- Very comfortable
- Top class comfort
- Luxury

2 Address and information about the hotel

3 Map references

4 Prices

- Lowest-highest price for a single room
- Lowest-highest price for a double or twin room
- suite Lowest-highest price for a suite
- Price for breakfast if not included

5 Hotel symbols

- Wheelchair access
- Interesting view from bedrooms
- Valet parking
- Car park
- No smoking bedrooms
- Conference rooms
- Swimming pool
- Spa
- Fitness

Cerulean Tower

Cerulean Tower

4
¥31 500-78 000
¥42 500-80 500
Suite ¥93 500-464 000
¥2 800

2 **TEL 03-3476-3000** / FAX 03-3476-3001
26-1 Sakuragaokacho, Shibuya-ku
www.ceruleantower-hotel.com

5

3 DOGENZAKA(1) SAKURAGAOKA See map p 12, C3

1 Rooms: 405
Suites: 9
Restaurants: 5

The hotel occupies a 40-story building near Shibuya Station. A high-rise hotel with convenient access to transportation, it opened in 2001. The guest rooms are on the 19th to 37th floors and all of them have views looking out over metropolitan Tokyo. Although the hotel is located next to Route 246, the rooms are quiet, and the modern interior design exudes serenity. On the top floor guests can enjoy Provençal cuisine in the tower restaurant Coucagno or relax at the Bello Visto bar with its view of the night lights of northern Tokyo. There are also a number of restaurants and bars off the lobby on the first floor. To relieve stress and enhance one's health and appearance there is also an indoor pool, a fitness center, and a beauty salon. A beacon of traditional culture both domestically and internationally, the Cerulean Tower Noh Theater is used for public performances of Noh, Kyogen, and other traditional performing arts. This is a hotel that takes its guests' comfort fully into account, placing greater emphasis on functionality and style than on showy accoutrements.

337

Where to eat

Michelin

Starred Restaurants

All the restaurants within the Tokyo Guide have one, two or three Michelin Stars and are our way of highlighting restaurants that offer particularly good food.
When awarding stars there are a number of factors we consider: the quality and freshness of the ingredients, the technical skill and flair that goes into their preparation, the clarity of the flavours, the value for money and, ultimately, the taste. Of equal importance is the ability to produce excellent food not once but time and time again. Our inspectors make as many visits as necessary so that you can be sure of this quality and consistency.
A two or three star restaurant has to offer something very special in its cooking that separates it from the rest. Three stars – our highest award – are given to the very best.
Cuisines in any style of restaurant and of any nationality are eligible for a star. The decoration, service and comfort levels have no bearing on the award.

✿✿✿

Exceptional cuisine, worth a special journey.

One always eats here extremely well, sometimes superbly. Distinctive dishes are precisely executed, using superlative ingredients.

✿✿

Excellent cuisine, worth a detour.

Skillfully and carefully crafted dishes of outsanding quality.

Starred Restaurants

A very good restaurant in its category.
A place offering cuisine prepared to a consistently high standard.

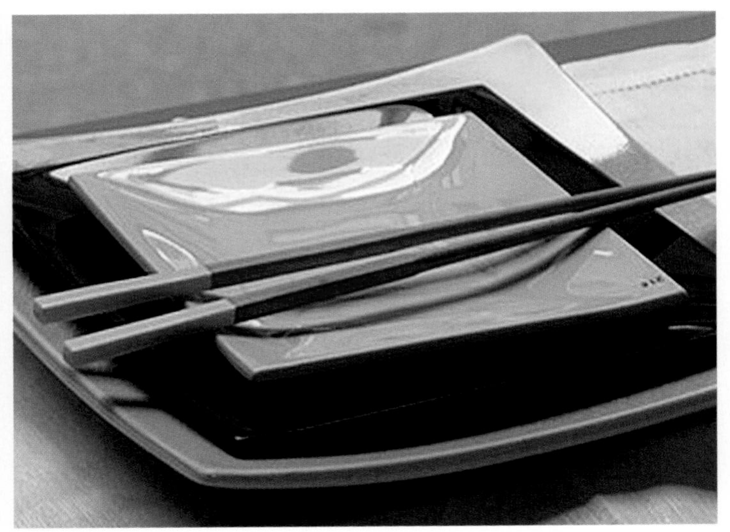

Restaurants by *ku*

Chiyoda-ku

Kioicho

Marunouchi

Nibancho

Uchisaiwaicho

Chuo-ku

Ginza

Kyobashi, Nihonbashi, Nihonbashi-Muromachi

Nihonbashi-Ningyocho

Tsukiji

Meguro-ku

Komaba

Minato-ku

Restaurants by *cuisine type*

Japanese

Contemporary

Fugu

Soba kaiseki

Sushi

Tempura

Teppan yaki

Unagi

Chinese

French

Contemporary

Italian

Contemporary

Spanish

Contemporary

Steakhouse

Restaurants particularly *pleasant*

Restaurants open
on Sunday

Restaurants to have *a late dinner*

Restaurants with *private rooms*

Abe 阿部

Abe

Lunch: menu ¥ 1,365
Dinner: menu ¥ 5,775-8,925
carte ¥ 3,000-8,600

TEL 03–3568–2350 / FAX 03–3568–2355
2-22-11 Akasaka, Minato-ku
www.kameya-net.com/akasaka-abe
6

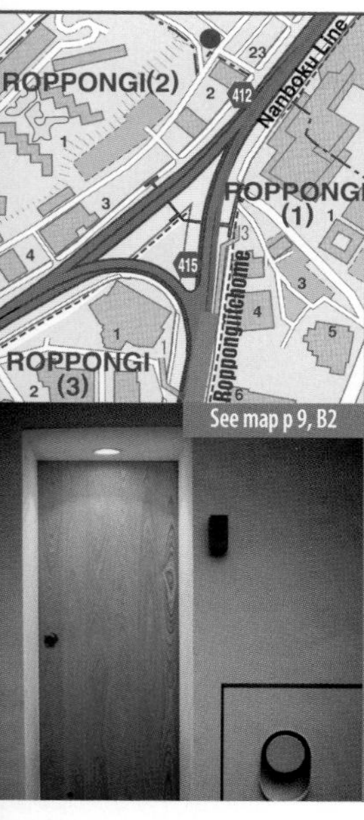

See map p 9, B2

Nestled in a back alleyway near Akasaka ARK Hills is a Japanese restaurant with a modest sign and an even more modest appearance. The owner, who runs two hot-spring inns in Yamagata Prefecture, opened Abe in Tokyo in July, 2006. Diners can savor the fresh vegetables, fish and Shonai beef brought in directly from Yamagata. With "authentic Japanese meals" as his concept, the owner puts a lot of care into creating seasonal dishes that showcase his fresh ingredients. The cozy interior features plain white walls and a floor laid with tiles in a subdued hue. There is a long table in the middle which seats ten to twelve people, as well as four private rooms of different sizes partitioned off by sliding doors. The cuisine is mainly traditional Japanese food, but several innovative ideas such as a meat dish with a curry sauce have been incorporated into the menu. Only one set-menu, with a choice of meat or fish, is offered for lunchtime. The dinner course is an *omakase* (chef's choice) course only. There is also a small but interesting selection of *sake* and wine.

Closed mid-August, late December-early January, Saturday, Sunday and Bank Holidays

Open:
lunch 11:30-14:30 L.O.14:00
dinner 18:00-23:00 L.O.22:00

Aimée Vibert

Aimée Vibert

Lunch: menu ¥5,800
Dinner: menu ¥11,600-22,000

TEL 03–5216–8585 / FAX 03–5216–7588
14-1 Nibancho, Chiyoda-ku
www.aimeevibert.com
10

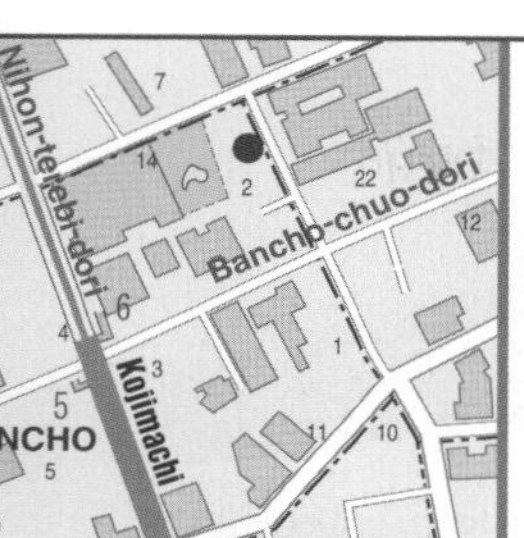

See map p 3, A2

Closed mid-August, late December-early January and Tuesday

Open:
lunch 11:30-14:00 (L.O.)
dinner 18:00-21:00 (L.O.)

Clusters of Aimée Vibert, also known as "Bouquet de la Mariée" in French, look like a wedding bouquet. This French restaurant that was named after this rose is located near Nihon Terebi Dori in Kojimachi, and consists of an elegant mansion and garden in the Île-de-France style. At night, the stone walls are lit up. When you pass through the lobby where you are greeted by a large number of staff and ascend to the second floor, you will find several salons furnished with Louis the 15th and 16th pieces, as well as with pieces from the Imperial Period. Wall frescoes and folding screens are used to set off the elegance of the dining area. The open veranda looks out on the lawn and gardens planted with trees. The extensive wine list features around 250 labels, mostly French wines, and the sommelier recommends various bottles. Clad in dark uniforms, the waiters provide impeccable service with customer satisfaction as their foremost concern. The facilities are often used for weddings, and the impression is of a well-organized team.

Ajiman 味満ん

Michelin

Dinner: menu ¥ 35,000-45,000
carte ¥ 30,000-40,000

TEL 03–3408–2910
3-8-8 Roppongi, Minato-ku
12

See map p 10, A4

In the simple, cozy interior of this Roppongi fugu restaurant are an L-shaped counter and three Japanese-style rooms. The restaurant, run by a family of five, has a homely atmosphere that attracts many regular customers. *Torafugu* is a high-grade fish, and the one with the white fin attached is particularly expensive. Ajiman uses wild *torafugu* caught at Shimonoseki. Its determination to satisfy its customers' demands for taste by providing only the most rigorously selected *fugu* is reflected in the restaurant's name: aji means taste and man means satisfy. Although the food served is primarily left up to the chef, efforts are made to accommodate customer preferences as to quantity and cooking methods. A typical dinner course consists of *kogori* (jellied fish broth), *sashimi, shirako* (fish milt), *fugu, age* (fried dish), *nabe* (hot pot), *zosui* (rice porridge) and fruit. During the *fugu* high season the restaurant never closes; in the off season one can eat other kinds of high-quality seafood.

Closed July, August, 31 December-4 January and Sunday from April-June

Open:
dinner 18:00-24:00 L.O.22:00

Aragawa 麤皮

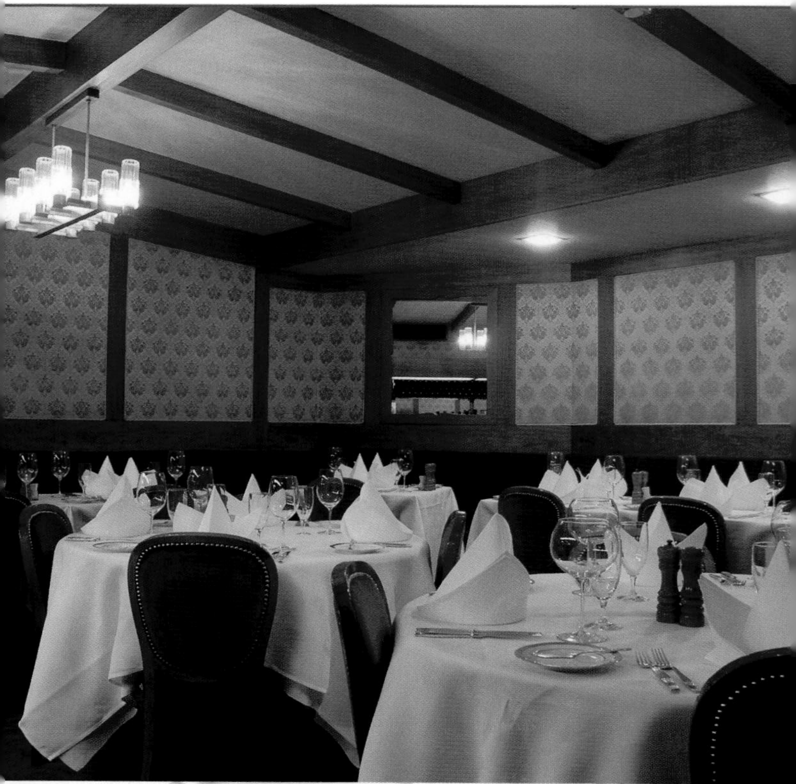

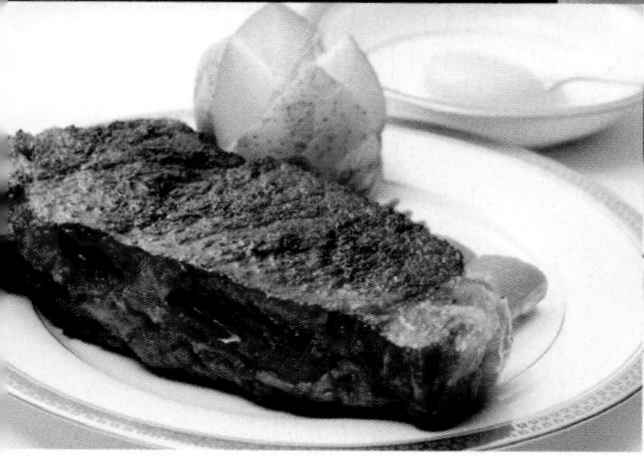

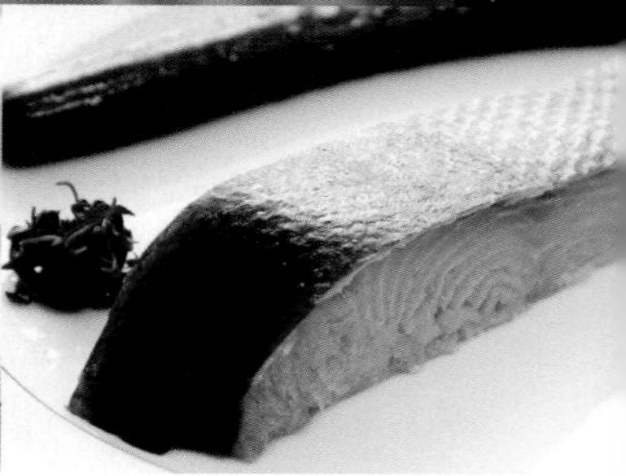

Aragawa, Michelin

Lunch: menu ¥ 56,000-78,400
carte ¥ 40,000-80,000

Dinner: menu ¥ 56,000-78,400
carte ¥ 40,000-80,000

TEL 03–3591–8765 / FAX 03–3591–8768
Hankyukotsusha Building B1F,
3-3-9 Shinbashi, Minato-ku

See map p 9, C1

Located in the first basement floor of the Hankyu Express Building, this steak kaiseki restaurant opened in 1967. Unchanging quality has been its watchword, and some of its regular patrons are now of the second or third generation. The difficult-to-find sign, the interior décor, the quality of the ingredients, and the special skills used to bring forth their flavor have all been maintained over the years. Inside, the entire place has the air of a pleasant old inn, thick red carpet, cherry wood chairs, and Swedish chandelier. The meat is lean, and only Sanada beef, a thoroughbred strain from Hyogo Prefecture, is used: of which only 1,000 head of cattle are produced annually. This impeccably selected basic ingredient is enhanced to perfection by careful use of salt and broiling in a brick oven fired with Bincho charcoal from Wakayama. Sink your teeth into it, and the flavor and texture of the meat and the subtle aroma of the charcoal will have you offering thanks for the bounties of nature.

Closed 30 December-3 January, Sunday and Bank Holidays

Open: 12:00-22:00 (L.O.)

Arai あら井

Michelin

Lunch: menu ¥ 5,775-32,340
Dinner: menu ¥ 20,790-32,340

TEL 03–3408–5588 / FAX 03–3408–5444
7-20-7 Roppongi, Minato-ku
26

See map p 10, A4

Closed mid-August, late December-early January, Sunday and Bank Holidays

Open:
lunch 11:30-15:30 L.O.13:00
dinner 17:30-22:30 L.O.20:00

In spring, a weeping cherry tree blooms near the entrance to this solitary, *sukiya*-style teahouse. Indirect lighting made from bamboo and Japanese paper bathes the rooms. Saryo Arai, whose mistress is proficient in flower arranging and the tea ceremony, moved to its present location in Roppongi in 1990 after four years as a tea house and *kaiseki* restaurant at Oiso in Kanagawa Prefecture. It has seven rooms, all of them private; the largest can accommodate a party of 50. The teahouse can be used for the tea ceremony and has a garden in which lovely tea flowers bloom. In addition to *kaiseki*, whose ingredients abound with seasonal appeal, the menu includes *shabu shabu* and *sukiyaki*. For the *ozashiki tempura* course, also popular with foreigners, the chef sets up a place to fry tempura in a Japanese-style room and makes it right before your eyes. The refined mistress's gracious and attentive touch can be sensed in every detail, making this a Japanese restaurant which is comfortable and which can also be used for business entertainment.

Arbace

Michelin

Dinner: menu ¥ 13,200
carte ¥ 10,000-16,500

TEL 03–3569–3386 / FAX 03–3569–3266
Ginza Hosono Building 3F,
6-7-6 Ginza, Chuo-ku

See map p 6, C3

Closed Golden week, mid-August, late December-early January, Sunday and Bank Holiday Mondays

Open:
dinner 17:30-1:00 (L.O.)

The owner of this restaurant is one of Japan's leading sommeliers. After working for twenty years in a French restaurant in Yurakucho he went independent and opened Arbace in Ginza. With a wine list with more than 500 labels, this is a restaurant where you can enjoy the combination of scrupulously selected wine and captivating French cuisine. The chef is young but puts his experience in famous restaurants in France, Australia, and Japan to work providing traditional French cooking with a reasonably light, refined touch. Japanese black cattle beef and veal are slowly pan-cooked. The aroma of the food is given serious attention, and a variety of oriental spices—cumin, coriander, and fennel—are used along with traditional French herbs. The décor has a natural feel, the main accents being wood and stone. Along with the contemporary art on the walls, it creates an adult, salon-like atmosphere. The service is at once communicative and thoroughly professional.

Argento Aso

Argento Aso, Michelin

Lunch: menu ¥ 5,650-9,605
carte ¥ 12,000-27,000

Dinner: menu ¥ 11,300-22,600
carte ¥ 12,000-27,000

TEL 03–5524–1270 / FAX 03–5524–1273
ZOE Ginza 8F,
3-3-1 Ginza, Chuo-ku
www.hiramatsu.co.jp

10

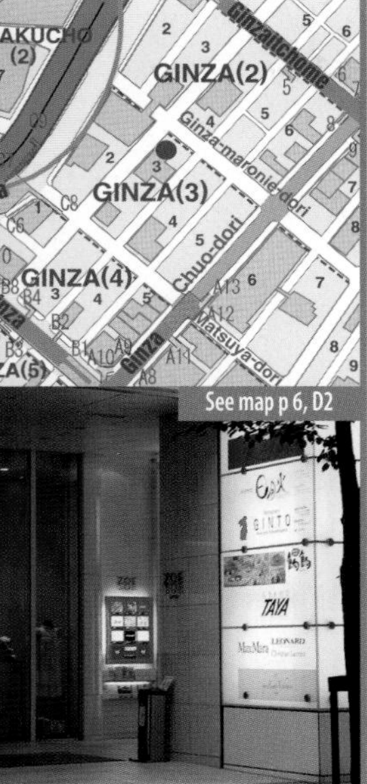

See map p 6, D2

Closed mid-August, late December-early January, Monday except Bank Holidays and Tuesday lunch

Open:
lunch 11:30-15:30 L.O.13:30
dinner 18:00-23:30 L.O.21:00

An Italian restaurant located behind Printemps Ginza. The 8th floor has a bar lounge, furnished with black sofas, as well as three private dining rooms, whose décor is accented by mirrors that reflect the chandeliers and tableware. On the 9th floor, the elegant main dining room's ambience is enhanced by an array of glassware from Austrian Lobmeyr, a collection of grappa decanters and Venetian chandeliers. The menu matches that of its sibling restaurant in Daikanyama. His French-accented techniques give a distinctive touch to specialties like seafood risottos and Iberian pork or beef casseroles in individual cocottes. Try his signature smoky butter blended with Tuscan olive oil, or his own tomato juice. The cellars offer 350 Italian and French wines and a superb collection of Armagnacs. With its own chapel and anterooms, the restaurant is also available for weddings.

Aroma-Frèsca

Michelin

Dinner: menu ¥ 11,550-20,350

TEL 03–5439–4010 / FAX 03–5439–4170
M Tower 2F,
1-7-31 Minami-Azabu, Minato-ku

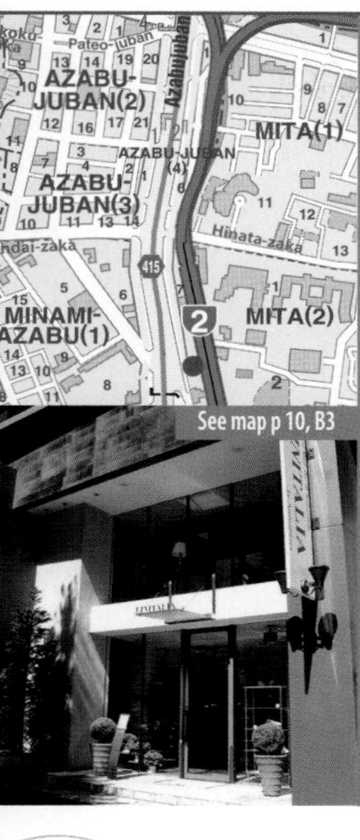

See map p 10, B3

This popular Italian restaurant opened in Minami Azabu in 2005. Wine bottles are displayed along the entire wall of the staircase leading up to the entrance on the second floor. The menu here consists of two types of dinner courses. The standard course does not change throughout the year. The seasonal course changes every three months. As the chef says, the distinctive feature here is "the straightforward approach to the ingredients;" the cuisine is lightly seasoned to bring out the natural, fresh flavor and is simply presented. He is uncompromising about selecting the best quality ingredients such as organically grown produce, seafood from Kyushu and Shikoku, and goatlings from Hokkaido. Particularly highly acclaimed are dishes that use fresh fish and large sea clams as well as the charcoal-broiled wagyu beef. The 100 percent Italian wine selection is also high quality. The wait staff provides deft and pleasant service. The restaurant is always full, and reservations are hard to come by, but if you call around 5 pm, there may be cancellations.

Closed mid-August, late December-early January, Sunday and Monday

Open:
dinner 18:00-22:30 (L.O.)

Asagi あさぎ

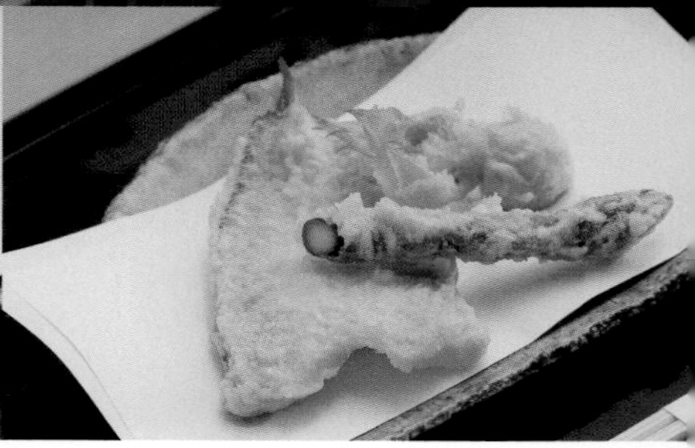

Michelin

Lunch: menu ¥ 2,100-7,350
Dinner: menu ¥ 10,500-15,750

TEL 03–3289–8188
6-4-13 Ginza, Chuo-ku

See map p 6, C2

To find this Ginza *tempura* place, head along Sotobori-dori from Ginza toward Shimbashi, turn right into the side street between Diamond Tiara and Nishi-Ginza Parking. Inside it's modern and high-ceilinged, seating just eight at a counter. The owner-chef and his wife are helped out by their daughter in the evenings. They're justly proud of their counter: a seamless slab of Japanese cypress, unplaned and well seasoned, it retains the rustic beauty of its natural lines. At the deep fryer that is the kitchen's centerpiece, the chef's skill captures the flavors of his materials. Using only sesame oil, he dips them, without a sound, for mere moments. Thus the coating of, say, a shrimp is permeated by the sweetness inside—it's more like eating shrimp than tempura. "I want to cook as if tempura is just the medium," says the chef. His first venture was in Sendagi, the next in Nishi-Azabu for 13 years. Since moving to Ginza in 1999, he visits the Tsukiji market each morning to buy the best fish.

Closed mid-August, late December-early January, Sunday and Bank Holiday Mondays

Open:
lunch 12:00-14:00 L.O.13:30
dinner 17:30-20:30 (L.O.)

FRENCH ✿

Au Goût du Jour Nouvelle Ēre

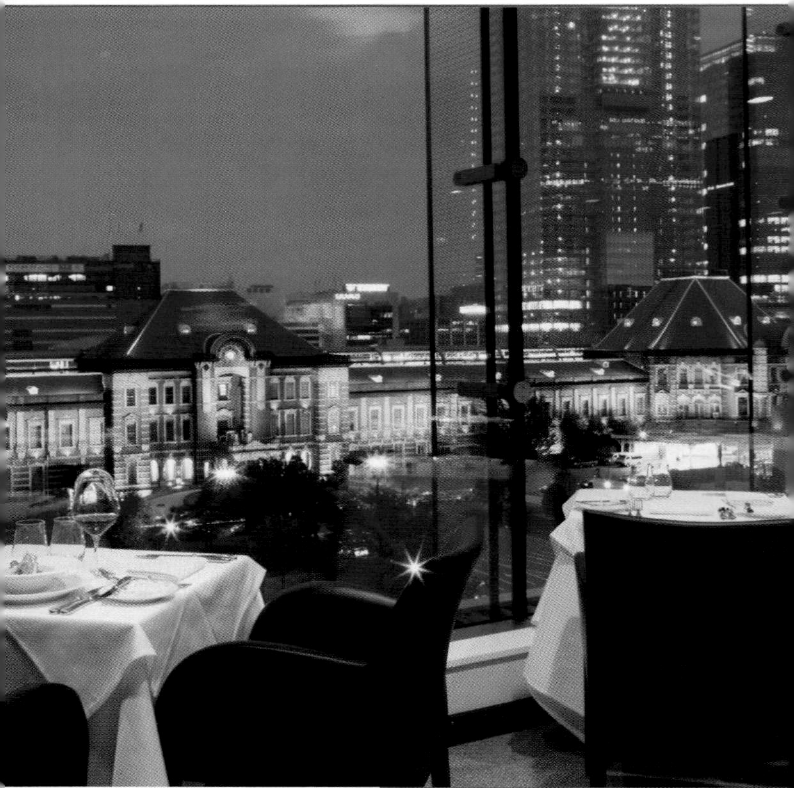

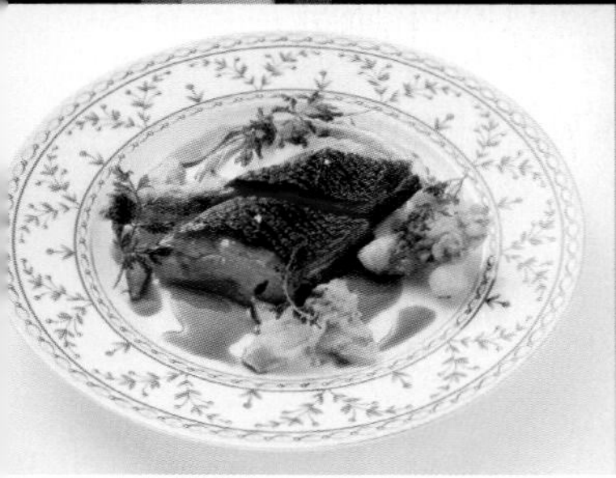

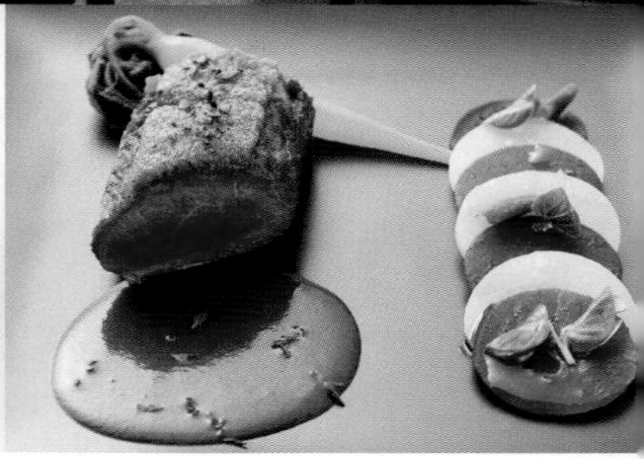

Au Goût du Jour Nouvelle Ēre

Lunch: menu ¥ 3,500-6,000
Dinner: menu ¥ 7,000-12,000
carte ¥ 8,000-9,500

TEL 03–5224–8070 / FAX 03–5224–8060
Shin-Marunouchi Building 5F,
1-5-1 Marunouchi, Chiyoda-ku
www.augoutdujour-group.com

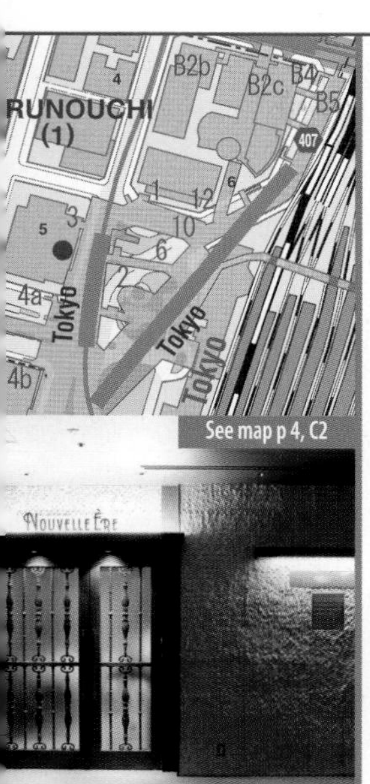

See map p 4, C2

This French restaurant looks down onto Tokyo Station. The chef, who was a pâtissier before changing careers, uses fresh ingredients and light, flavorful sauces. His cuisine has a refined, subtle taste that reflects the "Nouvelle Ère" of the restaurant's name. In addition to select seafood from Tsukiji, wild sea bream, sea bass and flounder are delivered straight from Ehime and tilefish come from Yamaguchi. For meat, the chef uses Lacan pigeon, Challans duck and other ingredients that he personally chooses while in France. In addition, sides of pork are delivered from the Basque region; the fat and meat-laden ribs and the meaty shoulder are cooked together into a kind of bacon for 48 hours. The thick fat intensifies the flavor. At dinnertime, guests can choose from ten or so contemporary desserts. The friendly service is impeccable.

Closed 1 January

Open:
lunch 11:00-13:30 (L.O.)
dinner 18:00-21:30 (L.O.)

Banrekiryukodo 万歴龍呼堂

Michelin

Lunch: menu ¥ 4,400-13,860
Dinner: menu ¥ 11,500-29,000

TEL 03–3505–5686 / FAX 03–3505–5693
2-33-5 Higashi-Azabu, Minato-ku
www.banreki.com
10

See map p 9, B2

Closed mid-August, late December-early January and Sunday

Open:
lunch 11:30-14:00 (L.O.)
dinner 18:00-21:30 (L.O.)

With the first two characters of its name, signifying "age-old," this Japanese restaurant, near Akabanebashi, expresses a desire to become a time-honored establishment, an embodiment of cultural heritage and history. The décor is modern and the fare and the tableware have a purely Japanese esthetic. The first-floor dining area has a large counter down the middle; a high-ceilinged private room in the back seats up to 10 people. The cavern-like basement has a low ceiling and secluded table seating in semi-private alcoves. The food is traditional Japanese, Tokyo-style. The chef worked for over ten years at a Gion restaurant in Kyoto. He cultivates a seasonal sensibility, bringing out the essential flavors of ingredients with a minimum of sugar and salt. The menu includes meat dishes and foie gras. While respecting tradition, the chef's new take on Japanese cuisine draws on Tokyo's resources, as a cosmopolitan food capital. Together with original ceramics, the tables are graced by lacquerware from Yamada Heiando, purveyors to the Imperial Household.

Beige

Michelin

Lunch: menu ¥ 6,600-12,100
carte ¥ 16,000-20,500

Dinner: menu ¥ 18,700-24,200
carte ¥ 16,000-20,500

TEL 03–5159–5500 / FAX 03–5159–5501
Chanel Building 10F,
3-5-3 Ginza, Chuo-ku
www.beige-tokyo.com

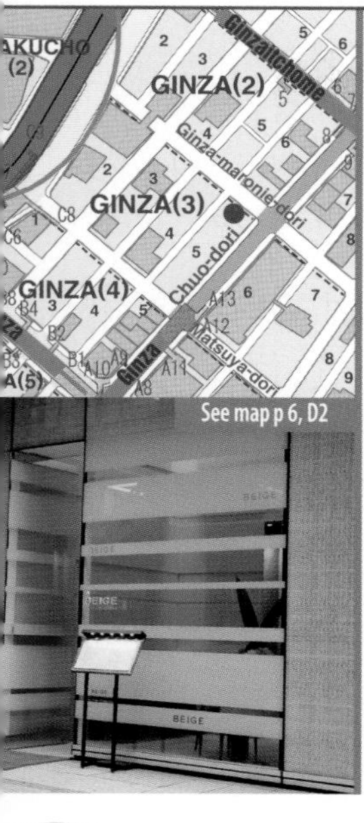

See map p 6, D2

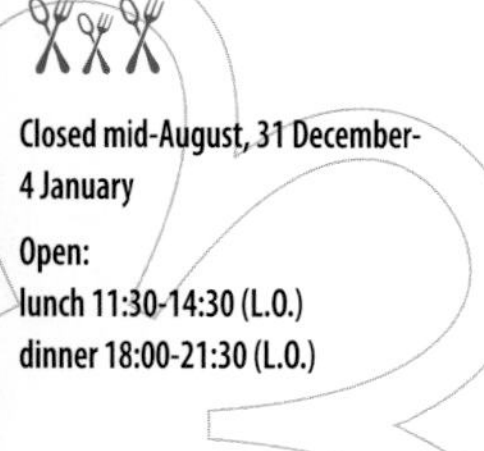

Closed mid-August, 31 December-4 January

Open:
lunch 11:30-14:30 (L.O.)
dinner 18:00-21:30 (L.O.)

The convergence of two top French brand names, Chanel and Alain Ducasse, gave rise to Beige. This restaurant, opened in December 2004, is located on the 10th floor of the Chanel Building at a prime site in Ginza. Here the concept that Alain Ducasse came up with was not cuisine à la française but rather contemporary French cooking using the finest Japanese ingredients. "Au fil des saisons" course at lunchtime can be savored in a relaxed atmosphere; it consists of three parts—végétal, mer, terre—and for dessert one can select "Carré Chanel, chocolat praliné, hazelnut ice cream." In the evening the mood is more elegant and refined; one can enjoy the "Collection course" at one's leisure. The chic main dining room is coordinated in tones of beige and brown to create a gorgeous interior surrounded by glass. From June until November, soft drinks and alcohol are served in Le Jardin de Tweed, the rooftop terrace. Complete with a small garden and pond and a view of Ginza below, this is a space well worth visiting.

Benoit

Benoit, Michelin

Lunch: menu ¥ 4,500-6,500
carte ¥ 6,200-7,200

Dinner: menu ¥ 8,000-14,000
carte ¥ 6,300-11,700

TEL 03–5468–0881 / FAX 03–5468–0883
La Porte Aoyama 10F,
5-51-8 Jingumae, Shibuya-ku
www.benoit-tokyo.com

See map p 12, C2

Closed 31 December and 1 January

Open:
lunch 11:30-14:30 (L.O.)
dinner 17:30-21:45 (L.O.)

A bistro-style restaurant where you can dine simply and without fuss in surroundings that make you feel as though you have been invited into a French home. It opened in 2005 as the Tokyo branch of the Paris restaurant Benoit, which was founded in 1912 and bought by Alain Ducasse in April 2005. In Tokyo, the French interior designer Pierre-Yves Rochon has coordinated plank flooring, terracotta style walls and the expansive views from the glass windows to create a harmonious space that is contemporary yet has the feel of the French countryside. The chef makes generous use of ingredients that he has rigorously selected himself and with contemporary flair has taken regional French cuisine to new heights. The menu is traditional French: beef tartare with quail's egg, grilled scallops in the shell Grenoble style, fricassee of chicken and crayfish. Wines are primarily French, from every part of the country.

Chemins

Michelin

Lunch: menu ¥ 3,080-5,830
carte ¥ 7,500-10,500

Dinner: menu ¥ 6,490-12,650
carte ¥ 7,500-10,500

TEL 03–3568–3344 / FAX 03–3568–3344
2-17-7 Akasaka, Minato-ku
www.chemins.jp
10

See map p 9, B1

The owner has a background in service. He trained in restaurants in Japan, studied in France for two years, and returned home, where after four years of working in other restaurants, he opened Chemins in 2002. The food is characterized by quality ingredients, skillful seasoning, and a light contemporary flavor. Produce is selected at the Tsukiji market, supplemented by once-a-week shipments of organic vegetables such as sweet carrots, baby turnips, and hatsuka radishes from Mishima in Shizuoka Prefecture. In summer, flounder, sardines, and plaice are brought in from Iwaki in Fukushima Prefecture. Winter fish, such as cod and anglerfish, also come from Iwaki. Kinmedai (alfonsin) from Choshi is served pan-fried with the scales on, accompanied by a shellfish sauce. There is an impressive 500 bins wine list, at good value. The simple modern interior has a light and graceful feel.

Closed late July-early August, late December-early January and Monday

Open:
lunch 11:30-16:00 L.O.13:30
dinner 18:00-24:00 L.O.21:30

Chez Inno

Tetsu Hayakawa

Lunch: menu ¥ 4,200-9,250
carte ¥ 12,000-17,500

Dinner: menu ¥ 15,000-23,100
carte ¥ 12,000-17,500

TEL 03–3274–2020 / FAX 03–3274–2452
2-4-16 Kyobashi, Chuo-ku
16

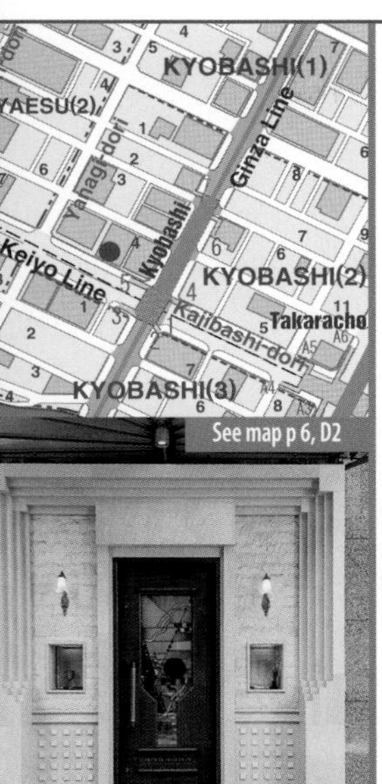

See map p 6, D2

Noboru Inoue, the owner-chef of this French restaurant in Kyobashi, is so famous that there is not a food connoisseur in Tokyo who does not hold him in high regard. After gaining experience at Troisgros in Roanne and Maxim's in Paris and serving as executive chef in several Tokyo restaurants, he opened his own place in 1984 and moved to his present location in 2004. Here with unremitting passion he serves classical French cuisine that wins the approval of his many patrons. Off the passageway from the entrance is the gorgeous art nouveau dining room as well as a private room. The menu includes, for instance, ravioli filled with truffles, braised sole sauce Albert, lamb en croute "Maria Callas" and marbré chocolat for dessert. The wine list selected by the chef sommelier contains more than 900 bins gathered from all over the world. Service by the wait staff is prompt and attentive.

Closed 31 December-5 January and Sunday

Open:
lunch 11:30-14:00 (L.O.)
dinner 18:00-21:00 (L.O.)

Chez Matsuo

Michelin

Lunch: menu ¥ 9,240
Dinner: menu ¥ 23,100-33,000

TEL 03–3485–0566 / FAX 03–3485–0766
1-23-15 Shoto, Shibuya-ku
www.chez-matsuo.co.jp

See map p 12, C2

Closed mid-August and late December-early January

Open:
lunch 12:00-15:00 L.O.13:00
dinner 18:00-23:00 L.O.20:30

A French restaurant in the upscale residential area of Shoto in Shibuya, in front of the Toguri Museum. This French style mansion (a former diplomatic residence) has been transformed as a restaurant in 1980. You'll enter into a salon bar equipped with a fireplace and furnishings from the early 20th century. Several private rooms continue off this, with their venerable wooden floors and paneling and antique lamps and mirrors which make for a calm and quiet atmosphere. Some face the lovely outside terrace, surrounded by greenery. There are also private rooms on the second floor, overlooking the trees in the courtyard. Beneath the trees flows a little brook with a small waterfall and you can have an aperitif at your table while enjoying the view of the seasonal blossoms. The menu consists only of set courses. Attention is given to securing the best regional ingredients, such as Mishima beef from Hagi in Yamaguchi Prefecture, vegetables from Ishikawa Prefecture, and fresh seafood from fishing ports all over Japan. Prices are rather high on dinner time.

Chez Tomo

Lunch: menu ¥ 3,180
carte ¥ 6,600-7,600

Dinner: menu ¥ 6,360
carte ¥ 6,600-7,600

TEL 03–5789–7731 / FAX 03–5789–7732
5-15-5 Shirokane, Minato-ku
www.chez-tomo.com

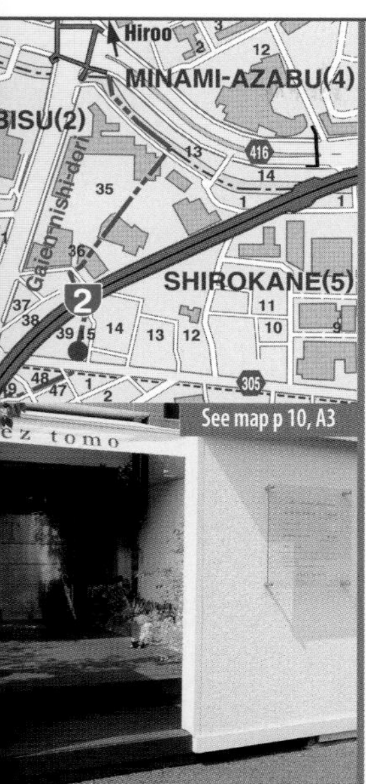

See map p 10, A3

Closed 2-7 August, 31 December-6 January and Monday

Open:
lunch 11:30-16:00 L.0.15:00
dinner 18:00-24:00 L.0.23:00

Although not very large, this restaurant in Shirokane serves French cuisine at good value. Day after day with unfailing enthusiasm the owner-chef prepares recipes with each and every customer in mind. Since about 80 percent of his diners are regulars, he changes the menu monthly so that they won't get bored. House specialties include egg dishes with sea urchin, black boudin snack, dishes (hot and cold) that use organic vegetables, fish and shrimp quenelles à la Paul Bocuse and brioche perdue for dessert. The chef worked in some famous, first-rate restaurants in France including Troisgros before returning to Japan and opening Chez Tomo in May 2002. Take a look into the small kitchen on the way to the dining table and you will see a homage signed and dated by Troisgros himself on the glass wall. Around 80 vintages have been selected to complement the food, and the wine, like the food itself, is reasonably priced. On clear days you can dine out on the small terrace surrounded by greenery.

Chikuyotei 竹葉亭

Michelin

Lunch: menu ¥ 8,085-11,550
carte ¥ 3,600-8,000
Dinner: menu ¥ 13,860-16,170
carte ¥ 3,600-8,000

TEL 03–3542–0789 / FAX 03–3542–0788
8-14-7 Ginza, Chuo-ku
25

See map p 6, D3

Chikuyotei, a seventh-generation restaurant specializing in *unagi,* was originally established near the end of the Edo period as a sword depository, but when swords were outlawed in 1876 the second-generation owner turned the establishment into an *unagi* restaurant. Housed in a lovely old building that escaped World War II unscathed, the restaurant features elegant *tatami* rooms throughout. The art and antiques placed here and there throughout the restaurant are from a collection started by the second-generation owner. Chikuyotei's *unagi* is plump and thick, with an excellent sauce made from a secret recipe. *Shirayaki, unagi* that is grilled without sauce and served with *wasabi* and soy sauce for a lighter touch, is also a specialty. Reservations are required for the *tatami* rooms, but for budget-conscious diners *unagi-don* (a large bowl of rice topped with *unagi*) can be enjoyed for either lunch or dinner in the table area accessed through a separate entrance.

Closed 31 December-3 January, Sunday and Bank Holidays

Open:
lunch 11:30-15:00 L.O.14:30
dinner 16:30-21:00 L.O.20:00

China Blue

China Blue, Conrad

Lunch: menu ¥ 3,800-9,000
carte ¥ 6,000-13,500

Dinner: menu ¥ 12,000-25,000
carte ¥ 6,000-13,500

TEL 03–6388–8000 / FAX 03–6388–8001
Conrad Hotel 28F,
1-9-1 Higashi-Shinbashi, Minato-ku
www.conradtokyo.co.jp

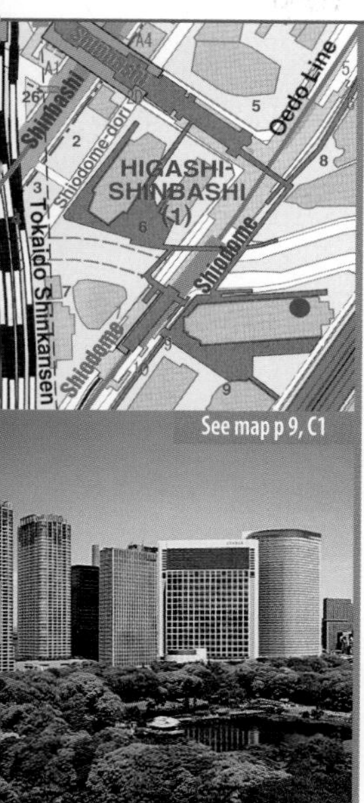

See map p 9, C1

This Chinese restaurant opened in January 2005 on the 28th floor of the Conrad Tokyo hotel, a modern tower building in Shiodome. To get to the restaurant one passes through the front lobby of the hotel and goes down a beautiful long corridor. At the entrance is a gate, one of many that are symbolically used as part of the concept for the hotel as a whole. In the main dining room light fixtures covered with blue cloth hang from the tall ceiling, bathing the tables in a soft glow. Tokyo Bay can be seen in the distance out of the windows. We recommend that you go at dinner to experience the dual pleasures of the lighting and the night-time views. There are three private rooms, two of which also have panoramic views. A huge glass wine cabinet, which holds 400 vintages, forms part of the decoration. The cuisine is contemporary Chinese, with influences from Canton, Singapore and Indonesia. Each dish is carefully prepared to bring out the foods' flavors and aromas.

Open:
lunch 11:30-14:30 (L.O.)
dinner 17:30-22:00 (L.O.)

Chugoku Hanten Fureika

中国飯店 富麗華

Chugoku Hanten Fureika

Lunch: menu ¥ 1,700-5,000
carte ¥ 6,000-12,000

Dinner: menu ¥ 15,015-34,650
carte ¥ 6,000-12,000

TEL 03–5561–7788 / FAX 03–5561–7878
3-7-5 Higashi-Azabu, Minato-ku
www.chuugokuhanten.com
150

See map p 10, A4

Closed 31 December-1 January

Open:
lunch 11:30-14:00 (L.O.)
dinner 17:30-22:00 (L.O.)

This is a restaurant where you can relax and enjoy the subtlety and depth of Chinese culture with all five senses. The theme of Chugoku Hanten Fureika is harmony between East and West, classical and modern, simplicity and sophistication. The cuisine is a fusion of lightly seasoned Cantonese and the stronger tasting Shanghai style. The chef is originally from Hong Kong, and the rest the full-time staff were all hired from Hong Kong and Shanghai. This theme also finds full expression in the interior design: the carved wooden screens against the beige walls, the Chinese vases and ornaments, and the ebony chopsticks and hemp plates on the tablecloth. Diners can enjoy performances of the erhu or a flute with their meals. The first floor is for general dining; a banquet hall that can accommodate up to 150 guests is on the second; and five private rooms occupy the third floor. A full complement of wait staff provide prompt and unerring service.

Cogito

Cogito

Lunch: menu ¥ 3,675-5,250
carte ¥ 6,000-8,000

Dinner: menu ¥ 8,800-16,500
carte ¥ 6,500-8,500

TEL 03–3796–3838 / FAX 03–3796–2277
3-2-15 Nishi-Azabu, Minato-ku

8

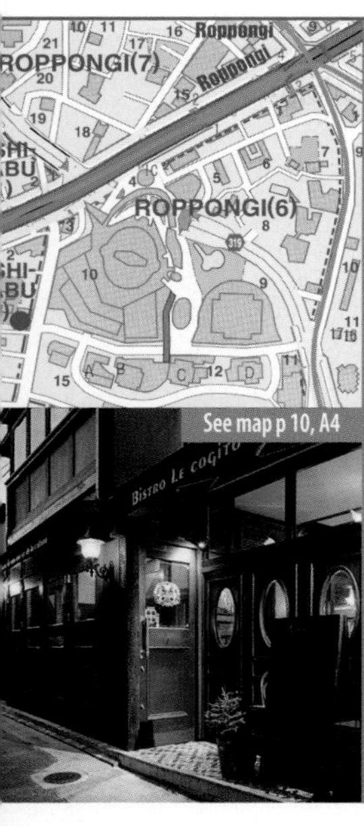

See map p 10, A4

Cogito is a French restaurant housed in detached, bistro-like premises in Roppongi Hills. After training in leading French and Swiss kitchens, the owner-chef launched his first solo venture on returning to Japan in 1994. Cogito, his third opus, opened in March 2006. The 1900 Vienna style interior, finished throughout with *muku* wood, is bathed in the warm light of chandeliers and bracket lamps. The cuisine—best sampled at dinner—features choice ingredients and classic techniques. The house specialty is game, shot by the chef himself on trips to Hokkaido during the hunting season. Unusual items include sika venison and hazel grouse. The prime cuts of venison are from the loin and thigh, suited for steaks. Nothing goes to waste, as the bones and offal are used for stock. The two-part wine list is a showpiece: the selection of 60 labels includes pre-1950 vintages. To conclude on a mellow note, visit the salon and wine cellar, hidden downstairs, for an after-dinner drink or cigar.

Closed late December-early January and Sunday

Open:
lunch 12:00-14:00 (L.O.)
dinner 18:00-22:30 (L.O.)

Coucagno

Coucagno, Cerulean Tower

Lunch: menu ¥ 4,050-9,820
carte ¥ 6,700-8,200

Dinner: menu ¥ 9,820-17,330
carte ¥ 8,600-12,000

TEL 03–3476–3000 / FAX 03–3476–3001
Cerulean Tower Tokyu Hotel 40F,
26-1 Sakuragaokacho, Shibuya-ku
www.ceruleantower-hotel.com

12

See map p 12, C3

Open:
lunch 11:30-14:00 (L.O.)
dinner 17:30-22:00 (L.O.)

This tower restaurant is on the 40th floor of the Cerulean Tower Tokyu Hotel, not far from Shibuya Station. The modern interior, in tones of brown and ivory, has large windows providing spectacular vistas of the southern part of Tokyo. In the dining area, good-sized tables are evenly spaced and embellished with contemporary silverware, crystal and porcelain vases. There is also a slightly raised circular bar from which to enjoy the view. There are two private rooms, only one of which shares the panoramic view, so be sure to specify when you book. The seasonal menu is basically Provençal (featuring the likes of tapenades, olive oil, and tomato confit), but with Japanese and contemporary twists depending on the chef's inspirations. The 200-label wine list focuses on France but includes offerings from Italy, Germany, California, Australia, New Zealand, and Japan. After feasting on dishes from the South of France, you might like to relax at the bar and gaze at the city lights. "Coucagno" means "land of plenty."

Crescent

Michelin

Dinner: menu ¥ 28,875-34,650

TEL 03–3436–3211
1-8-20 Shiba-Koen, Minato-ku
www.restaurantcrescent.com

24

See map p 9, B2

Closed mid-August, late December-early January, Sunday and Bank Holidays

Open:
dinner 17:30-22:30 L.O.20:30

Standing sedately next to the lush greenery of Shiba Koen. This five-story English-looking building in a late Victorian style is well maintained if somewhat old fashioned and "aristocratic" atmosphere. When it opened in 1957, it was fashionable among politicians, business leaders and members of the upper class, winning for it the soubriquet "a modern-day Rokumeikan." The present chef trained at Troisgros and Girardet. He believes in two things: the best ingredients and being particular about those who produce them. He has built a network based on trust and communication and primarily uses what is brought in from agricultural cooperatives or sent to him directly from growers nationwide. Seafood is delivered in season: from winter to spring there is Ezo abalone from the Sanriku district and trout from Aomori; from May there is abalone from Chiba. The superior quality of the desserts also merits attention. There is a wine cellar in the basement, and a spectacular wine list, including some valuable bins not found elsewhere.

ITALIAN 

Cucina Hirata

Michelin

Dinner: carte ¥ 6,300-12,000

TEL 03–3457–0094 / FAX 03–3457–0074
Endo Building 3F,
2-13-10 Azabu-Juban, Minato-ku

See map p 10, A4

A five-minute walk from the Tokyo Metro Azabujuban station brings you to Cucina Hirata, a small Itaiian restaurant. The barber shop on the first floor serves as a landmark. The restaurant's name is Italian for "Hirata's Kitchen" and reflects the owner/chef's notion of having visitors to his restaurant eat what he considers to be tasty, without being bound by convention. He brings out the best in the fresh, flavorsome ingredients, and many of his dishes are comparatively simple, without a single superfluous ingredient. Coming from a farming family in Miyagi Prefecture, he took an interest in the cultivation of pesticide-free organic vegetables from an early age, is very particular about seasonal ingredients and where they are produced, and only buys seasonal fish that have been caught off the coast of Zushi after checking them with his own eyes. Moreover, the roast pork from Akita pigs brought up on feed containing wholesome, enzyme-enhanced vegetables is superb. The menu is refreshingly unassuming, and the wine list with more than 200 bins is also top-notch.

Closed Golden week, mid-August, late December-early January, Sunday and Bank Holidays

Open:
dinner 18:00-22:00 (L.O.)

FRENCH CONTEMPORARY 

Cuisine(s) Michel Troisgros

Cuisine(s) Michel Troisgros, Hyatt Regency

Lunch: menu ¥ 4,620-11,550
carte ¥ 12,300-18,400

Dinner: menu ¥ 13,860-23,100
carte ¥ 12,300-18,400

TEL 03–5321–3915 / FAX 03–3340–3722
Hyatt Regency Hotel 1F,
2-7-2 Nishi-Shinjuku, Shinjuku-ku
www.hyattregencytokyo.com

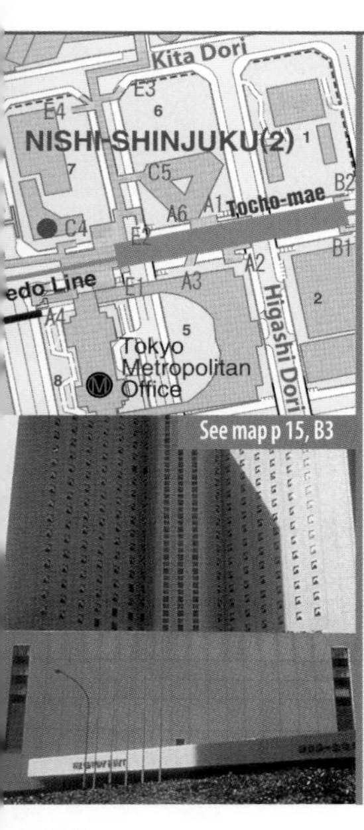

See map p 15, B3

Open:
lunch 11:30-15:00 L.O.14:00
dinner 18:00-23:00 L.O.21:30

Cuisine(s) Michel Troisgros opened in September, 2006 in the Hyatt Regency hotel in Shinjuku, and is the brainchild of Michel Troisgros, the third-generation owner/chef of Troisgros, a first-class restaurant in Roanne (North West of Lyons). Said to have been influenced by Japanese cuisine, Troisgros offers contemporary French cuisine with a soupçon of Japanese flavor and style. Next to the reception area with its comfortable waiting room, you can see the glass-enclosed kitchen located in the middle of the restaurant. There are two dining areas—a chic, contemporary area that is also glass-sided, and a second area with wood that evokes a French auberge. Super Potato, the interior design firm headed by Takashi Sugimoto, was responsible for the décor. The menu changes every two months, and with the exception of the poultry that is brought in from France, all the ingredients used are produced in Japan. French wines make up the bulk of the extensive wine list.

Daigo 醍醐

Daigo

Lunch: menu ¥ 11,500-21,850

Dinner: menu ¥ 17,250-21,850

TEL 03–3431–0811 / FAX 03–3431–1382
Forest Tower 2F,
2-3-1 Atago, Minato-ku

See map p 9, B2

Closed 1 January

Open:
lunch 12:00-15:00 L.O.14:00
dinner 17:00-22:00 L.O.20:00

A *shojin ryori* restaurant that has been in operation since 1950 at the foot of Atago Hill in Tokyo. *Shojin ryori,* a cuisine with deep ties to Zen Buddhism and grounded in its austere culture, offers a rich taste of vegetarian dishes including root vegetables and beans. Daigo's cuisine is what they call *shojin kaiseki,* a course comprising a succession of small individual dishes featuring seasonal ingredients: fresh *tofu* served in bamboo sections, a light soup of puréed corn, *soba* noodles freshly prepared by the owner, and a mushroom porridge. When Daigo opened, it was located on the grounds of the Soto Zen temple Seishoji. In 2002, Daigo moved to the second floor of the Forest Tower. The interior is a blend of *wabi* and *sabi,* refinement and elegance in the spirit of a Zen temple, complete with *ikebana* beautifully matched with their ceramic containers. Hanging scrolls and other decorative elements complete the sense of being in a uniquely Japanese space.

Dons de la Nature

Michelin

Dinner: menu ¥ 23,100
carte ¥ 23,000-37,000

TEL 03–3563–4129 / FAX 03–3563–4130
B1F,
1-7-6 Ginza, Chuo-ku
www.dons-nature.jp

See map p 6, D2

Closed mid-August, late December-early January, Sunday and Bank Holidays

Open:
dinner 17:00-22:00 L.O.21:00

The name of this steakhouse is French for "gifts of nature." The layout features an open kitchen, sleek counter, and table seating. The owner-chef, a veteran of French cuisine, opened Dons de la Nature after training at a famous Tokyo steakhouse. The beef, from black-haired crossbred cattle, is the star attraction, and the chef is very particular about its quality. Instead of *teppanyaki,* he proposes a less familiar form of steak with real substance. First, he carefully checks the texture and condition of the meat he purchases, which comes from heifers at around 33 months old. After about two weeks' aging in a meat locker, the cuts are carved and swathed in cloth to absorb excess juices, then they spend another seven to ten days aging in a vacuum to boost the taste by melding the fat and meat flavors. To ensure the best results, orders start at 400 grams—we suggest you bring a friend. The walls are hung with landscapes of Amsterdam and La Rochelle in France, and the quiet background music is classical.

 ✿✿

Esaki えさき

Michelin

Lunch: menu ¥ 3,675-5,250
Dinner: menu ¥ 9,240-11,550

TEL 03–3408–5056 / FAX 03–3408–5056
Hills Aoyama B1F,
3-39-9 Jingumae, Shibuya-ku
www.aoyamaesaki.net
10

See map p 12, D2

Be sure to look out for the illuminated name stand facing the street as this basement restaurant in a quiet residential area of Jingumae is a little hard to find. Esaki offers a dining area that seats ten, two private rooms that each seat four, and a counter that seats six. Raw concrete feature walls, marble flooring and dark-hued tables combine to create a beautiful, chic décor. Two sandstone wall frescos carved by an artisan from Bali are focal points of the interior. The owner uses only natural, fresh ingredients and his organic vegetable dishes are an important part of the menu. To maintain a consistent taste, he is very particular about his seafood—sea bream from Sado Island, striped horse mackerel from Awaji Island, and, in the summer, sea bass from the Joban coast. His signature dish is a deep-fried lily bulb dumpling wrapped with a thin coating made from rice cracker crumble—an aromatic, elegant dish. In the summer he substitutes a sweetfish soup.

Closed Golden week, mid-August, late December-early January, Sunday and Bank Holidays

Open:
lunch 12:00-14:00 L.O.13:30
dinner 18:00-23:00 L.O.21:30

Fukamachi 深町

Michelin

Lunch: menu ¥ 5,250-7,350
carte ¥ 5,000-10,000

Dinner: menu ¥ 8,400-15,650
carte ¥ 5,000-10,000

TEL 03–5250–8777 / FAX 03–5250–8777
2-5-2 Kyobashi, Chuo-ku

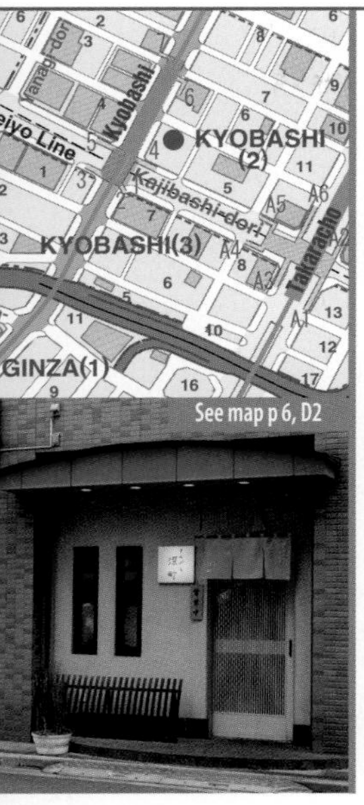

See map p 6, D2

Tempura restaurant Fukamachi's door curtain says "From the Hilltop Hotel" because that is where the owner cooked *tempura* for 35 years. Fukamachi's superb fare, thinly battered and lightly fried, does the tasty ingredients justice. In proper Edo style, the high-quality sesame oil is changed often. Using two deep fryers, the chef watches the oil temperature closely to obtain soft morsels in a crisp, fragrant coating. He performs this sleight of hand with thrilling deftness. The family-run place serves its tempura on round Negoro lacquer trays on a cypress counter. The décor is minimal; the large Tokoname water jars were acquired for the owner's antique collection. In fact, he chose Kyobashi for its antique shops as well as its proximity to the Tsukiji fish market, where he buys fish every morning. Besides whiting and sea eel, he finds the now hard-to-come-by flathead uniquely suited to Edomae *tempura*. At lunchtime he caters to business types with *kakiage tendon* (mixed vegetable and shrimp *tempura* on rice).

Closed mid-August, late December-early January and Monday

Open:
lunch 11:30-14:00 L.O.13:30
dinner 17:00-21:00 (L.O.)

Fukudaya 福田家

Fukudaya, Michelin

Lunch: menu ¥ 31,500-37,800
Dinner: menu ¥ 35,280-50,400

TEL 03–3261–8577 / FAX 03–3261–1518
6-12 Kioicho, Chiyoda-ku

  40

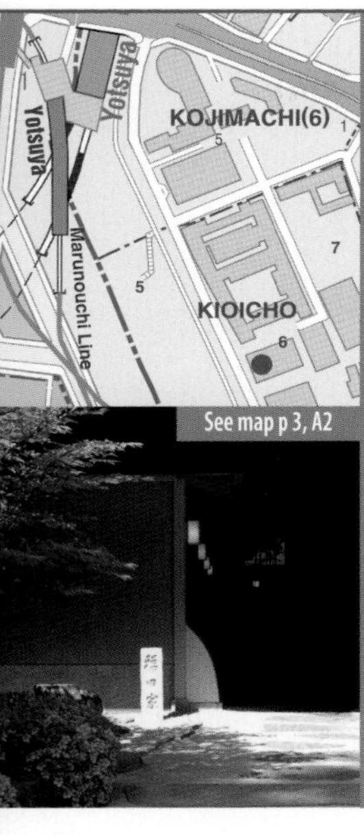

See map p 3, A2

Closed late December-early January, Sunday and Bank Holidays

Open:
lunch 11:00-15:00
dinner 17:30-22:30

This exclusive traditional Japanese restaurant opened as an inn and restaurant in Toranomon in 1939 and subsequently moved to Kioicho. It underwent a complete renovation in 1995. Ownership has been passed down within a single family, and the present owner is the third generation to run it. Located in an office building on a prime piece of real estate, the spacious restaurant has seven Japanese-style rooms on two floors. The way in which the room layout has a view of the garden framed by sliding doors, the numerous antiques and the aroma of wood and *tatami* could be called the very essence of Japanese architecture. The grand hall can accommodate up to 40 people; there is even a 750-year-old thatched-roof house on the second floor. The cuisine is orthodox *kaiseki* composed of rigorously selected seasonal ingredients expertly prepared by the owner. A meal here, of course, is not simply pleasing to the palate but a gift of the seasons to be savored with all five senses. The quality of the service is excellent.

Fukuju 福樹

Michelin

Lunch: menu ¥ 17,325-23,100
Dinner: menu ¥ 20,790-55,000

TEL 03–3571–8596 / FAX 03–3571–8596
5F,
8-8-19 Ginza, Chuo-ku
8

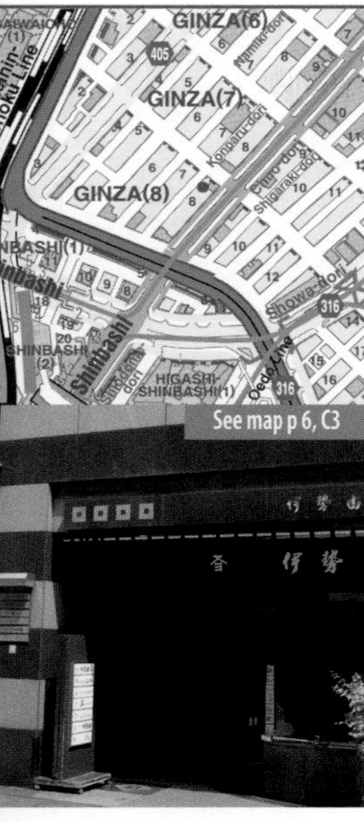

See map p 6, C3

Fukuju is a cosy Japanese restaurant run by the owner and his wife. The evocative name (fuku means happiness; ju means forest) was given by the chief priest of Kaneiji in Ueno. Located off Ginza Chuo-dori on the fifth floor of a building on Komparu-dori, it is not easy to find. Inside there is a counter made from a single thick board of Japanese cypress and a Japanese-style private room that looks like a tearoom. If reserved in advance, this room can be used exclusively for a tea ceremony at which a meal is served. All the food is prepared by the owner himself, who takes his creed from the aesthetic principle of *shingyoso*: orthodox style and its elegant variations. The fish comes direct from Sanriku, Kesennuma, Ehime and Oita, and includes salmon, pike eel, spotted halibut, sea urchins, tilefish and *fugu*. In addition to shark fin dishes and boiled abalone, we recommend hot pots of tortoise or *fugu* and seasoned steamed rice. Only one reservation for lunch is accepted each day.

Closed mid-August, late December-early January, Sunday and Bank Holidays

Open:
lunch 12:00-15:00 L.O.13:00
dinner 17:30-22:30 L.O.20:30

Gastronomie Française Tateru Yoshino

Gastronomie Française Tateru Yoshino, Michelin

Lunch: menu ¥ 4,050-9,500
Dinner: menu ¥ 8,660-17,330

TEL 03–6252–1155 / FAX 03–6252–1156
Park Hotel Shiodome Media Tower 25F,
1-7-1 Higashi-Shinbashi, Minato-ku
www.tateruyoshino.com

28

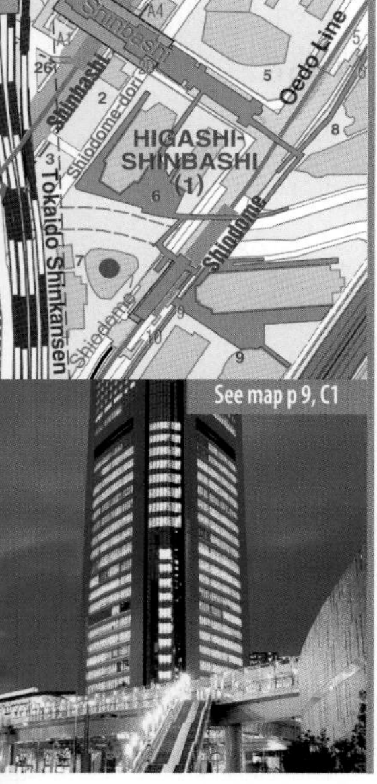

See map p 9, C1

Tateru Yoshino, the owner-chef of the restaurants Stella Maris in Paris and "Tateru Yoshino" in Shiba-Koen, Tokyo, opened this "Gastronomie Française Tateru Yoshino" in the Park Hotel in 2003. The hotel is housed in the Shiodome Media Tower, a Shiodome area landmark, and the restaurant is located on the 25th floor of the hotel, which is the also the lobby floor. Seating only 22 people, this modern, elegant salon features spacious windows, white walls accented with contemporary paintings, crystal and pottery objets d'art and chestnut-hued seats. The cuisine is inspired contemporary French with a wide spectrum of flavors. Small plates can also be enjoyed at the salon bar in the vicinity of the counter. "Bar à vins Tateru Yoshino" also offers an interesting wine menu. The floor staff provides impeccable service. Although not large, this pleasant restaurant run by the skilled Tateru Yoshino and his team is well worth a visit.

Open:
lunch 11:30-15:00 L.O.14:00
dinner 18:00-23:00 L.O.21:00

Ginza La Tour

Michelin

Lunch: menu ¥ 4,950-8,800
carte ¥ 15,000-20,000

Dinner: menu ¥ 13,750-20,350
carte ¥ 15,000-20,000

TEL 03–3569–2211 / FAX 03–3569–2219
Kojun Building 5F,
6-8-7 Ginza, Chuo-ku
www.ginzalatour.com

12

See map p 6, C3

This French restaurant, on the fifth floor of the Kojun Building in Ginza, opened in 2006 and its classical décor has a Baroque feel. You can sip an aperitif at the bar in the lobby while awaiting your dinner companion. The owner-chef honed his skills at La Tour D'Argent, first in Paris, then in Tokyo; he went solo in 1993, in Kagurazaka, before fulfilling his dream with the move to Ginza. Rather than rely on regular suppliers, he scouts the markets, buying only the choicest products. Superior beef is supplied by Ogata Farm in Iwate; the fillet is sautéed, the rump is prepared *au jus de viande,* while the rib meat is stewed with a red burgundy. For the house specialty hors d'oeuvre, *"Foie Gras Royale,"* foie gras is heated slowly for four hours, then infused with Sauternes and softly perfumed with Sicilian oranges and honey. The chef's signature meat dish is *canard rôti* or *grillé*. The main course can be followed with a superb selection of French cheeses. At Ginza La Tour, solid technique and old-world French style prevail.

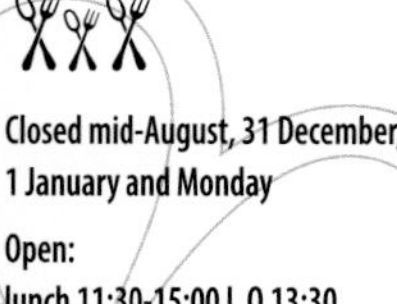

Closed mid-August, 31 December, 1 January and Monday

Open:
lunch 11:30-15:00 L.O.13:30
dinner 18:00-23:00 L.O.20:30

Ginza Sushiko Honten
銀座寿司幸本店

Michelin

Lunch: menu ¥ 9,450-26,250
Dinner: menu ¥ 16,800-27,500

TEL 03–3571–1968 / FAX 03–3571–1907
6-3-8 Ginza, Chuo-ku
10

See map p 6, C2

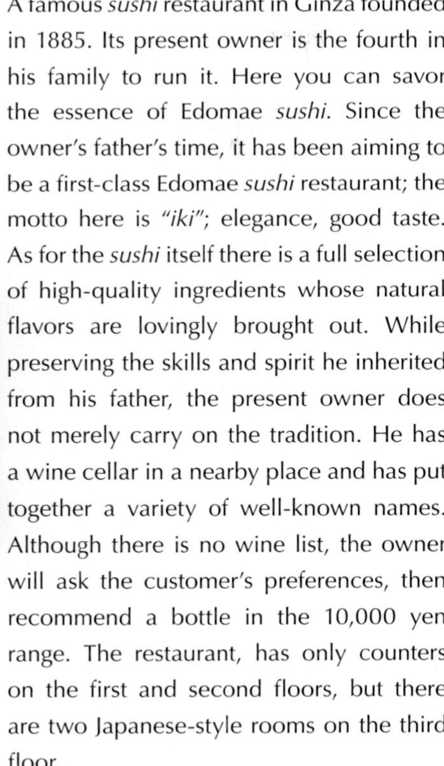

A famous *sushi* restaurant in Ginza founded in 1885. Its present owner is the fourth in his family to run it. Here you can savor the essence of Edomae *sushi*. Since the owner's father's time, it has been aiming to be a first-class Edomae *sushi* restaurant; the motto here is *"iki"*; elegance, good taste. As for the *sushi* itself there is a full selection of high-quality ingredients whose natural flavors are lovingly brought out. While preserving the skills and spirit he inherited from his father, the present owner does not merely carry on the tradition. He has a wine cellar in a nearby place and has put together a variety of well-known names. Although there is no wine list, the owner will ask the customer's preferences, then recommend a bottle in the 10,000 yen range. The restaurant, has only counters on the first and second floors, but there are two Japanese-style rooms on the third floor.

Closed mid-August and late December-early January

Open: 11:30-23:00 L.0.21:45

✿✿✿

Hamadaya 濱田家

Hamadaya

Lunch: menu ¥ 16,500-25,300

Dinner: menu ¥ 30,000-42,000

TEL 03–3661–5940 / FAX 03–3808–0801
3-13-5 Nihonbashi-Ningyocho, Chuo-ku
www.hamadaya.info

  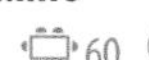 60

See map p 5, B1

Closed mid-August, late December-early January, Sunday and Bank Holidays

Open:
lunch 11:00-15:00 L.O.14:00
dinner 17:30-23:00 L.O.21:00

This Japanese restaurant was founded in 1912. During the Edo era, it was also a *geisha* house, and the *geisha* of Hamadaya were the celebrities of their day. The historic building is in traditional *sukiya*-style architecture, only a few examples of which still remain. All 11 Japanese-style rooms are private dining rooms, each of which has a tastefully laid out Japanese garden. The doors and flower arrangements change with the seasons: in summer, for example, there are bamboo screen doors instead of *shoji*; the dedication to good service here is apparent in even the minutest detail. The cuisine is *kaiseki* that makes generous use of seasonal ingredients and is prepared in a strictly orthodox Edo style. The menu changes weekly, and, if so desired, the same ingredients can be prepared and served in different ways to suit the diners' preferences. As befits a traditional *ryotei* restaurant, Hamadaya allows one to call in *geisha* and other companions to add to the pleasure of a banquet or for business entertainment.

Hanasanshou 花山椒

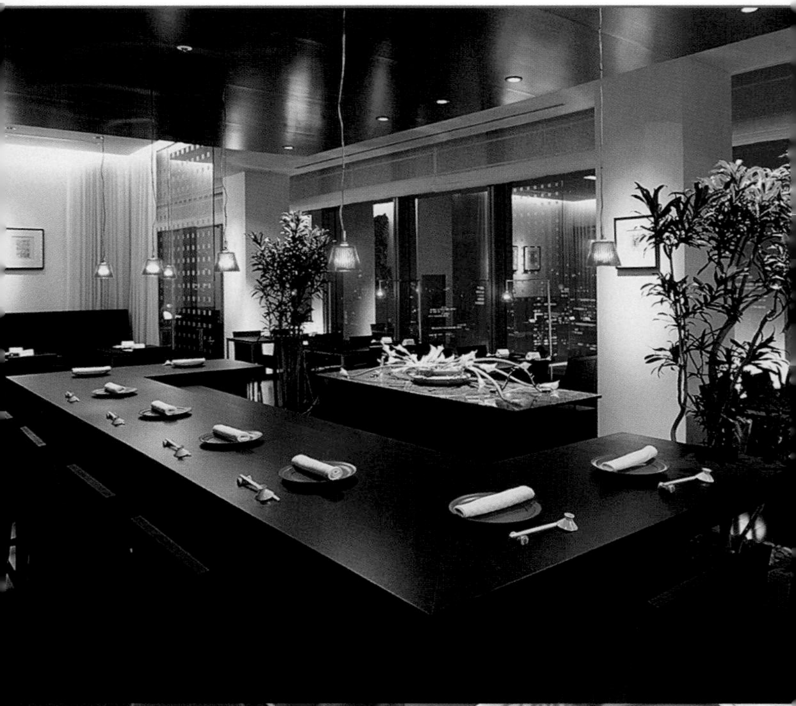

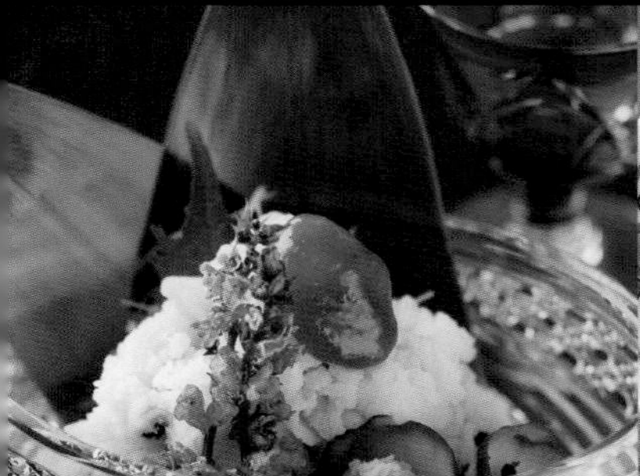

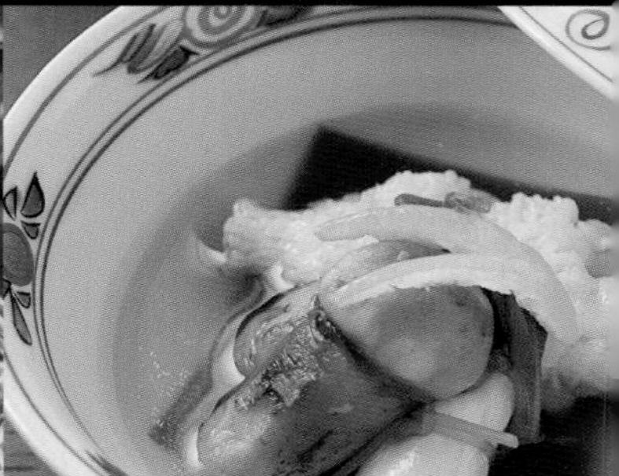

Hanasanshou, Park Hotel

Lunch: menu ¥ 2,800-8,100

Dinner: menu ¥ 6,400-11,600
carte ¥ 4,800-7,400

TEL 03–6252–1177 / FAX 03–6252–1178
Park Hotel Shiodome Media Tower 25F,
1-7-1 Higashi-Shinbashi, Minato-ku
www.parkhoteltokyo.com

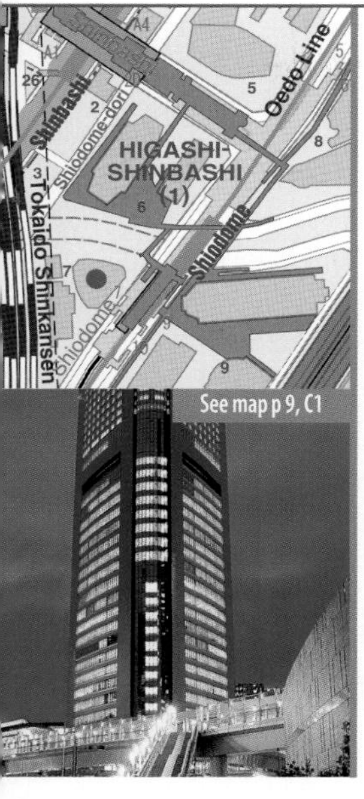

See map p 9, C1

A Japanese-style restaurant in the Park Hotel Tokyo in the Shiodome Media Tower. There is a spacious lounge on the lobby floor (25th floor) where you can listen to live jazz on certain nights of the week. Hanasanshou features a rather modern décor, with white walls and a chic, wood-trimmed interior. Seating at the long, narrow table faces the windows so you can enjoy the night-time view of the Shimbashi district during your meal. The cuisine is traditional Kyoto-style *kaiseki*. The head chef at this restaurant is committed not only to the flavor of fresh seasonal foods, but to healthy eating as well. The vegetables essential to Kyoto cuisine are procured directly from the farms producing them. The lunchtime menu features two traditional box lunches, the *Shokado Bento* and the *Daitokuji Bento*, *kaiseki* and *tempura* courses, beefsteak and *sushi* sets, and other dishes. At night, only *kaiseki* is offered. The drinks menu is headed by a good selection of *shochu*.

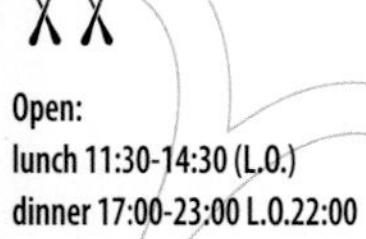

Open:
lunch 11:30-14:30 (L.O.)
dinner 17:00-23:00 L.O.22:00

Harutaka 青空

Michelin

Dinner: menu ¥ 15,000-20,000

TEL 03–3573–1144 / FAX 03–3573–1144
Kawabata Building 3F,
8-5-8 Ginza, Chuo-ku

4

See map p 6, C3

This restaurant was opened in Ginza in 2006 by a *sushi* master who apprenticed for 12 years at Sukiyabashi Jiro. His innate aesthetic sensibilities are on display in the design and appurtenances of the restaurant: the counter made of cypress from Kiso and the flower arrangement done by the owner himself. But his keen eye for discerning and selecting only the finest ingredients goes well beyond that. He begins each day with a trip to Tsukiji. Hokkaido-born, he is a shrewd judge of the best fish in every category. In May it's bonito; lightly grilled over straw - the flavor and aroma of a plate of this is incomparable. Between then and June there is fresh abalone from Ohara in Chiba. Mantis shrimp are brought in alive and steamed briefly before being served to the customer. The *shari—sushi* rice—is a specially ordered blend of sweet-tasting rice and one that is not too sticky. Harutaka has brought a breath of fresh air to the Ginza district and is already establishing a reputation for itself for the taste of its *sushi*.

Closed Golden week, mid-August, late December-early January, Sunday and Bank Holidays

Open:
dinner 17:30-1:30 (L.O.)

Higuchi 樋口

Michelin

Dinner: menu ¥ 11,000-16,500

TEL 03–3402–7038 / FAX 03–3402–7038
2-19-12 Jingumae, Shibuya-ku

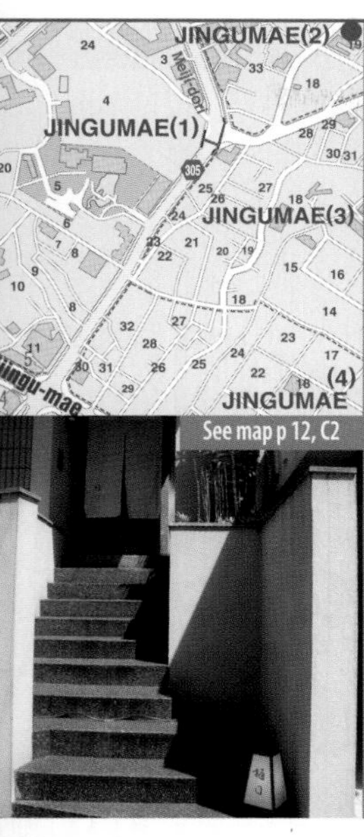

See map p 12, C2

Ascend the stone staircase set into the building and pass through an entrance hung with a *noren* and you find yourself in a purely traditional interior, with the greenish-brown earthen walls providing a subdued effect. The owner trained in a variety of traditional Japanese restaurants before opening Higuchi in 2000. He is committed to presenting the flavor of fresh ingredients straight up, with no compromises. Seafood, especially, is kept alive until the last moment. Sea bream is steamed in *sake*, and the head and bones are used in *aradaki*. It is also grilled using an aromatic combination of marinade and *sansho* (Japanese pepper). In spring, stock is made form the bones of *hamo* (pike eel). In autumn, when fresh *matsutake* from the Shinshu and Chugoku regions are added to *hamo shabu-shabu*, you can enjoy the apt pairing of these ingredients. In addition to sake there is a well-selected and appropriately priced wine list centering on some 20 different varieties of French wine.

Closed Golden week, mid-August, late December-early January, Sunday and Bank Holidays

Open:
dinner 18:00-21:00 (L.O.)

Hinokizaka ひのきざか

Hinokizaka, The Ritz-Carlton

Lunch: menu ¥ 4,950-19,800
Dinner: menu ¥ 13,200-33,000

TEL 03–3423–8000 / FAX 03–3423–8001
The Ritz-Carlton Hotel 45F,
9-7-1 Akasaka, Minato-ku
www.ritzcarlton.co.jp

See map p 9, B2

The Japanese restaurant Hinokizaka is on the 45th floor of The Ritz-Carlton, which opened in March 2007 in Roppongi's Tokyo Midtown complex. When making reservations it is best to say what kind of food you have in mind, since many genres - kaiseki, teppanyaki, tempura, sushi - are available at Hinokizaka. The principal cuisine is kaiseki, a superb, multi-course meal, aromatic, carefully prepared and served with due respect for the season. In the traditional Japanese-style dining room, diners can enjoy a view of Shinjuku and Yotsuya through wide glass windows. Here, the interior décor is beautiful, and guests can watch in comfortable surroundings as the chefs and their assistants busily prepare the food. Cuisine other than kaiseki is also served in the small rooms. There are four private rooms. The lunch course is reasonably priced.

Open:
lunch 11:30-14:30 (L.O.)
dinner 17:30-21:30 (L.O.)

Hiramatsu

Hiramatsu

Lunch: menu ¥ 7,500-9,800
carte ¥ 16,000-20,000

Dinner: menu ¥ 18,500-23,000
carte ¥ 16,000-20,000

TEL 03–3444–3967 / FAX 03–3444–3991
5-15-13 Minami-Azabu, Minato-ku
www.hiramatsu.co.jp

14

See map p 9, A2

A French restaurant in Minami Azabu. It opened in Nishi Azabu in 1982 and moved to its present location in 1988. The owner-chef Hiramatsu Hiroyuki, has loved France ever since he read the works of Jean-Jacques Rousseau as a boy; his subsequent encounter with the cookbook of the renowned, early-20th-century French chef, Fernand Point, instilled a passion for French cooking. Restaurant Hiramatsu has an elegant reception area surrounded by French antiques on the first floor; in the first-floor basement is a gallery that displays many paintings by the chef's brother. There are a bar and private rooms on the second floor, and the main dining room is on the third. The cuisine is traditional French with some contemporary touches. The menu changes with the seasons, and the course at lunchtime changes weekly. There is also a superb wine list with some 750 kinds of French wine.

Closed mid-August, late December-early January, Monday except Bank Holidays, Tuesday lunch and Wednesday lunch

Open:
lunch 12:00-14:30 (L.O.)
dinner 18:00-21:30 (L.O.)

Hirosaku ひろ作

Michelin

Lunch: menu ¥ 5,000-20,000
Dinner: menu ¥ 21,000

TEL 03–3591–0901 / FAX 03–3593–3886
3-6-13 Shinbashi, Minato-ku
4

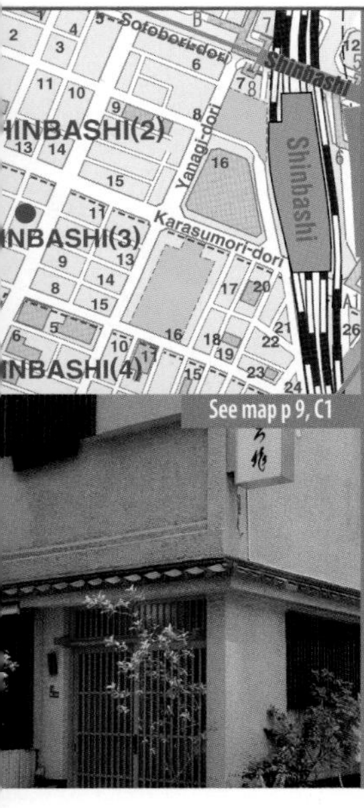

See map p 9, C1

In an old, freestanding house in Shimbashi, a friendly husband and wife team runs this Japanese *kappo* restaurant. The owner apprenticed at a traditional Japanese restaurant in Akasaka during his 20s and, after working at a number of other restaurants, opened his own place in 1973. Hirosaku is a place where one can enjoy food cooked to perfection in simple surroundings. Its distinctive feature is the unparalleled seasonings that draw out the goodness of the ingredients to the utmost degree and take the art of plain style cooking to new heights. The focus of these seasonings is always precisely defined. The *soba* that concludes the meal is perfection; the light buckwheat flour, a blend of flours from Hokkaido and Nagano, has a sheen that makes the noodles seem almost transparent. The dipping sauce made from a high-quality bonito *dashi* is flavorful without being too strong and complements the velvety *soba* which goes down perfectly. This is a restaurant that is at its best during its nighttime operating hours.

Closed mid-August, late December-early January, Saturday, Sunday and Bank Holidays

Open:
lunch 11:45-13:30 (L.O.)
dinner 18:00-20:00 (L.O.)

Hishinuma 菱沼

Michelin

Lunch: menu ¥ 3,927-8,085
Dinner: menu ¥ 13,860-20,790

TEL 03–3568–6588 / FAX 03–3568–6335
Axis Building B1F,
5-17-1 Roppongi, Minato-ku

See map p 10, A4

Having operated for 21 years in Mita, this Japanese restaurant moved to its present location in the basement of the Axis Building in 2005. Hishinuma is a "barrier-free" restaurant in all senses of the word: there is wheelchair access, and the cuisine transcends the usual stylistic boundaries, offering vegetable *kaiseki* as well as snapping turtle and blowfish courses. Making extensive use of fresh seasonal ingredients, it provides a genuine Japanese taste of the four seasons. The owner's aspiration is "to serve society through food," and he has prepared a special course for children that he hopes will encourage them to enjoy food and be conscious of nutrition from a young age. The quiet interior, with its wood floors and indirect lighting, has a contemporary Japanese flavor. The owner himself is fond of wine, so the matching of wines to the Japanese cuisine is imaginative, and the wine selection interesting. From seats at the counter you can watch the staff at work at a long cutting board, a station for rolling out and cutting *soba* noodles, and a charcoal grill.

Closed mid-August, late December-early January, Sunday and Bank Holidays

Open:
lunch 11:30-13:30 (L.O.)
dinner 17:30-22:00 (L.O.)

Ichimonji 一文字

Michelin

Lunch: menu ¥ 9,240-18,480
Dinner: menu ¥ 13,860-23,100

TEL 03–5206–8223 / FAX 03–5206–8227
3-6 Kagurazaka, Shinjuku-ku

See map p 16, D1

Kagurazaka still bears traces of its geisha heyday. Hidden away on a street that runs alongside Zenkokuji temple is Ichimonji, an old-style *kaiseki* restaurant. The owner-chef catered *kaiseki* courses for tea ceremonies for 13 years before opening his own restaurant in Kagurazaka in 2005, and has mastered the tea rituals of several different schools. "Ichimonji" is the name of the narrow strips of cloth used in the horizontal area immediately above and below the calligraphy itself on a hanging scroll, and they play an important role in determining the overall quality of the scroll. After you have removed your shoes in the entranceway, a young employee leads you indoors, where there is a counter built in the *sukiya* style (architectural style based on an aesthetic of naturalness). On the second floor is a graceful, traditional-style Japanese room with an alcove. The fine quality delicacies from the sea and the mountains used in each dish harmonize with the hues and textures of the utensils, and with the season.

Open:
lunch 12:00-14:00 (L.O.)
dinner 18:00-21:00 (L.O.)

Ishikawa 石かわ

Michelin

Dinner: menu ¥ 16,600

TEL 03–5225–0173 / FAX 03–5225–0173
3-4 Kagurazaka, Shinjuku-ku

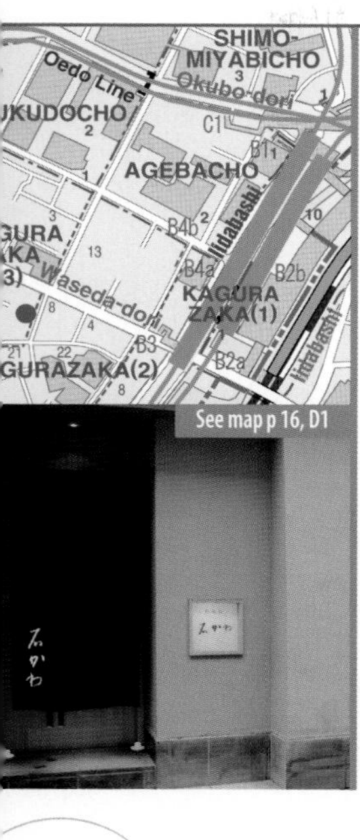

See map p 16, D1

After three years at the above address, the young chef-owner of Ishikawa will transfer his restaurant to 5-37 Kagurazaka late 2007. Note that photos and map describe his old establishment, but the phone number will be the same. In his new location, the owner-chef will prepare exactly the same type of seasonal dishes as before. His menu is a carefully thought-out *omakase* course which carries on the tradition of *kappo*-style cuisine, and delights his regular patrons with an array of pleasant flavours. His choice of ingredients and the tableware in a variety of styles reflect his conscientiousness. A small collection of *sake* and wine complements the food perfectly. The best features of this restaurant are the consistent hospitality and the owner-chef's single-minded enthusiasm for his craft. The counter and private rooms are all designed for a small number of people, and the attention to detail is evident in the attractive and effective use of space.

Closed mid-August, late December-early January, Sunday and Bank Holidays

Open:
dinner 18:00-23:00 L.O.22:00

Joël Robuchon

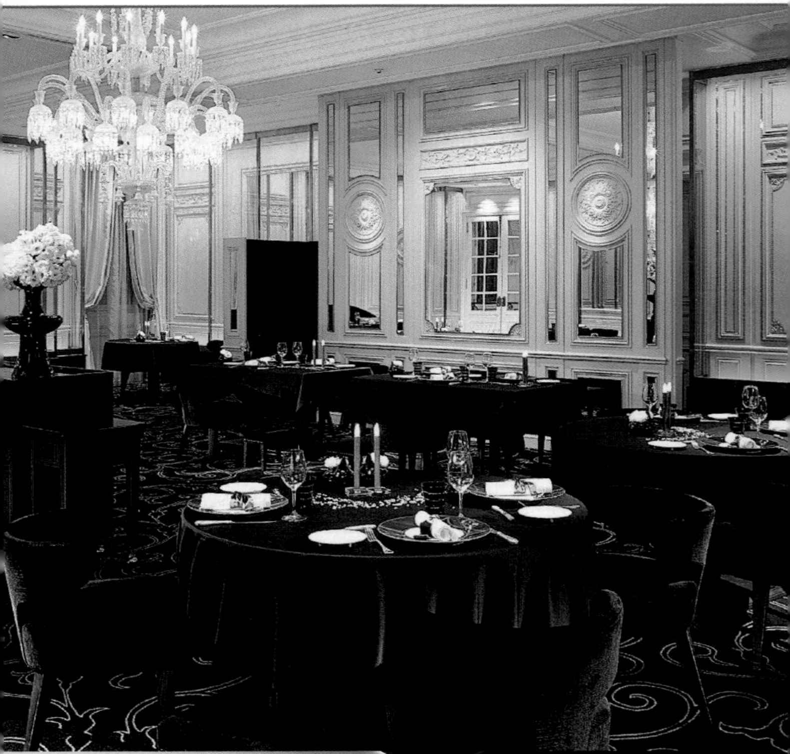

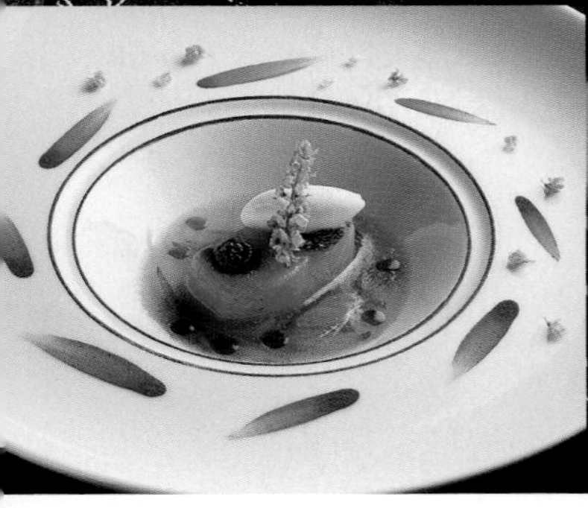

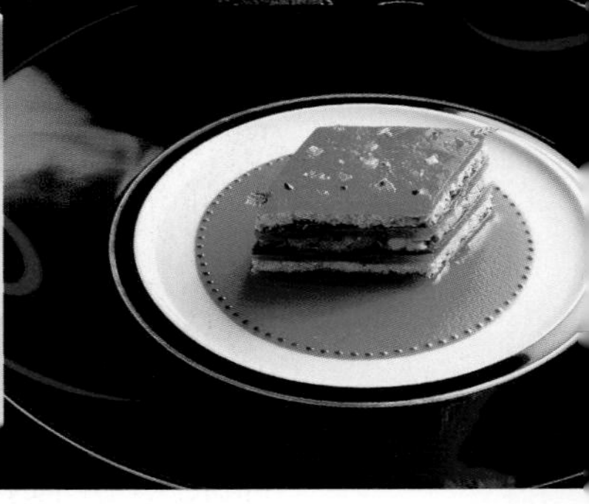

Joël Robuchon

Lunch: menu ¥ 8,960-39,200
carte ¥ 17,600-22,600

Dinner: menu ¥ 24,650-39,200
carte ¥ 17,600-22,600

TEL 03–5424–1347
Yebisu Garden Place,
1-13-1 Mita, Meguro-ku
www.robuchon.jp

30

See map p 7, C2

Open:
lunch 11:30-14:30 (L.O.)
dinner 18:00-22:00 (L.O.)

In the center of Yebizu Garden Place is a three-story replica of an 18th-century French château. The restaurant on the second floor is Joël Robuchon; named after the famous French chef himself. On the first floor is La Table de Joël Robuchon, a simpler version of the same restaurant. In the second-floor dining room, the walls are decorated with Swarovski crystal glass and a Baccarat glass chandelier hangs from the ceiling, allowing guests to enjoy the illusion of dining in an old castle in France. The cuisine has a contemporary taste, and its gorgeous colors are quintessentially French. The menu changes frequently, but the specialties like caviar gelée, millefeuille of tomato and crab and langoustine ravioli with truffle are recommended. There are some 1,200 different vintages on the wine list, an unrivalled attraction for wine lovers. Also a delight is the deft and solicitous service provided by the sommelier, maitre d' and the rest of the staff. On the third floor are beautiful private rooms.

✿✿✿

Kanda 神田

Michelin

Dinner: menu ¥ 11,550-23,100

TEL 03–5786–0150 / FAX 03–5786–0150
3-6-34 Moto-Azabu, Minato-ku

See map p 10, A4

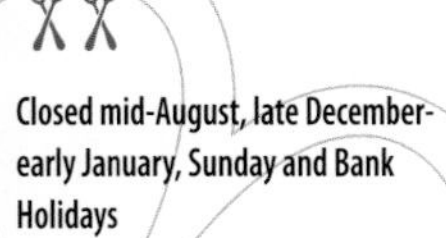

Closed mid-August, late December-early January, Sunday and Bank Holidays

Open:
dinner 18:00-22:30 (L.O.)

The pleasures of sampling Kanda's menu reflect its focus on premium seasonal ingredients—bream and bonito in spring; sweetfish, pike eel, and flounder in early summer; tuna and mackerel in autumn; sole and anglerfish in winter. The vegetables, too, have a sunny intensity in spring and summer and an earthy robustness in winter; and their preparation taps into that vitality. Every dish, while very simply presented, shows evident care. The staff tune in to customers' tastes: conger eel arrives plain-broiled for *sake* drinkers, but comes with a soy-based sauce for those drinking red wine. The closer he feels to the customer, says the owner, the better his creations will please. The out-of-the-way location in the upscale Moto-Azabu neighborhood is not easy to find at first, and the sign is very discreet. The 100-item wine list ranges from relatively inexpensive labels to fine vintages. The cooks lend a lively vibe to the bright, relaxed dining area.

Keyakizaka

Keyakizaka, Grand Hyatt

Lunch: menu ¥ 4,400-8,700
Dinner: menu ¥ 18,500-24,200
carte ¥ 8,500-21,200

TEL 03–4333–8782
Grand Hyatt 6F,
6-10-3 Roppongi, Minato-ku
www.grandhyatttokyo.com

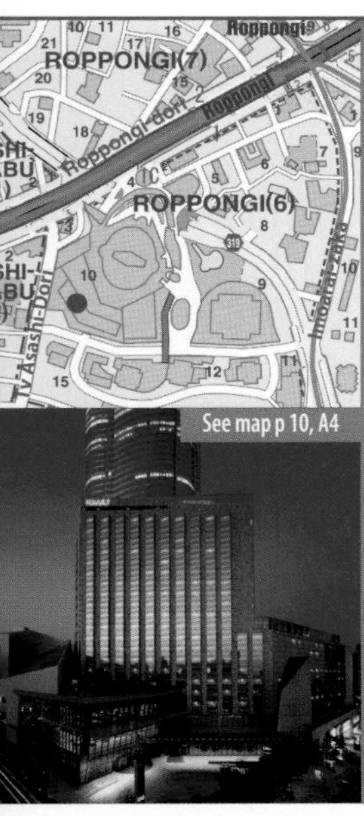

See map p 10, A4

Open:
lunch 11:30-14:30 (L.O.)
dinner 18:00-22:00 (L.O.)

A *teppanyaki* restaurant in Grand Hyatt in the Roppongi Hills complex. The distinguishing feature of this restaurant is its new concept of *teppanyaki*, incorporating the sensibilities of French and Spanish cuisine. On the menu you will see *teppanyaki* standards like seafood and steak, but there is a uniqueness to their preparation. For example, wild sea bass is paired with chorizo, and squid with endive salad, to excellent effect. Another dish features warm foie gras with carmelized figs, and prawns are served in an omelet. The prompt and skillful service is another satisfying aspect of this restaurant. The wine list has a selection of some 500 labels from around the world. The high-ceilinged interior has wood floors and beautifully designed modern lighting. Decorations featuring the *keyaki* (zelkova) tree also contribute to the overall aesthetic. In the center of the open kitchen is a display of seasonal vegetables in a bamboo tub like those traditionally used in the marketplace.

Kikumi きくみ

Michelin

Lunch: menu ¥ 10,080-25,200
Dinner: menu ¥ 25,200-31,500

TEL 03–3583–3600 / FAX 03–3583–3635
1-9-25 Akasaka, Minato-ku
30

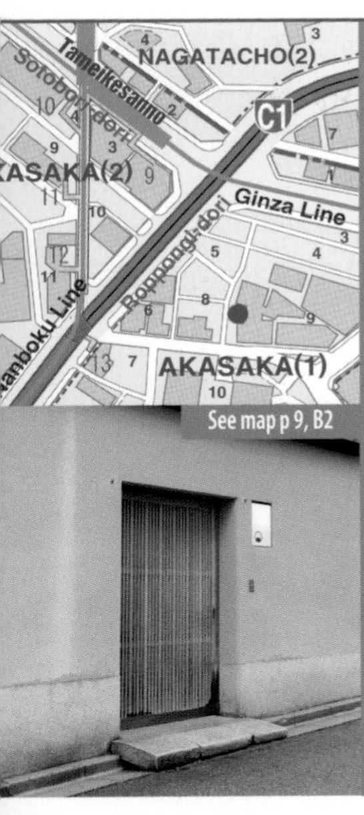

See map p 9, B2

An established traditional Japanese restaurant in Akasaka. The owner is a woman from Fukuoka whose parents ran a restaurant-inn in Hakata. In 1962 they opened Kikumi in Akasaka and put their daughter in charge. The interior is done in a purely Japanese style; there is a large hall on the first floor and four private rooms on the second. The chef, who took up the post in 2003, selects ingredients in Tsukiji to complement each day's reservations. The quality of each dish is superb and gives clear evidence of the chef's solid culinary craftsmanship. The pike eel from Mie Prefecture is a pale amber color; it is cooked and seasoned to perfection. Another dish combines *kuchiko* (dried sea cucumber ovaries) and very fresh squid. Deep green young ginkgo nuts and *samatsu* (early crop *matsutake* mushrooms) have a firm texture and taste. Carefully carved squash and *ishikawaimo* (a kind of potato) combined with *yuba* (*tofu* skin) make for an elegant simmered dish. The menu changes twice a month. Kikumi is a restaurant that avoids faddish innovations and sticks with traditional cuisine.

Closed Golden week, mid-August, late December-early January, Sunday and Bank Holidays

Open:
lunch 12:00-13:00 (L.O.)
dinner 17:30-20:00 (L.O.)

Kikunoi 菊の井

Kikunoi

Dinner: menu ¥ 17,325-23,100

TEL 03–3568–6055 / FAX 03–3568–6056
6-13-8 Akasaka, Minato-ku
www.kikunoi.jp
10

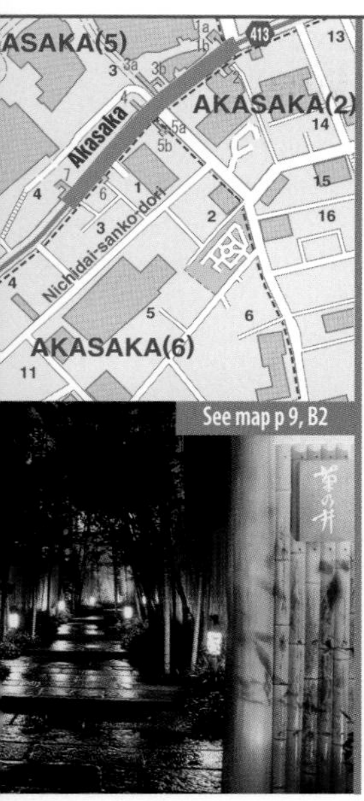

See map p 9, B2

This restaurant, which combines both *ryotei* and *kappo*, is a venerable establishment whose main branch is located next to Kodaiji in Kyoto. The owner's ancestor was a tea-server in the employ of the wife of Toyotomi Hideyoshi, Kitanomandokoro; his descendants began serving *kaiseki* after the Meiji Restoration. The present owner, Yoshihiro Murata, is a third-generation chef; yet while he carries on the family tradition, he is always making changes to his cooking style. He uses ingredients from all over the world to create his own original *kaiseki*, in which a Japanese sense of the seasons is valued above all else. The restaurant is a traditional Japanese-style building; the first floor has a counter from which a small Japanese garden can be seen and another Japanese *tatami* counter. On the second floor are a tea room and Japanese-style rooms. The aim of this restaurantl is to make diners in Tokyo feel as though they were in Kyoto. The owner's dream is to proselytize Japanese cuisine throughout the world. He has held a food fair in Paris and contributes to other international activities.

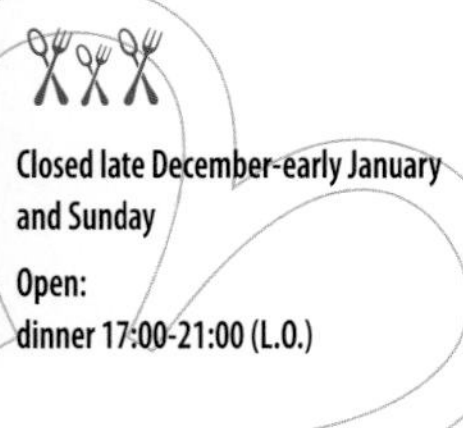

Closed late December-early January and Sunday

Open:
dinner 17:00-21:00 (L.O.)

Kogetsu 湖月

Michelin

Dinner: menu ¥ 15,750

TEL 03–3407–3033
5-50-10 Jingumae, Shibuya-ku

See map p 12, C2

Kogetsu, a restaurant offering Kyoto-style cuisine, is located near the United Nations University. The name was originally given to a restaurant run in Hamburg, Germany in the 1960s by the former owner and its current proprietress. In 1967, they opened Kogetsu at its current location. Up to nine people can be seated at the counter, and there is also a *tatami* area with sunken *kotatsu* at the back. The congenial head chef serves food directly to the diners seated at the counter, while the *kimono*-clad proprietress and her assistant provide table service. Every detail of the menu, from the initial preparation to the finishing touches, is overseen by the head chef. Kogetsu's cuisine makes the most of fresh seasonal ingredients brought in from Kyoto—bamboo shoots in spring, pike eel in summer, and *mizuna-nabe* in winter—and gives diners a sense of the season. The subtle yet profound arrangement of delicacies from the mountains and the sea, and the pleasant interaction between the staff and the diners are distinctive characteristics of this restaurant.

Closed mid-August, late December-early January, Sunday and Bank Holidays

Open:
dinner 18:00-21:30

✿✿✿

Koju 小十

Michelin

Dinner: menu ¥ 15,015-20,790
carte ¥ 9,000-18,000

TEL 03–6215–9544 / FAX 03–6215–9545
8-5-25 Ginza, Chuo-ku
www.kojyu.jp

10

See map p 6, C3

The owner, Toru Okuda, apprenticed at a famous restaurant in Tokushima and he achieved his heart's desire in 2003 when he opened this place in Ginza. The name Koju was given by the late Nishioka Koju, a potter who had been a close friend of the owner. "I want you to sense the energy that good quality ingredients have," says the owner, whose culinary creed is "natural." This is refined cuisine; each and every dish uses the best natural ingredients. He is so fussy about ensuring freshness that he even tells the dealers where to place the ice during transit. One specialty is a dish of prawns and summer vegetables. Eel is delicious either broiled plain or roasted with sugared soy sauce. Crabs from Kobe and Tottori are charcoal grilled and eaten with a sauce made from crab butter and boiled *sake*. This is Japanese cuisine made with a contemporary sensibility but based on traditional techniques. Another attraction is the selection of wines and Japanese *sake* made by the owner, who is both a qualified sommelier and a *sake* connoisseur.

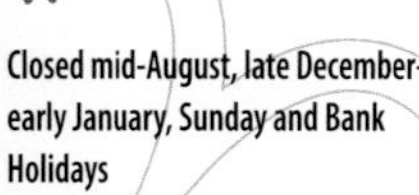

Closed mid-August, late December-early January, Sunday and Bank Holidays

Open:
dinner 17:30-2:00 L.O.1:00 (Saturday 17:30-24:00 L.O.21:30)

Komuro 小室

Michelin

Lunch: menu ¥ 6,930-13,860
Dinner: menu ¥ 13,860-34,650

TEL 03–3235–3332 / FAX 03–3235–3338
13 Wakamiyacho, Shinjuku-ku

4

See map p 16, D1

Closed mid-August, 21 December-16 January, Sunday, Monday lunch and Bank Holidays

Open:
lunch 12:00-13:00 (L.O.)
dinner 18:30-20:00 (L.O.)

After years of training in a famous restaurant in Mejiro, the owner of the Japanese *kaiseki* restaurant Komuro opened for business in Kagurazaka in 2000. When you enter the restaurant, which has only an eight-seat counter and a single private room, you are gently greeted by wife of the owner. In the kitchen, the owner divides cooking duties between four members of staff. The restaurant's philosophy is to use the best ingredients to provide delicious food through which guests can savor the changing seasons. But flavor is not everything, the owner says. "A pleasant atmosphere, beautiful tableware, and *sake* that can further bring out the essence of the food are also important elements." Conger eel from Akashi is now difficult to obtain, but its smooth flavor, refined aroma, and pleasant aftertaste are a treat. In autumn come the earliest shipments of *matsutake* mushrooms from Yamaguchi, Shimane and Tamba. The owner, a large and good-natured man, is all smiles whenever the conversation comes to food.

Kondo 近藤

Michelin

Lunch: menu ¥ 5,250-7,350
Dinner: menu ¥ 8,400-15,750

TEL 03–5568–0923
Sakaguchi Building 9F,
5-5-13 Ginza, Chuo-ku

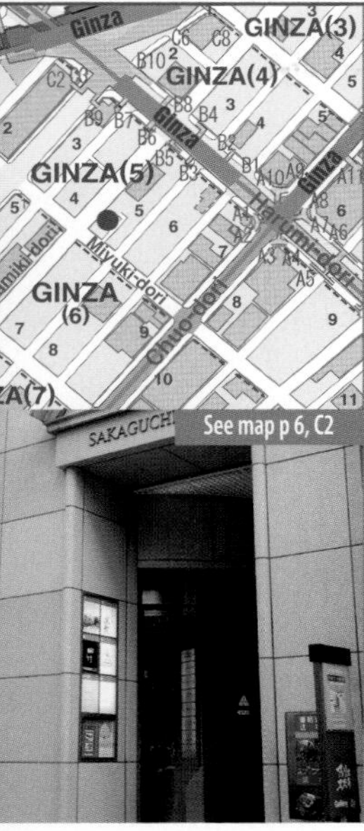

See map p 6, C2

In order to provide his many customers with vegetables that are in season and the freshest ingredients, a chef will go to the growing areas and buy only those that meet his standards. The owner of the *tempura* restaurant Kondo is a chef who does just that. He is especially well known for the quality of his vegetables. He sprinkles the vegetables lightly in batter, then fries them with a craftsman's skill using his own original sesame oil to bring out the natural flavors to perfection. The ingredients are kept on ice instead of in a refrigerator to produce the freshest possible taste. The interior—a plain wood counter and two bright, chic rooms—goes well with the ambiance of the elegant Ginza building in which the restaurant is located. On the walls are paintings by the author and well-known gourmet Ikenami Shotaro, who especially loved this part of town.

Closed Golden week, mid-August, late December-early January, Sunday and Bank Holiday Mondays

Open:
lunch 12:00-15:00 L.O.13:30
dinner 17:00-22:30 L.O.20:30

Kosetsu 古拙

Michelin

Lunch: menu ¥ 5,500
carte ¥ 1,050-1,680
Dinner: menu ¥ 11,000

TEL 03–3543–6565 / FAX 03–3543–6565
Toni Building 2F,
2-13-6 Ginza, Chuo-ku

See map p 6, D2

Located off Showa-dori, Kosetsu can be recommended to anyone who wishes to relax and enjoy *soba* in quiet surroundings. Since its opening in 2005, it has become known and loved as a restaurant that uses *soba* to express the essence of Japanese cuisine. A typical five-course meal might include a *soba* dish composed of abalone and seaweed, followed by *soba sushi*, a *soba* hotpot with eel and egg, fried *soba* and crab dressed with vegetables prepared in cornstarch, and a *soba* rollcake for dessert—a culinary experience both highly original and intensely flavorful. Only fish and vegetables that complement the taste of the *soba* are used. The owner prefers to use vegetables from Tochigi and Kyoto and orders lots of mountain vegetables from Akita when they are in season. But the undisputed star here is the *soba*. "*Soba* is a difficult dish to prepare," the owner says. "Whatever mood you are in that day immediately comes out in the texture." He studied *soba* on his own after working in various restaurants, including one that specialized in eel. The *soba* kaiseki at lunch is good value.

Closed mid-August, late December-early January and Sunday

Open:
lunch 11:30-14:00 L.O.13:30
dinner 18:00-22:30 L.O.20:30

Kyubey 久兵衛

Kyubey, Michelin

Lunch: menu ¥ 6,300-24,150
Dinner: menu ¥ 11,550-34,650

TEL 03–3571–6523 / FAX 03–3571–6552
8-7-6 Ginza, Chuo-ku
www.kyubey.jp
24

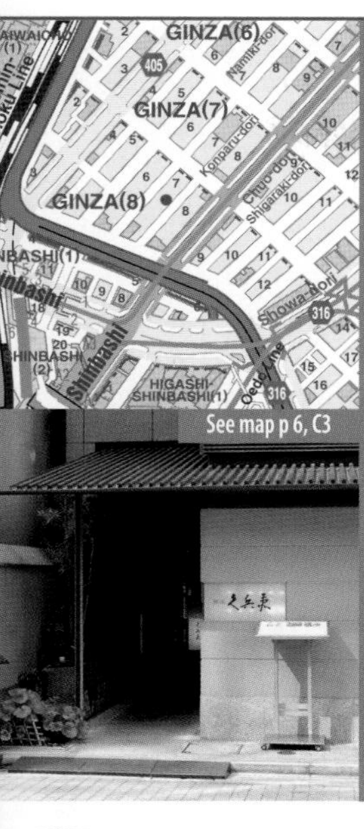

See map p 6, C3

This *sushi* restaurant was founded in 1935, and the present (second-generation) owner-chef has worked at the restaurant since 1964, the year of the Tokyo Olympics. It has been at its present location since 1993. Kyubey is famous for having been frequented by Kitaoji Rosanjin, the famous potter, and the Kitaoji Rosanjin Gallery on the fourth floor of the building is testimony to the friendship between the original master and Rosanjin. The building itself won a prize for excellence in the Tokyo Architecture Awards, and though the exterior is contemporary, the interior is traditional. Kyubey is well known for the freshness of the ingredients used in its *sushi*. It is also said that this restaurant was the first to use ingredients such as salmon roe and sea urchin for *sushi*. There are several different types of dining rooms, and depending on the number of your party you may be able to use a private room. The name Kyubey comes from the nickname of the original master.

Closed mid-August, late December-early January, Sunday and Bank Holidays

Open:
lunch 11:30-13:45 (L.O.)
dinner 17:00-21:30(L.O.)

JAPANESE CONTEMPORARY 

La Bombance

Michelin

Dinner: menu ¥ 11,000

TEL 03–5778–6511 / FAX 03–5778–6511
B1F,
2-25-24 Nishi-Azabu, Minato-ku
www.bombance.com

See map p 9, A2

Located in the first-floor basement of a condominium slightly past the Nishi Azabu crossing on the right heading toward Shibuya. The interior is cozy, consisting only of a counter and a table, but the light gently filtering through the wooden lattices gives it a modern feel. Serious thought has been given not just to the interior but to comfort. After apprenticing for four years at Fukudaya in Kioicho, the chef opened this restaurant in 2004 with the idea of providing food not found elsewhere. Though the underlying style is Japanese, the cuisine incorporates a variety of ingredients like foie gras, Iberian pork and mozzarella cheese and defies simple categorization as French, Italian etc. The menu is a set course that changes monthly. The price is kept down and the portions are more than adequate. The restaurant's name actually means "feasting" in French.

Closed mid-August, late December-early January, Sunday and Bank Holidays

Open:
dinner 18:00-22:00 (L.O.)

La Cave Hiramatsu

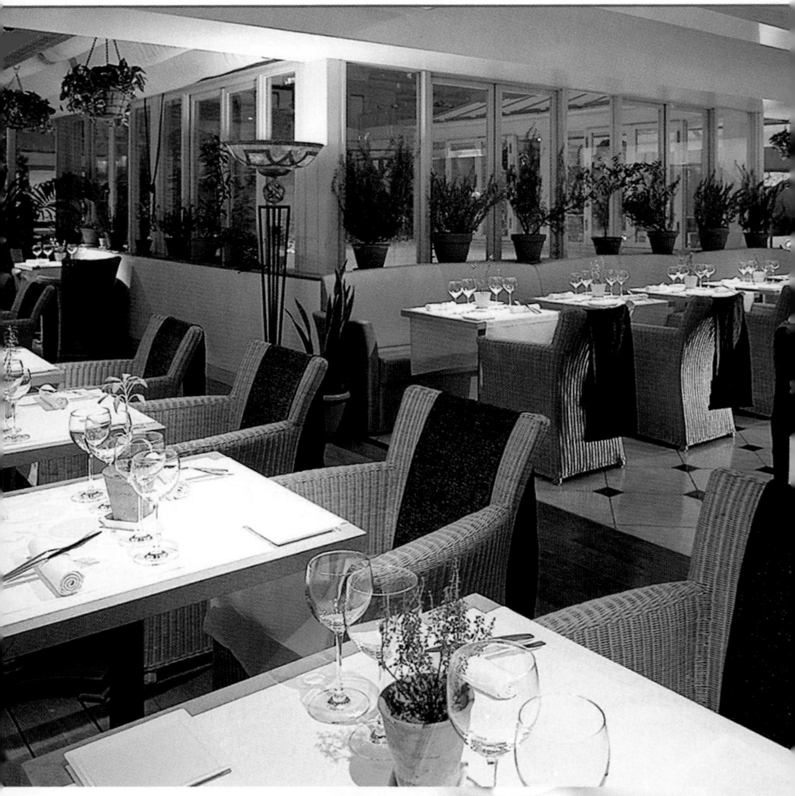

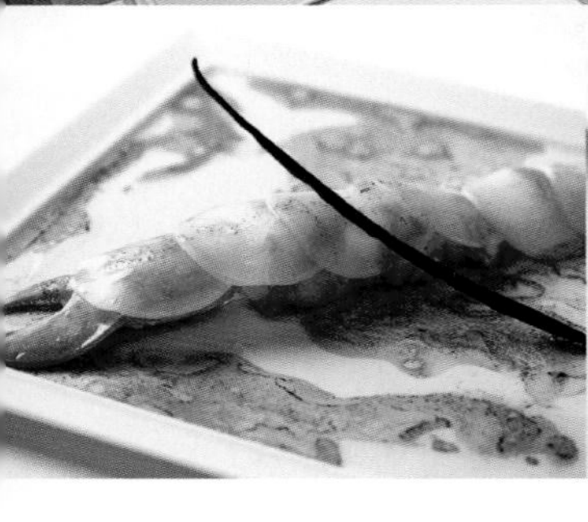

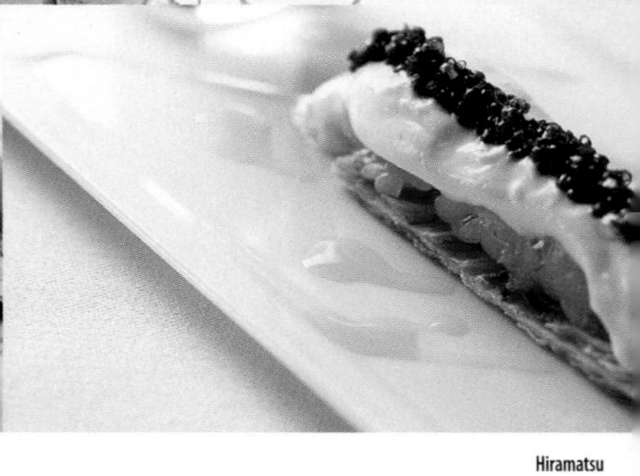

Hiramatsu

Dinner: menu ¥ 7,700
carte ¥ 7,000-10,000

TEL 03–5766–6880 / FAX 03–5766–6882
4-3-7 Nishi-Azabu, Minato-ku
www.hiramatsu.co.jp

80

See map p 9, A2

Closed 1-3 January and Monday except Bank Holidays

Open:
dinner 18:00-23:00 (L.O.)

Next to the site in Nishi Azabu where Restaurant Hiramatsu first opened; one of Hiramatsu Hiroyuki's favorite students now serves as chef. It used to be mainly for weddings, but in June 2007, it underwent a complete change of style based on a brand new concept. First, the cuisine changed from contemporary to classic French. The menu includes such traditional dishes as terrine of beef cheek and tongue topped with jelly, a selection of charcuterie, rabbit rillettes, foie gras ravioli, seafood bouillabaisse, Challans duck feuilleté in a juniper berry flavored red wine sauce, a selection of cheese from Alléosse in Paris, Grand Marnier soufflé and rum savarin. The wine list has also changed; carefully selected bottles and glasses of wine are offered at reasonable prices so it is now possible to relax and enjoy one's wine as if at a wine bar. The stylish, modern four-story building has a reception area, two private rooms and the bar on the second floor, and the main dining room on the third.

L'Alliance

L'Alliance

Lunch: menu ¥ 3,900-10,000
Dinner: menu ¥ 9,350-16,500
carte ¥ 9,000-20,000

TEL 03–3269–0007 / FAX 03–3269–0242
2-11 Kagurazaka, Shinjuku-ku
www.lalliance.jp

20

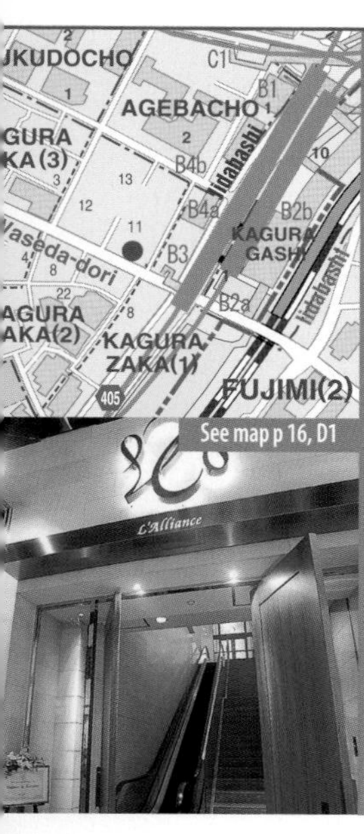

See map p 16, D1

Closed 31December-4 January, Saturday, Sunday and Bank Holidays

Open:
lunch 11:30-15:00 L.0.14:00
dinner 18:00-22:00 L.0.21:00

A French restaurant that opened in Kagurazaka in 2003. The chef, experienced in a variety of French regional cuisines, provides a new style of French cooking attuned both to the seasons and to the incorporation of Japanese ingredients. Fish is prepared in a manner that brings out the best of its natural flavor, and sauces and garnishes emphasize the sense of the seasons. Sometimes the restaurant uses light Japanese flavorings such as stock made from *kombu* seaweed, and expresses the beauty of Japanese cooking in a French context. A specialty of the house is a dome of foie gras slow-cooked after being marinated for an entire day, served in a brioche baked on the premises, and set off with a 20-year-old balsamic vinegar. The roast rack of lamb is cooked in a southern French style with a tapenade. The food is enhanced by a stellar selection of wines, including old vintages going back as far as 1918. The spacious interior, a renovated disco, is a melding of Asian and European styles, and the high ceiling gives an open-air feeling. We recommend this restaurant as a dinner venue.

L'Anneau d'Or

Michelin

Lunch: menu ¥ 4,200-26,250
Dinner: menu ¥ 7,700-27,500

TEL 03–5919–0141 / FAX 03–5919–0152
Yotsuya Sun Heights B1F,
4-6-1 Yotsuya, Shinjuku-ku

See map p 16, C3

This French restaurant overflows with the warmth of the inseparable husband-and-wife team that runs it. The owner-chef, trained in several famous restaurants in Japan and in Europe, opened this restaurant in 2005 after fourteen years at Chez Tani in Shimokitazawa. "The most important thing with cooking is the aroma. If the aroma is good the food will naturally taste good as well," says the chef, who brings in fresh seasonal ingredients from all over the country and creates from them a cuisine that is richly flavorful but not overly heavy. A specialty of the house is a meticulously prepared poached egg in a lovely ceramic cup with a sauce of truffles and foie gras. Quality wines are available at reasonable prices. "At our place our guests are always number one," says the chef's wife, and her skill and care as a hostess bears that out.

Closed late December-early January and Wednesday

Open:
lunch 12:30-15:00 L.O.13:30
dinner 18:30-22:30 L.O.20:30

La Primula

Michelin

Lunch: menu ¥ 3,850-6,050

Dinner: menu ¥ 9,240-11,550

TEL 03–5439–9470 / FAX 03–5439–9469
3F,
2-8-10 Azabu-Juban, Minato-ku

See map p 10, A4

La Primula's chef spent three years training in various regions of Italy, including Emilia-Romagna, Lombardy, and Piedmont. He named La Primula ("primrose") after the restaurant in Friuli where he ended his Italian sojourn. In April 2007, La Primula moved to Azabu Juban from its former address in Moto Azabu. The entrance features an eye-catching Venetian lamp. Modern Italian food is offered in two fixed price menus only. Among the signature Friulian fare is *cjalçons*, pasta envelopes filled with potato purée, cinnamon, mint, and raisins, topped with Parmesan. Another winner is the goulash, paprika-stewed beef cheeks served with polenta. Flavors are enhanced by Italian techniques such as charcoal grilling, or seasoning that leaves a lingering scent of lemon and olives. The two menus, each consisting of an *amuse-bouche*, two antipasti, pasta, fish and meat courses, and dessert, offer variety and ample quantity.

Closed late December-early January, Sunday and third Monday

Open:

lunch 12:00-15:00 L.O.13:30

dinner 18:00-23:00 L.O.21:30

FRENCH CONTEMPORARY ✿

La Table de Joël Robuchon

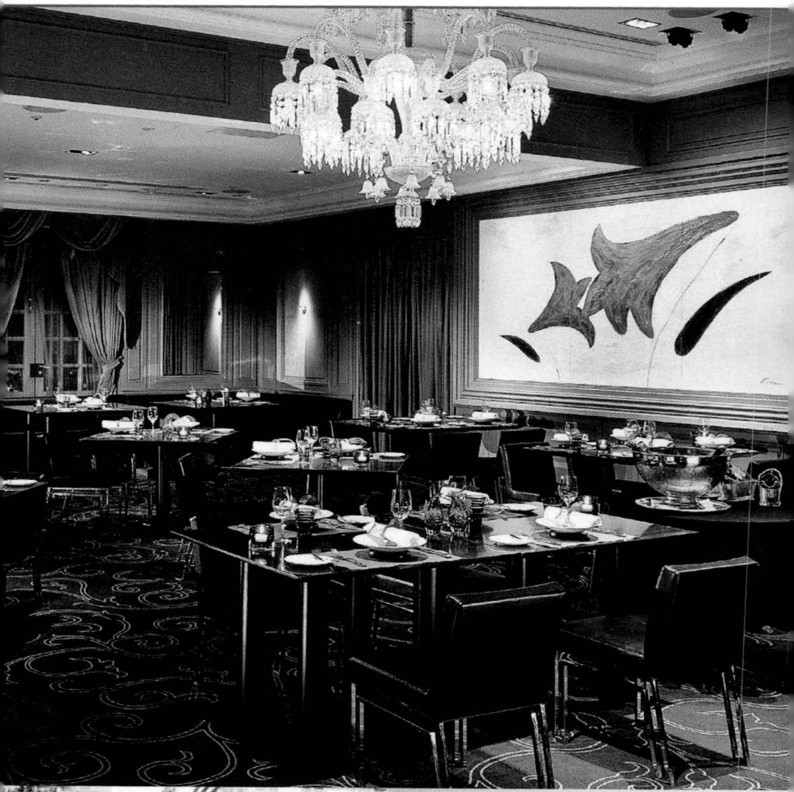

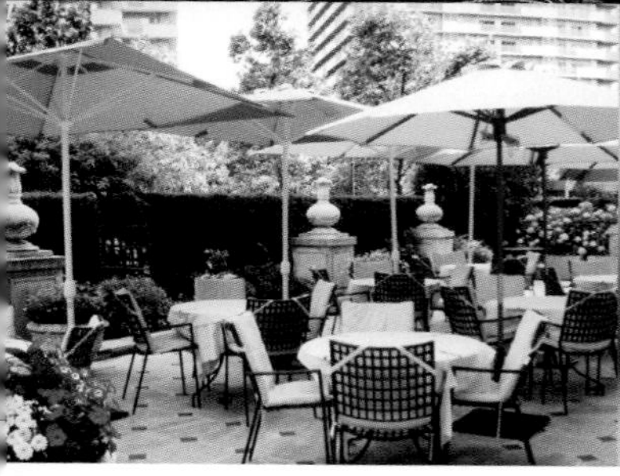

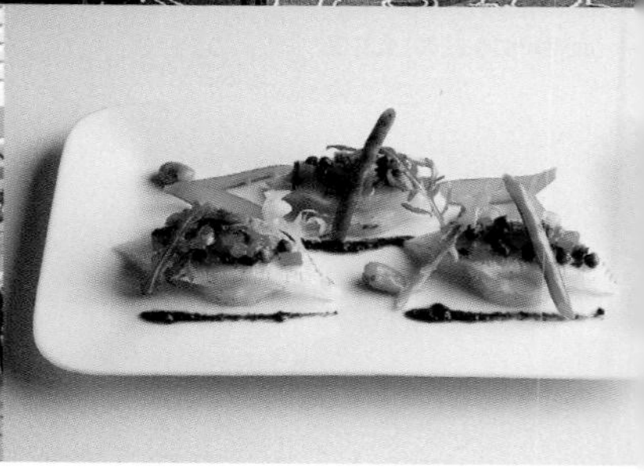

La Table de Joël Robuchon, Michelin

Lunch: menu ¥ 4,070-5,500
carte ¥ 8,000-15,000

Dinner: menu ¥ 6,600-13,200
carte ¥ 8,000-15,000

TEL 03–5424–1338 / FAX 03–5424–1339
Yebisu Garden Place,
1-13-1 Mita, Meguro-ku
www.robuchon.jp

See map p 7, C2

Open:
lunch 11:30-14:30 (L.O.)
dinner 18:00-22:00 (L.O.)

Joël Robuchon likes to use the word *convivialité* to describe the concept of his first-floor restaurant, housed in a replica 18th-century French château in the midst of Yebisu Garden Place. The ambience in the main dining area—with its violet walls dressed with modern art, its large chandelier of Baccarat glass, and its contemporary furniture—does indeed encourage guests to relax and enjoy. La Table's modern French cuisine is solidly grounded in the 21st century, as Robuchon mingles French, Spanish, Italian and Japanese influences in his original recipes. The set courses are very reasonably priced. The sommelier will advise on a good selection of wines by the glass; about 100 labels are also available by the bottle. After dining, you might like to retire to the elegant yet friendly second-floor bar or head off for some shopping in the boutique downstairs. In summer, a pleasant terrace seating set with greenery is available.

FRENCH CONTEMPORARY 

L'Atelier de Joël Robuchon

L'Atelier de Joël Robuchon

Lunch: menu ¥ 4,350-6,950
carte ¥ 8,300-13,700

Dinner: menu ¥ 6,950-13,860
carte ¥ 8,300-13,700

TEL 03–5772–7500 / FAX 03–5772–7789
Roppongi Hills Hillside 2F,
6-10-1 Roppongi, Minato-ku
www.robuchon.jp

See map p 10, A4

L'ATELIER de Joël Robuchon

Open:
lunch 11:30-14:00 (L.O.)
dinner 18:00-22:00 (L.O.)

Joël Robuchon, the famous French chef has created this new restaurant concept in 2003 in Tokyo. Although restaurants bearing his name can now be found in international cities throughout the world. L'Atelier de Joël Robuchon has a striking red and black interior, and a wide counter that seats 44. In the open kitchen one can see the many chefs hard at work preparing cuisine that fuses the culinary cultures of France, Spain and Japan. From France there is foie gras, asparagus and poultry; there's Iberian ham from Spain; and fish, fruits and vegetables from Japan. In every case only the finest ingredients are used in the fixed price menu, which changes with the seasons. There is also a menu entitled "Petites portions dégustations" that allows one to sample several dishes prepared from original recipes. Another specialty of this restaurant might be said to be its wine selection with labels from all over the world. There is also a bakery and a boutique; the items for which were all selected by Joël Robuchon himself.

La Tour d'Argent

La Tour d'Argent

Dinner: menu ¥ 23,000-32,000
carte ¥ 15,000-24,000

TEL 03–3239–3111 / FAX 03–3221–2874
New Otani Hotel,
4-1 Kioicho, Chiyoda-ku
www.newotani.co.jp

30

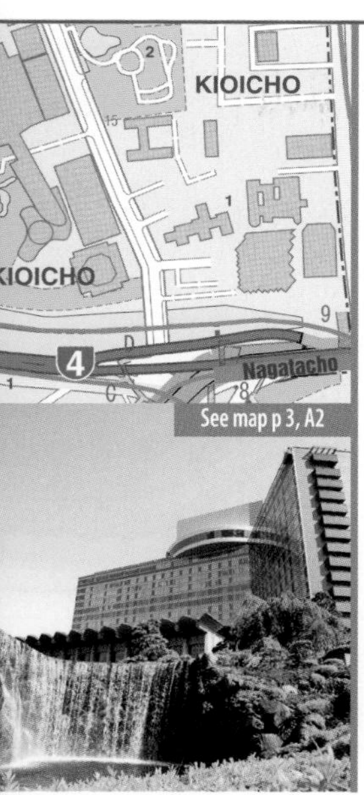

See map p 3, A2

Opened in 1984 in the Hotel New Otani, La Tour D'Argent Tokyo is the sister restaurant of La Tour D'Argent, the high-class Parisian restaurant founded in 1582. After you have viewed the portrait of Henri IV astride his steed and the antique collection in the blue-carpeted entrance hall, make your way to the dining salon, where you are greeted by splendid décor reminiscent of La Tour D'Argent in Paris. The spacious, oval room is redolent of luxury at every turn — with large chandeliers, opulent oak-panelled walls, Louis XV furniture, and elegant, understated curtains. While the cuisine bears a close resemblance to that served in La Tour D'Argent in Paris, it has original flourishes. The signature dish is duckling that is flown in directly from the Vendée, in France. Diners who select this dish receive a certificate which gives the number of the duckling consumed as a memento. Around 600 bins, most of which are French, are offered in the extensive wine list. La Tour D'Argent Tokyo is the place for special occasions, one of the most elegant dining room in Tokyo.

Closed Monday

Open:
dinner 17:30-22:30 L.O.21:00

La Tourelle

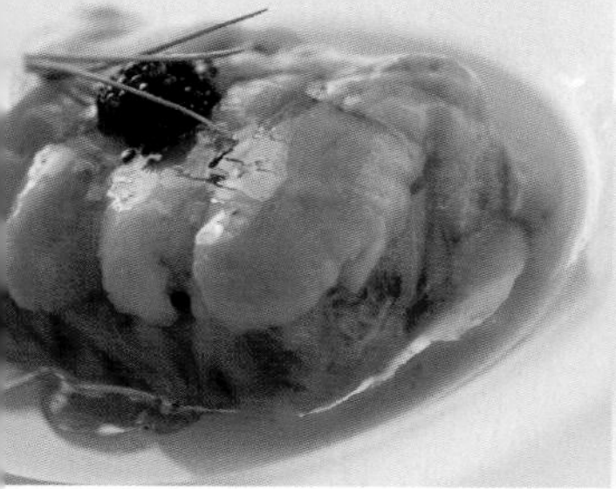

Michelin

Lunch: menu ¥ 2,730-6,700
Dinner: menu ¥ 9,000-15,400
carte ¥ 12,000-17,000

TEL 03–3267–2120 / FAX 03–3267–2120
6-8 Kagurazaka, Shinjuku-ku
www.tourelle.jp

See map p 16, D1

A French restaurant located on a residential sidestreet off Kagurazaka. You'll see a tricolor flag, and then climb a staircase lined with potted plants to reach an interior that, with its beamed ceiling and wood floor, has the look of a classic French restaurant. The owner and the chef worked together before at La Tour d'Argent in Tokyo. The values they share with regard to food are a great strength of this restaurant. The chef carefully selects his seafood and vegetables from trusted suppliers. The result is colorful, well-harmonized French cooking using traditional techniques rather than making a display of his originality, and because of this, the genuine flavor of the ingredients can be savored. The chef says the basics of cooking all come down to one thing: "Does it taste good, or not?" The restaurant also has a good reputation for value, given the unstinting use of top-quality ingredients – and the set courses are a particular bargain. The service is bright and attentive.

Closed mid-August, late December-early January, Monday and 1st and 3rd Tuesday

Open:
lunch 11:30-14:30 L.O.13:30
dinner 18:00-22:00 L.O.20:30

FRENCH CONTEMPORARY 

Le Jeu de l'Assiette

Michelin

Lunch: menu ¥3,850-6,050
Dinner: menu ¥8,800-13,200
carte ¥9,100-11,000

TEL 03–6415–5100 / FAX 03–6415–5101
Sun Village Daikanyama 2F,
2-17-5 Ebisu-Nishi, Shibuya-ku
www.lejeudelassiette.com

See map p 12, C3

A French restaurant midway between Daikanyama and Ebisu stations, opened in 2007. Its young chef trained in restaurants in Japan and France, and offers a fresh and lively take on French cuisine. His philosophy is to bring out the natural flavor and aroma of the ingredients, with nothing unessential added. Sea perch, grouper, sea urchins, tilefish, and other seafood come directly from the chef's hometown of Hagi in Yamaguchi Prefecture; squab and Charente duck from France. The specialty of the house is foie gras wrapped in citron-infused rabbit. Another excellent offering is a colorful marriage of goose breast with fresh beets. The extensive wine list runs to some 200 bins, at reasonable prices. The wide selection of inexpensive champagnes is particularly pleasing. The table arrangements and settings are lovely, and a Venetian glass chandelier illumines the interior.

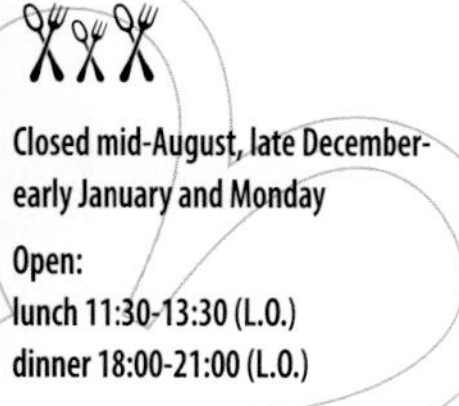

Closed mid-August, late December-early January and Monday

Open:
lunch 11:30-13:30 (L.O.)
dinner 18:00-21:00 (L.O.)

Le Mange-Tout

Michelin

Dinner: menu ¥ 13,860

TEL 03–3268–5911 / FAX 03–3268–5911
22 Nandomachi, Shinjuku-ku
www.le-mange-tout.com

See map p 16, C2

This French restaurant opened in 1994 in a townhouse, and was renovated for a grand reopening in 2006. The interior, decorated in a simple and clean modern Italian style, has an open kitchen on the ground floor and a fourteen-seat dining room on the second. The chef speaks of wanting to pass these techniques on to the next generation of chefs. He has a deep love of the ingredients and materials of cooking. The chef is particularly fussy when it comes to truffles and foie gras, ingredients symbolic of French cuisine. Add to this his extraordinary skill with terrines, and you know you will be able to savor some of the finest foie gras available. From Alpes' lakes comes the omble chevalier, a fish resembling the Japanese iwana or the char, which is lightly smoked and given a medium-rare quality. Escoffier's famous Peach Melba makes splendid use of juicy fresh peaches beautifully matched with vanilla ice cream and a raspberry sauce.

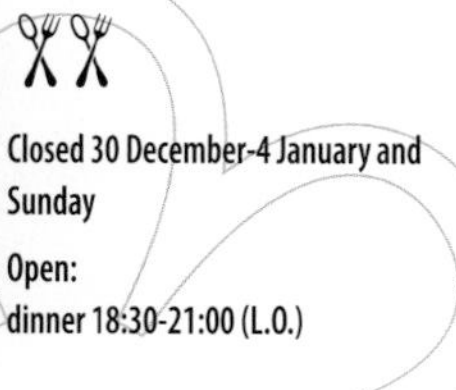

Closed 30 December-4 January and Sunday

Open:
dinner 18:30-21:00 (L.O.)

FRENCH CONTEMPORARY 

L'Embellir

Michelin

Lunch: menu ¥ 4,850-7,500
carte ¥ 10,000-20,000

Dinner: menu ¥ 17,325
carte ¥ 10,000-20,000

TEL 03–3423–0131
B1F,
4-17-33 Minami-Aoyama, Minato-ku
www.lembellir.com

See map p 9, A2

This French restaurant in Minami Aoyama has a modern interior. In keeping with the theme of "beauty and health," they have a way with organic vegetables. At the Tsukiji market, the chef sources fragrant produce from Ibaraki, Gunma, Tochigi, and Yamanashi. His *légumes en terrine* combines 14 to 17 different kinds of vegetable, each with its own light seasoning. Among the seafood dishes, a whole horse crab from the Sea of Okhotsk makes a fresh, delicately flavored hors d'oeuvre, in which carefully shelled crabmeat is prepared salad-style, with crab butter and paprika, and garnished with tiny, moist grapefruit tartlets. In spring and summer, milk-fed Hokkaido lamb is roasted and the jus is accented with, among other things, a homemade coffee liqueur. Winter offerings include *suppon* (soft-shelled turtle) consommé, and baby squid stuffed with scallop mousse and pig's trotter meat. The food is not too heavy, and its hallmarks are tempting aromas, refined flavors, and creative seasoning. Some of the à la carte dishes are available in half portions.

Closed mid-August, late December-early January and Sunday

Open:
lunch 11:30-14:00 (L.O.)
dinner 18:00-21:30 (L.O.)

FRENCH CONTEMPORARY 

Les Créations de Narisawa

Les Créations de Narisawa

Lunch: menu ¥ 5,200-8,100
carte ¥ 13,000-16,000

Dinner: menu ¥ 17,350-28,900
carte ¥ 13,000-16,000

TEL 03–5785–0799
2-6-15 Minami-Aoyama, Minato-ku
www.narisawa-yoshihiro.com

See map p 9, A1

This French restaurant opened in 2003; and is located in Minami Aoyam, behind the Sony Computer Entertainment building. Its logo is a honeybee because the image of the hard-working bee flying in search of the blessings of nature reflects the spirit of the owner chef, Narisawa Yoshihiro. Inside, the white walls, the chic, elegant flooring and the contemporary furniture are coordinated to brilliant effect. The chef owns a vegetable garden at Mochizuki in Shinshu and uses the vegetables grown there, in addition to the organic vegetables brought in directly from a farm in Nagano Prefecture. The fixed price menu changes daily depending on the produce received. The cuisine is based on French recipes and is arranged with contemporary flair, expressive of the chef's creative sense. House specialties include the pairing of foie gras with strawberries, lobster roasted with vanilla and tomato, lamb prepared with lavender, and chocolate fondant and rosewater sherbet; novel combinations which have won the chef many fans.

Closed Golden week, 1 week in October, 31 December-5 January, Sunday and 1st and 3rd Monday

Open:
lunch 12:00-13:30 (L.O.)
dinner 18:30-21:00 (L.O.)

FRENCH 

Les Enfants Gâtés

Michelin

Lunch: menu ¥ 3,465-6,350
carte ¥ 6,000-11,000

Dinner: menu ¥ 7,510-11,550
carte ¥ 6,000-11,000

TEL 03–3476–2929 / FAX 03–3476–2928
2-3 Sarugakucho, Shibuya-ku
www.club-nyx.com

See map p 12, C3

Every day the chef prepares eight kinds of original terrines. The simple country-style terrine is allowed to age for more than two weeks to seal in the flavor of the meat. Organic vegetables from Fukuoka Prefecture are used in the soup. Fish is shipped directly from Tsukune Bay in Kagoshima. Sea bass à la nage is sautéed with its skin on until fragrant, then bathed in a stock made from clam bouillon seasoned with tomatoes and basil, and garnished with burdock. The house specialties are winter game dishes and include such old favorites as *lièvre* (hare) *à la royale, colvert* (mallard), and *perdreau* (young partridge). In each case, contemporary techniques have been applied to traditional recipes. The bar at the entrance is decorated in a mid-20th century style, while the dining room evokes the Art Deco era of 1915-1935, and the two rooms are partitioned by black and white stained glass. The restaurant gets its name from a Parisian café that the chef used to frequent while he was gaining experience at famous restaurants in France.

Closed late December-early January and Monday

Open:
lunch 12:00-14:00 (L.O.)
dinner 18:00-21:30 (L.O.)

Le 6ème Sens

Le 6ème Sens

Lunch: menu ¥ 4,500-10,000
carte ¥ 11,500-17,000

Dinner: menu ¥ 12,000-18,000
carte ¥ 11,500-17,000

TEL 03–3575–2767 / FAX 03–3289–5937
6-2-10 Ginza, Chuo-ku
www.6eme.com

12

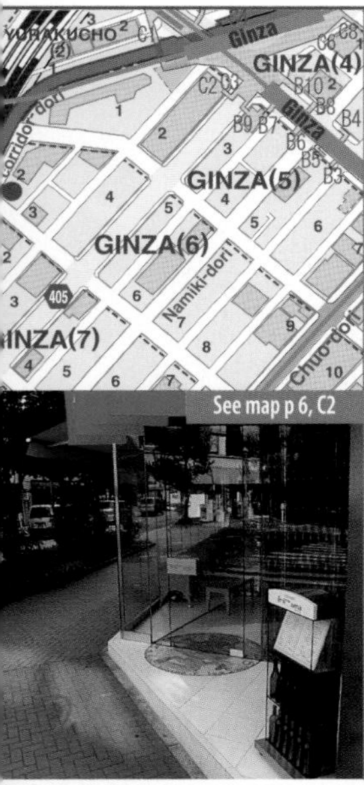

See map p 6, C2

Closed mid-August, late December-early January, Sunday and Bank Holidays

Open:
lunch 12:00-14:00 (L.O.)
dinner 18:00-21:00 (L.O.)

A small dining room café serving casual food occupies the first part of this French restaurant hidden behind a nice and original wine bottles wall. In the main dining room are tables from Bali, a fireplace hand-made by an Italian craftsman, a Bizen-ware floor, and feather-covered lighting fixtures. The mosaic at the entrance depicts the goddess Oeno, a follower of the wine god Bacchus in Roman mythology. In the basement is a private room with a chef's table. There is also a glass-panelled wine cellar housing 10,000 bottles of wine and representing nearly 350 vintages. The cuisine is produced by Dominique Corby, who was once the chef at La Tour D'Argent in Tokyo, and its theme is classic modern. Japanese ingredients are skillfully used together with those found only in France, and the presentation is painstakingly perfect. House specialties include a caviar pyramid, lobster sabayon, duck and, for dessert, soufflé. The fixed price menu changes monthly.

Les Saisons

Les Saisons, Imperial Hotel

Lunch: menu ¥ 7,510-8,670
carte ¥ 13,000-28,000

Dinner: menu ¥ 18,500-28,900
carte ¥ 13,000-28,000

TEL 03–3539–8087 / FAX 03–3581–9146
Imperial Hotel-Main building,
1-1-1 Uchisaiwaicho, Chiyoda-ku
www.imperialhotel.co.jp

16

See map p 4, C3

A French restaurant in the Imperial Hotel. Located on the second-floor mezzanine immediately above the main lobby, Les Saisons might be called the Imperial's star restaurant. The interior was completely redesigned by Francois Le Grix in 2005 in a "classical modern" style that fuses the gravity of tradition with contemporary elegance. The spacious and comfortable dining room, with its warm-toned lighting, is carpeted in beige and furnished with big tables and velvet armchairs. There are four private rooms plus a cigar salon. The large staff of first-class cooks working in the main dining room is supervised by a head chef from Reims, the principal city of the Champagne region. The well-prepared, delectable food is in the traditional French style but is also infused with a modern sensibility. The menu changes every two months. The lunch course can be enjoyed relatively inexpensively. The wine list is outstanding, containing some 700 bins from France and other nations in the world.

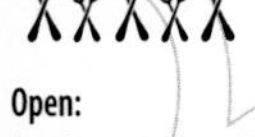

Open:
lunch 11:30-14:30 (L.O.)
dinner 17:30-22:00 (L.O.)

L'Osier

L'Osier

Lunch: menu ¥ 6,720-11,200
carte ¥ 19,000-27,500

Dinner: menu ¥ 20,160-39,200
carte ¥ 19,000-27,500

TEL 03–3571–6050 / FAX 03–3571–6080
Shiseido Building,
7-5-5 Ginza, Chuo-ku
www.shiseido.co.jp/losier

   10 

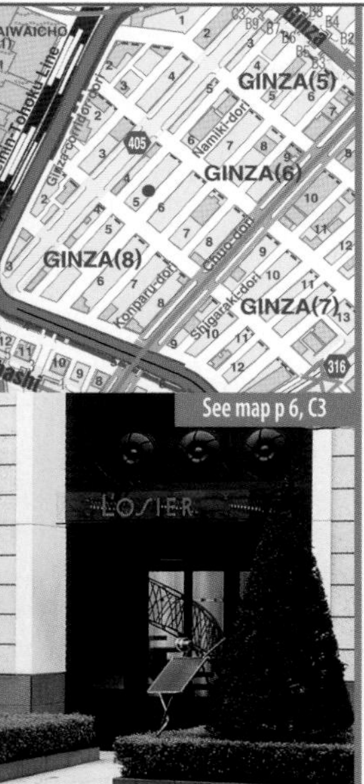

See map p 6, C3

Closed Golden week, 2 weeks mid-August, 30 December-8 January, Sunday and Bank Holiday Mondays

Open:
lunch 12:00-14:30 (L.O.)
dinner 18:00-21:00 (L.O.)

"To delight our customers": this is the ambition of chef Bruno Menard and his staff at L'Osier. The restaurant is located in the House of Shiseido (its owner company) in Ginza. Your eyes will be delighted, first of all, by the magnificent Art Deco interior. A glassed-in spiral staircase ascends to the dining area, its ambience enhanced by modern Aubusson tapestries, Daum Frères glass (works by Salvador Dali and Jean Cocteau), and paintings by French artists. Consummate pleasure is provided here by richly flavored dishes, crafted from premium French and Japanese ingredients with the talented chef's contemporary touch. The constantly evolving menu features the likes of Breton lobster salad, shellfish *tartare*, roast suckling pig with truffle-scented polenta, and, for dessert, *tarte soufflée au chocolat*. The professional service is another delight. Choose from a fine wine list with the aid of the knowledgeable sommelier. A trolley offering over twenty kinds of *petits fours* rounds off the meal with a flourish.

Maison d'Umemoto Shang-hai

Michelin

Lunch: menu ¥ 11,550
Dinner: menu ¥ 17,325-34,650

TEL 03–5467–2837 / FAX 03–5467–2838
New city Residence Nishi-Azabu Twin Tower II B1F,
2-26-20 Nishi-Azabu, Minato-ku

See map p 9, A2

Closed mid-August, late December-early January, Sunday and Bank Holidays

Open:
lunch 11:30-13:00 (L.O.)
dinner 18:00-22:00 (L.O.)

Head toward Aoyama at Nishi-Azabu crossing, look out for an ice cream shop in a residential tower, and you'll find Maison d'Umemoto Shang-hai hidden away in the basement. The cooking here is up market home-style, à la French Concession in old Shanghai. The chef recreates dishes he was taught by the Chinese owner of the Shinjuku restaurant where he trained. Using premium ingredients and a soupçon of seasoning, it brings out simple, essential tastes. Condiments and portion sizes can be adjusted on request. The chef makes bi-monthly trips to Hong Kong to secure the likes of dried abalone and swallows' nests, and he insists on seeing before he buys. He also employs French products such as Bresse chicken and white asparagus. Try the Shanghai crab dishes, especially the fried rice or spicy noodles with crab butter. The menu is fixed price only. The décor evokes an upscale French home in old Shanghai; the tableware is Limoges porcelain, Baccarat chopstick rests and Christofle chopsticks.

Maison Paul Bocuse

Maison Paul Bocuse

Lunch: menu ¥ 2,750-3,850
carte ¥ 13,000-21,000

Dinner: menu ¥ 13,200-27,500
carte ¥ 13,000-21,000

TEL 03–5458–6324 / FAX 03–5458–6328
Daikanyama Forum B1F,
17-16 Sarugakucho, Shibuya-ku
www.hiramatsu.co.jp

See map p 12, C3

The Hiramatsu group's restaurant Symposion in Daikanyama was renovated and endowed with the spirit of the brasseries that Bocuse runs in Lyon. The cuisine is truly French and celebrates traditional tastes. Vegetables, foie gras, beef cheek and truffles are added to a consommé made from beef cheek and vegetables; the dish is then covered with pie dough to seal in the flavor and cooked in an oven. Sole from the Straits of Dover is roasted and served with a choice of either a brown butter sauce or olive oil. Black-haired *wagyu* beef is served à la Rossini: beef fillet and foie gras are grilled to perfection, then garnished with an intensely aromatic truffle sauce. The interior consists of a mosaic-tiled dining room and a more modern-looking dining room in the back. The layout in the mosaic room is striking: tables face the open kitchen as if in a theater. Since there are many weddings here at weekends, it is best to reconfirm whether the restaurant is booked.

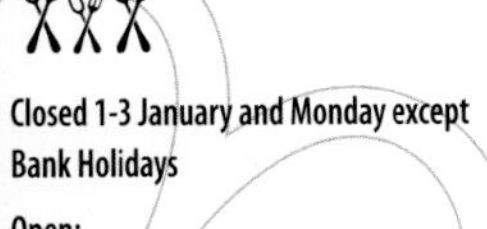

Closed 1-3 January and Monday except Bank Holidays

Open:
lunch 11:30-14:00 (L.O.)
dinner 18:00-21:30 (L.O.)

Makimura まき村

Michelin

Lunch: menu ¥ 6,615-8,820
Dinner: menu ¥ 11,025-14,340

TEL 03–3768–6388 / FAX 03–3768–4822
6-19-10 Minami-Oi, Shinagawa-ku

See map p 13, B3

A Japanese restaurant a five-minute walk from Omori Station. Separated by the *shoji* partition, the interior consists of three tables and a counter that seats six. We recommend the counter (but it's only available in the evenings). The owner never selects the ingredients for a menu he has decided upon in advance but rather puts together that day's meal based on the best ingredients available in the market. In order to bring out the natural taste, he is restrained in his seasoning, holding down the amount of *kombu* and dried bonito in his *dashi* so that it will blend in with the ingredients. The decisive element in the *dashi* is the dried bonito. After long years of study, the specialty here is sea bream *chazuke* (boiled rice with tea) with its rich aroma and taste; the sesame sauce based on a secret traditional recipe complements the wild sea bream from Sajima and Katsuura and the *nori* from Ariake. The owner believes that there is no contradiction between changing with the times and carrying on a tradition.

Closed Golden week, mid-August, late December-early January and Sunday

Open:
lunch 12:00-14:00 L.O.13:00
dinner 17:30-22:00 L.O.21:00

Minoichi 未能一

Michelin

Lunch: menu ¥ 5,775-28,875

Dinner: menu ¥ 11,550-28,875

TEL 03–3289–3011 / FAX 03–3289–3011
Suzuryu Building 5F,
8-7-19 Ginza, Chuo-ku

See map p 6, C3

This *kappo* restaurant is located on the fifth floor of a mixed-use building in Ginza. It operated in this part of Ginza for 14 years, before moving to Odawara. But Ginza was hard to forget and the restaurant's faithful clientele kept asking for its return, so in 2006 Minoichi came back. Today, this small restaurant run by a husband and wife team exudes a feeling of harmony. "We are always doing things that are not immediately apparent," the owner says. In spring red sea bream is seasoned with salt and steamed with natural mineral water. In summer there are salted innards of sweetfish or pike eel from the Seto Inland Sea done Yanagawa style. Fall brings a hot pot using *matsutake* mushrooms; in winter there is *fugu* as well as horse mackerel and mackerel from Saganoseki in Oita Prefecture. Most diners order the chef's choice, but there is also an ample number of individual dishes. *Bozushi* (stick sushi, pressed into a bar-like shape) and *chirimen sansho* (white bait and Japanese peppers) to take home are also popular; when making reservations, be sure to order them in advance.

Closed mid-August, late December-early January and Sunday

Open:
lunch 12:00-15:00 L.O.13:00
dinner 17:00-22:30 L.O.21:00

Miravile

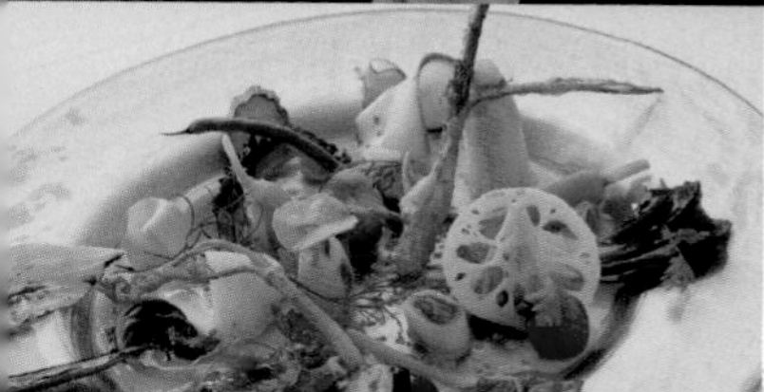

Michelin

Lunch: menu ¥ 2,940-4,095
Dinner: menu ¥ 5,500-7,700
carte ¥ 6,000-11,000

TEL 03–5738–0418 / FAX 03–5738–0418
1-16-9 Komaba, Meguro-ku
www.miravile.net

Miravile's chef loves motorbikes and cars, paintings and music. Beginning in 1989 he spent six years gaining experience in France, where he worked in a local restaurant as its first Japanese apprentice. The cuisine of the restaurant influenced him enough that in 2000, he opened a restaurant with the same name here in Japan. Wanting to "serve people truly delicious food," he dedicates himself to "cooking that expresses who I am." Born and raised in Hiroshima, he loves fish from the Seto Inland Sea, and he gets his vegetables only from producers he knows by sight. Since he puts a premium on the originality and combination of ingredients in crafting each individual dish, be prepared to wait awhile between courses. Specialties of the house include beef tongue and foie gras Saint Marc style, sausage made with wild sea bream from the Seto Inland Sea and pork, oxtails and pig's feet in a pastry crust. Prices are reasonable, and the staff takes good care of you.

Closed 1-5 January and Wednesday

Open:
lunch 12:00-15:00 L.O.14:00
dinner 18:30-23:00 L.O.21:30

Momonoki 桃の木

Momonoki

Lunch: menu ¥ 2,500-15,000
carte ¥ 3,000-6,500

Dinner: menu ¥ 7,000-15,000
carte ¥ 3,000-6,500

TEL 03–5443–1309 / FAX 03–5443–1309
2-17-29 Mita, Minato-ku
www.mitamachi-momonoki.com

See map p 10, B3

Closed mid-August, late December-early January and Wednesday

Open:
lunch 11:30-14:30 L.0.14:00
dinner 17:30-22:30 L.0.21:30

The principal players on the menu at Momonoki are Canton and Shanghai, but Beijing and Szechuan cuisines also make frequent guest appearances. The chef is intent on bringing out the natural flavor of the ingredients and is sparing in his use of oil. "It's healthier than the old Chinese cooking," he says, "and I've adapted it a bit to Japanese tastes." But he is obviously not a slave to fashion, and his passion for the pursuit of food that is delicious in every sense comes across quite clearly. From spring into summer, the large crabs known as *watarigani* are dropped briefly into boiling oil and then slow-simmered in soy sauce. There is a deliciously salty stir-fry of fermented *tofu* and *esai,* a Chinese green imported from Taiwan. Giant prawns from Aichi are served in a Shanghai-style chili sauce flavored solely with red chili peppers and there is an unusual dish featuring duck's tongue, which uses chilis and a variety of other herbs and spices in the Beijing style. The décor is unpretentious and contemporary.

Monnalisa

Monnalisa

Lunch: menu ¥ 5,570-11,605
Dinner: menu ¥ 7,890-18,570
carte ¥ 8,500-16,000

TEL 03–3240–5775 / FAX 03–3240–5776
Marunouchi Building 36F,
2-4-1 Marunouchi, Chiyoda-ku
12

See map p 4, C2

Closed 1 January
Open:
lunch 11:30-15:30 L.O.14:00
dinner 17:30-23:30 L.O.21:30

A French restaurant at the top of the Marunouchi Building (the 36th floor). The interior is divided into two sections. One has sweeping views on the woodlands of the Imperial Palace; the other, in unpainted wood and beige, offers a nice panorama of the city. Oil paintings by Fujinaga Shoji are hung throughout the restaurant. The chef went to France when he was 25 and after apprenticing at one of France's most prestigious restaurants, he returned to Japan and served as chef at a famous restaurant here before managing Monnalisa. He rigorously selects all the ingredients himself and will even go to the growing areas to check up on the quality. Using seasonal ingredients like scorpion fish and prawns from Nagasaki, crab and unshucked scallops from Hokkaido, he takes care that neither the cooking techniques nor the seasonings overlap, then finishes them off with a light touch.

Morimoto XEX

Morimoto XEX

Dinner: menu ¥ 11,000-22,000
carte ¥ 5,500-30,000

TEL 03–3479–0065 / FAX 03–3479–1696
7-21-19 Roppongi, Minato-ku
6

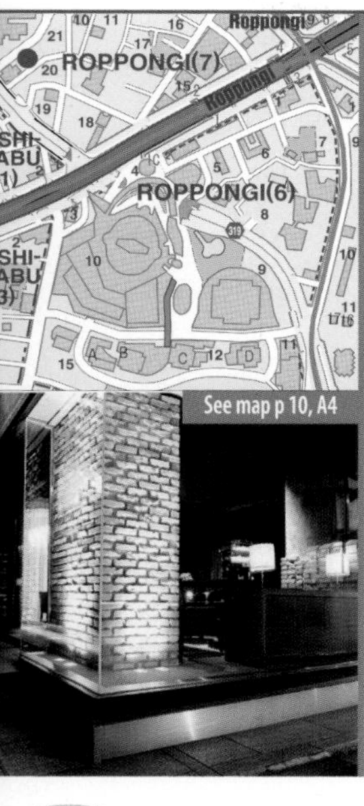

See map p 10, A4

This restaurant that opened in September 2005 near the Roppongi Tunnel, is a collaboration between Masaharu Morimoto, the New York owner-chef, and Y's Table Corporation. The emphasis here is on dining and entertainment, bringing together *teppanyaki, sushi* (not included in this guide) and a bar in a single complex consisting of a basement and two higher floors. Descending by a futuristic metal spiral staircase from the first floor, you emerge into the main *teppanyaki* dining area. Here, you can see cuts of quality Kobe beef and an antique ham slicer in a glass-fronted refrigeration case. Lobsters and black abalone produced and shipped after the restaurant places an order and Date chicken from Chiba tempt the appetite. On the second floor is a lounge where you can relax after dinner and enjoy dessert and a drink.

Closed 31 December-3 January

Open:
dinner 18:00-24:30 L.O.23:00

Muroi 室井

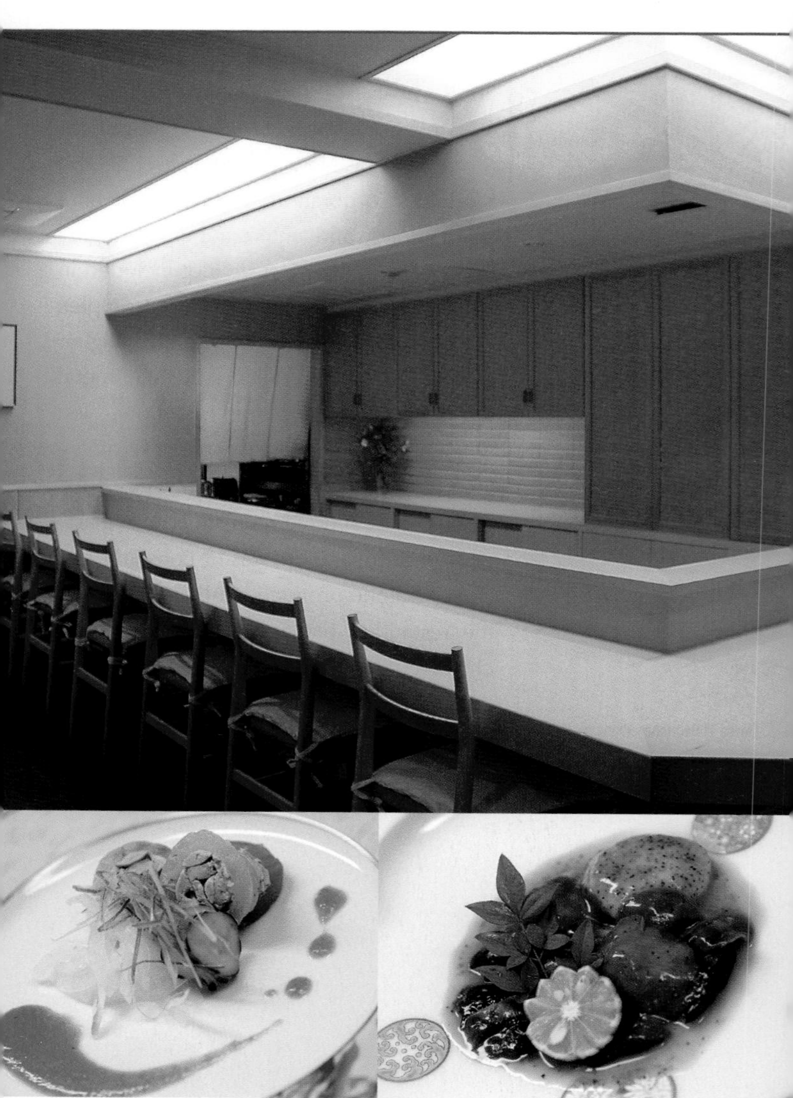

Michelin

Dinner: menu ¥ 17,325-34,650

TEL 03–3571–1421 / FAX 03–3571–1423
Suzuryu Building 2F,
8-7-19 Ginza, Chuo-ku
8

See map p 6, C3

After training in another traditional Japanese restaurant in Ginza, the owner opened Muroi in 1980. From home-style comfort food to startlingly innovative contemporary dishes, Muroi provides imaginative cooking unbound by adherence to a single style. For example: from spring into summer, you might try fresh wild vegetables from all over Japan; a carpaccio of flounder accompanied by a plum dressing; or a curry with a traditional Japanese stock base using seaweed and dried bonito. New flavors are eagerly investigated. The highlight of the restaurant's offerings is undoubtedly the wild mushrooms of autumn. Every year the owner and the chefs travel to the mountains of Aizu and the Nasu Highlands to harvest about 40 kilograms a day of wild mushrooms. In addition to a delightful menu of mushroom pastas, risottos, and soups, the tour de force is a dish marrying a wild mushroom sauce with the milt of *fugu*. The service, overseen by the owner's wife, is attentive. From mid-June until the end of November the weekend schedule is irregular, so advance reservations are required.

Closed Golden week, mid-August, late December-early January, Sunday and Bank Holidays

Open:
dinner 17:30-22:00 (L.O.)

Mutsukari 六雁

Mutsukari, Michelin

Dinner: menu ¥ 13,860-17,325

TEL 03–5568–6266 / FAX 03–5568–6267
Ginza Pony Building 6F,
5-5-19 Ginza, Chuo-ku
www.ponygroup.com/mutsukari/

See map p 6, C,D2

Mutsukari takes its name from the originator of Japanese cooking mentioned in the eighth-century "Chronicles of Japan." Fragrant aromas greet the nose on arrival at the sixth floor entrance; inside are an open kitchen with two wide counters, two tables and a private room. There are five tables on the seventh floor, and a private room with a kitchen on the eighth. The interior décor, which makes one feel one has entered a very special space, is contemporary, but the materials—wood, earth, stone and iron—are mostly traditional Japanese. Only set courses are offered: a 10-course meal consisting primarily of fish and vegetables and a 12-course vegetarian meal. All the food is artistically arranged and exquisitely served on beautiful tableware. Some of the vegetables used are brought in directly from the restaurant's own farm in Chiba. The owner's own wine collection is in the cellar, and if asked he will serve some to suit the diner's taste.

Closed 1-3 January, mid-August, Sunday and Bank Holidays

Open:
dinner 17:00-23:00 L.O.20:30

JAPANESE

Nadaman New Otani
なだ万 ホテルニューオータニ店

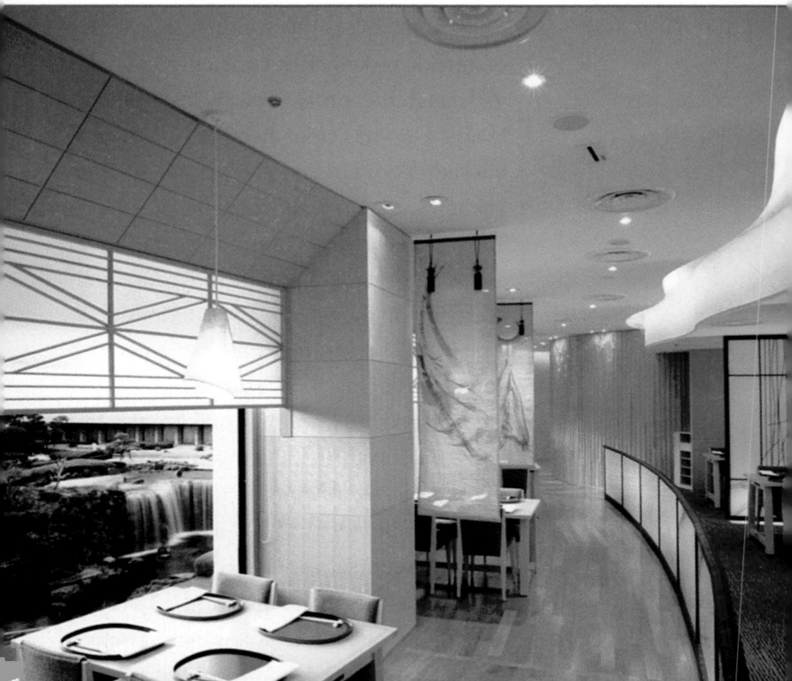

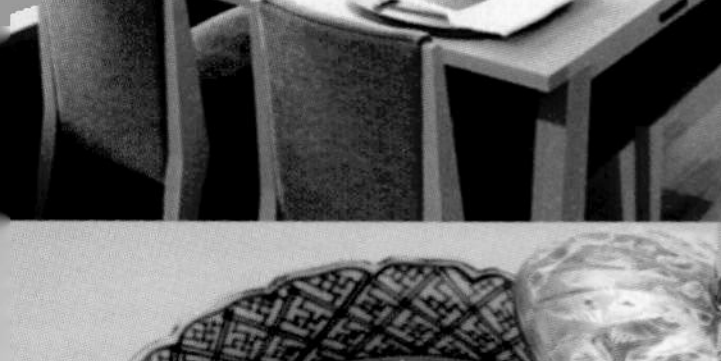

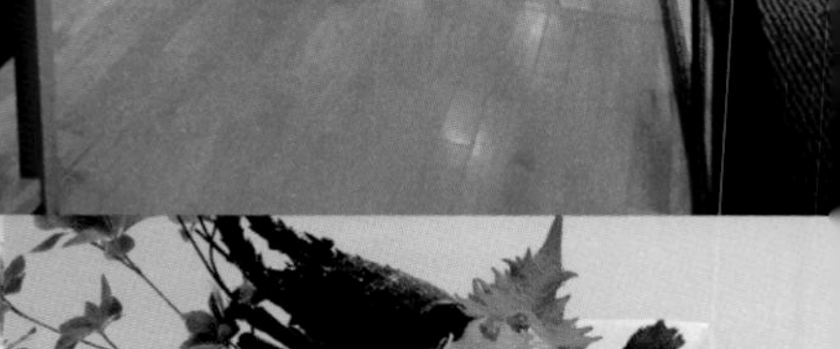

Nadaman, New Otani, Michelin

Lunch: menu ¥ 4,300-25,400
Dinner: menu ¥ 12,650-25,400

TEL 03–3265–7591
New Otani Hotel Tower Lobby 6F,
4-1 Kioicho, Chiyoda-ku
www.nadaman.co.jp

See map p 3, A2

A Japanese restaurant on the sixth floor of the new Tower at the Hotel New Otani. The entrance is a little hard to find, but once inside, you have a panoramic view of the Hotel New Otani's 10,000 tsubo (nine acre) Japanese garden. In that garden is Nadaman's main branch, Sazanka-so. The tables by the window are ideally suited for viewing the garden. There are also four Japanese-style and three Western-style private dining rooms. The restaurant's menu features a variety of courses oriented towards special occasions, also offering a wide variety of dishes from *tempura* to steaks from prime Japanese beef, *shabu-shabu*, and assorted Nodate *bento* boxes. All offer quality ingredients skillfully prepared into refined, varied, and superb cuisine. The service, by staff wearing traditional Japanese dress, is relaxed but attentive and professional. The prices are somewhat more reasonable than Sazanka-so, and the mini-*kaiseki* course on the lunch menu is particularly good value.

Open: 11:30-22:00 (L.O.)

JAPANESE

Nadaman Sazanka So
なだ万 山茶花荘

Nadaman, Michelin

Lunch: menu ¥ 25,200-31,500
Dinner: menu ¥ 60,000

TEL 03–3264–7921 / FAX 03–3264–7938
New Otani Hotel Japanese-Garden,
4-1 Kioicho, Chiyoda-ku
www.nadaman.co.jp

16

See map p 3, A2

A traditional Japanese restaurant in the garden of the Hotel New Otani. Appropriate to a garden with a history of over four hundred years, Nadaman is a restaurant with a pedigree, founded in Osaka in 1830. It moved from Osaka to the Hotel New Otani in 1974. Surrounded by a bamboo grove and other plantings, the traditional *sukiya*-style building is the work of the late Murano Togo. In the four Japanese-style rooms, the snow-viewing Japanese sliding doors and the skylights covered with Japanese paper emit a soft natural light that beautifully sets off the gold and silver decorated sliding door panels; the overall atmosphere is of being seated in an elegant traditional teahouse. The *kimono*-clad waitresses are experienced and inspire confidence. The cuisine is traditional kaiseki, emphasizing the flavors and sensibilities of the four seasons. The prices put this restaurant outside the realm of casual pleasure, but it should be somewhat easier to visit at lunchtime.

Closed 27 December-5 January

Open:
lunch 11:30-15:00
dinner 17:00-22:00

 ✿

Nakajima 中嶋

Nakajima, Michelin

Lunch: menu ¥ 840-5,150

Dinner: menu ¥ 8,400-13,650

TEL 03–3356–7962 / FAX 03–3356–7962
Hihara Building B1F,
3-32-5 Shinjuku, Shinjuku-ku
www.shinjyuku-nakajima.com
20

See map p 15, B3

A Japanese restaurant in Shinjuku 3-chome. The owner's grandfather, the first chef at a restaurant run by the potter and restaurateur, Kitaoji Rosanjin, opened his own restaurant in Ginza in the late 1920s. In 1962 the owner's father branched out on his own and opened the restaurant in Shinjuku that is now run by the present owner. While inheriting the dishes originated by his grandfather, he has introduced his own innovations rooted in traditional Kansai cuisine. Endowed with a personality that fulfills all the three requisites for a chef—concern for the cuisine, concern for the customer and concern for the next generation—he is in great demand at cooking schools and on television cooking shows, and is also well known as an author of cookbooks. The interior is cozy and always lively. A business lunch is offered at noontime; a *kaiseki* course can also be enjoyed if ordered in advance.

Closed mid-August, late December-early January, Sunday and Bank Holidays

Open:
lunch 11:30-14:30 L.O.13:45
dinner 17:30-22:00 L.O.20:30

Narukami

Michelin

Lunch: menu ¥ 4,042-9,240
Dinner: menu ¥ 6,930-15,015

TEL 03–6226–2225 / FAX 03–6226–2244
Shinbo Building B1F,
6-13-7 Ginza, Chuo-ku
www.restaurant-narukami.com

See map p 6, D3

Closed mid-September, late December-early January and Monday
Open:
lunch 11:30-14:00 (L.O.)
dinner 18:00-21:00 (L.O.)

The chef-owner started out in Italian cuisine but switched to French and, after a stint in France, went solo in 2003. He treats local products with respect. Conger and pike eel, bream, sea bass, and flounder are flown in from his native Ako in Hyogo. A hunter friend sends him game from Tamba. In winter, he obtains raw oysters grown in the calm waters of Setouchi. He prepares these products as simply as possible, crafting dishes with depth and balance. In summer, finely sliced pike eel is wrapped around wild *maitake* mushrooms from Saku, Nagano, fragrantly broiled and served with a dipping sauce of pike eel liver and green *sansho* pepper. These local ingredients imbue the chef's creations with a Japanese sensibility. Fixed price only; the three menus vary in the number of dishes and seasonal features. The décor of a red ceiling, black chairs and exposed-brick walls is striking. Modern Italian cutlery, Limoges china and Japanese dishware grace the tables.

SPANISH CONTEMPORARY 

Ogasawara Hakushakutei

小笠原伯爵邸

Ogasawara Hakushakutei

Lunch: menu ¥ 8,085

Dinner: menu ¥ 11,550

TEL 03–3359–5830 / FAX 03–3359–5831
10-10 Kawadacho, Shinjuku-ku
www.ogasawaratei.com
20

See map p 16, C2

Behind Wakamatsu Kawada station, there is a 1927 Spanish style villa once owned by the Ogasawara family, lords of the domain of Kokura, and known as the hereditary arbiters of etiquette among the Samurai elite. In 2002, it was restored, and now you can enjoy fine Spanish dining there. The first floor contains the main dining room, two private rooms, a salon-gallery, a lounge, a courtyard patio with dining tables, and an ornate cigar room decorated in an Islamic style. The second floor features VIP rooms and a roof garden. Only set courses are offered, and the menu changes every two months. The chef trained for eight years in Andalusia, Catalonia, and Barcelona. Pigeons, Iberian pork, fresh ham, red sweet peppers, and spices are imported from Spain, and herbs are grown in a garden on the premises. The chef uses the most advanced techniques and equipment to create Spanish cuisine which brings forth the intense flavors and aromas of these natural ingredients.

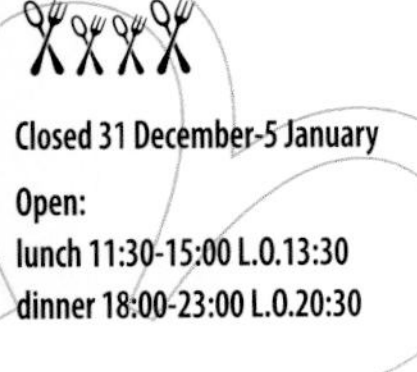

Closed 31 December-5 January

Open:
lunch 11:30-15:00 L.O.13:30
dinner 18:00-23:00 L.O.20:30

Ohara et Cie

Ohara et Cie

Lunch: menu ¥ 2,940-6,300
Dinner: menu ¥ 5,500-11,000

TEL 03–5785–3485 / FAX 03–5785–3485
Y-Flat B1F,
1-11-15 Nishi-Azabu, Minato-ku

See map p 9, A2

Closed 1 January, 7-13 January, mid-August and Monday

Open:
lunch 12:00-15:30 L.O.13:30
dinner 18:00-23:00 L.O.22:00

Ohara et Cie is a restaurant off Roppongi-dori that opened in 2000. Inside, the painted wood-grained walls, the marble floor and, of course, the tablecloths are all coordinated in immaculate shades of white. Here it is possible to savor French cuisine that is put together simply and without excess. “I want this to be a place where diners can drop by informally on a regular basis,” the owner chef says. A native of Ibaraki, he uses vegetables grown at his family home. The attention to detail and the inventiveness that he brings to the food are an expression of his love for it. In winter the mousse he makes from wild snipe delivered to him by his uncle has a delicious aroma and a rich taste. The entree of shrimp and cauliflower topped with caviar is really pleasant. For dessert there is a chocolate fondant flambéed with Grand Marnier, which is beautifully executed.

Ohara's

Michelin

Lunch: menu ¥ 3,465-8,085
carte ¥ 8,000-14,000

Dinner: menu ¥ 8,085-11,550
carte ¥ 8,000-14,000

TEL 03–5436–3255 / FAX 03–5436–3255
Yacmo Building B1F,
5-4-18 Osaki, Shinagawa-ku

See map p 13, B1,2

A French restaurant located in a quiet residential neighborhood about midway between JR Osaki Station and Gotanda Station. Look out for a white-awning at the entrance and then descend the entryway into the basement. You emerge into an interior also themed in white that exudes a fresh, clean feeling. The owner-chef trained in a number of famous restaurants in France and operated his own restaurant in Sapporo for 23 years before opening Ohara's in Tokyo in 2001. The cuisine is traditional French regional cooking, meticulously prepared and expertly sauced. Red sea bream from Bungo in Oita Prefecture is prepared with white wine and saffron. There is a varied palette of seasonal flavors: in spring, instantly smoked Hokkaido trout is paired with salad; in summer you can try a cumin-scented gazpacho, or in winter, a terrine of Ezo deer. The warm service provided by the German hostess, chef's wife, is an additional flourish, complementing both the cuisine and the restaurant's ambience.

Closed 28 December-4 January, 15-18 January, Monday and 1st and 3rd Tuesday

Open:
lunch 11:30-15:30 L.O.14:00
dinner 18:00-23:30 L.O.21:30

Ohno 大野

Michelin

Dinner: menu ¥ 6,930-13,860
carte ¥ 6,000-12,000

TEL 03–3571–4120
7-2-20 Ginza, Chuo-ku
www.auxamis.com

See map p 6, C3

In a cul-de-sac to the left as you head from Yurakucho toward Shimbashi, just off Ginza's Corridor Street, you will find Japanese restaurant Ohno - owned by a true devotee of wine and food. The ambience is bright and homely; the first floor seats eight at an unvarnished wood counter, the second has three tables and a private room for four. The ebullient chef took the helm when the place opened in 2006, having met the owner while working at a Japanese restaurant near the Paris Opéra. He says of his traditional Japanese fare, "The goal is to create simple, tasty dishes that bring out the genuine flavors of the ingredients." Try the seasonal hotpots, cooked at the table and good any time of year. The 200 wines range from those which are reasonably priced to those which cost several hundred thousand yen a bottle. They offer an à la carte menu after 8 p.m. and are open until 2 a.m. It's a convenient spot for singles. Many patrons drop in for one à la carte dish and some wine.

Closed 31 December-5 January and Sunday

Open:

weekday dinner 17:30-2:00 (L.O.)

Saturday and Bank Holidays dinner 17:00-23:00 (L.O.)

Okina 翁

Michelin

Dinner: menu ¥ 11,550-28,875

TEL 03–3477–2648 / FAX 03–3477–2649
B1F,
1-3-10 Ebisu-Nishi, Shibuya-ku
8

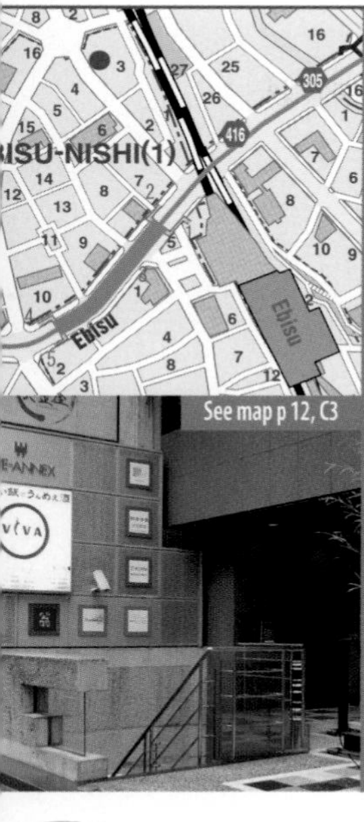

See map p 12, C3

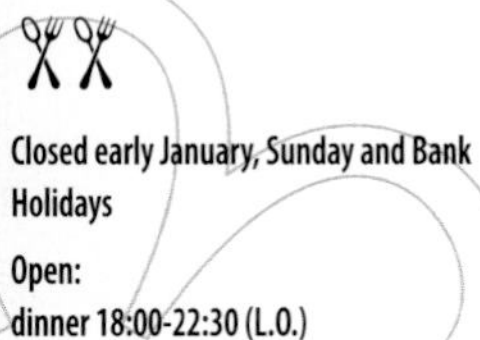

A traditional Japanese restaurant in Ebisu Nishi famous for its *soba*, which is no surprise since the mistress of the house is an eighth-generation member of a family that runs a historic Sarashina *soba* restaurant. Only the heart of the buckwheat kernel is used to produce the snow-white noodles known as Sarashina *soba,* which is characterized by its smooth texture and hint of sweetness. The dipping sauce, a trade secret, uses three different varieties of dried bonito and is a perfect match for the noodles, neither too thick nor overly assertive. Specialties of the house include *soba* flavored with *yuzu* and green tea kneaded together into the dough, and an original winter *soba* in which white and black truffles are similarly added to the noodles before they are cooked. Nor is the menu limited to *soba*; there are other delicious dishes using the freshest ingredients: seafood from Toyama and Hokkaido, sweetfish and pike eel from Kyoto.

Closed early January, Sunday and Bank Holidays

Open:
dinner 18:00-22:30 (L.O.)

Ozaki おざき

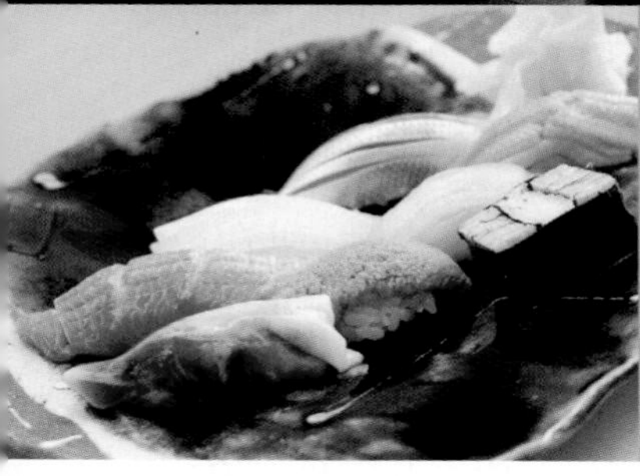

Michelin

Dinner: menu ¥ 15,015

TEL 03–3454–1682 / FAX 03–3454–1682
3-4-5 Azabu-Juban, Minato-ku

See map p 10, A4

Closed 29 December-5 January and Sunday

Open:
dinner 18:00-24:00 L.O.22:00

Off on a quiet sidestreet, you will find an understated sign, with "Ozaki" written in hiragana script, and a dark boarded entrance. The restaurant is particularly scrupulous about the quality of its tuna, always purchasing the choicest domestic tuna available first thing in the morning at the Tsukiji fish market. The owner comes from a family engaged in managing a sushi restaurant, and will only use the best as far as tuna is concerned. Ozaki offers only a set course menu, partly based on *sushi,* with one of the specialties being crab roasted in its shell, a dish that you may savor all year round. The decor is based on a refreshingly simple palette of beiges and earth tones. Along one wall decorated with bamboo is a counter, where the owner-chef prepares the food and happy to answer any questions you might have about it. Two waitresses round out the staff, providing decent and pleasant service. The owner is fond of wine, and this shows in the good selection of champagnes and wines on his list.

ITALIAN

Piatto Suzuki

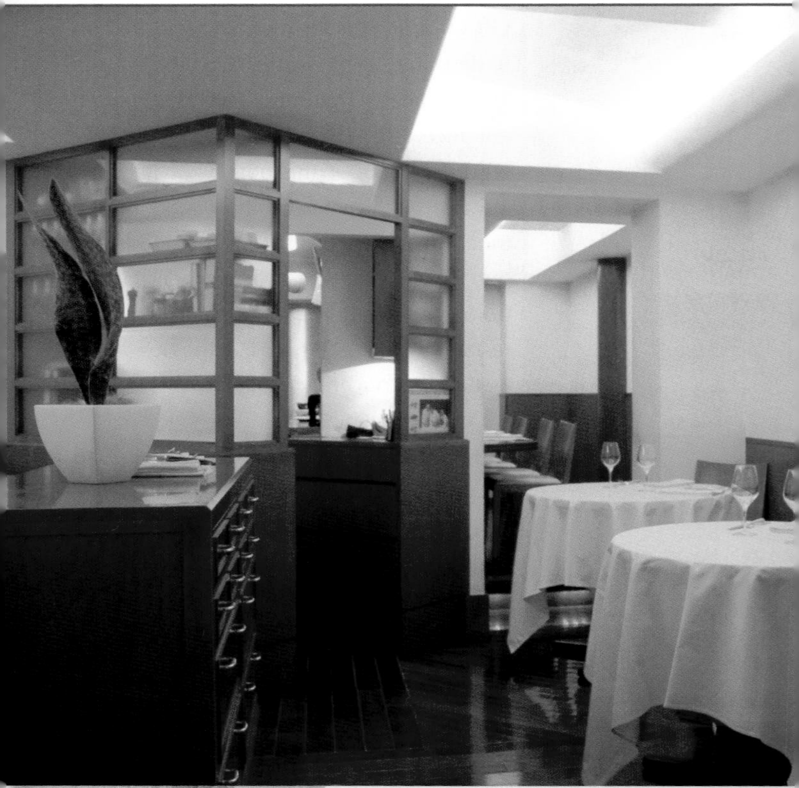

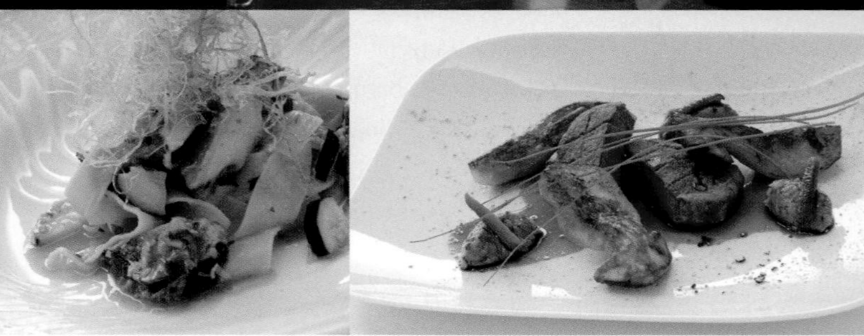

Michelin

Dinner: menu ¥ 10,500
carte ¥ 6,300-12,000

TEL 03–5414–2116 / FAX 03–5414–2116
4F,
1-7-7 Azabu-Juban, Minato-ku

See map p 10, A4

The signage of this Italian restaurant is understated and the dining room itself is not terribly spacious, with a six-person counter and five tables, but is filled every night with a lively crowd. What makes this restaurant special is that the food conveys very directly both the quality of the ingredients and the passion and careful attention that went into its preparation. The menu, from a solid base in traditional Italian cooking, adds a little here and subtracts a little there to arrive at its array of individual dishes. The chef personally and painstakingly selects the finest ingredients: prized Agu pork from Okinawa, chicken from Miyazaki, and fillet of beef from Hitachi in Ibaraki. Vegetables are also direct from the farm, mainly from the Kyoto area. To purchase fresh seafood the chef goes straight to "Tokyo's stomach"—the Tsukiji fish market. Every year during the Golden Week holidays he heads for Italy, making the rounds of the restaurants to sample the food and hone his palate.

Closed Golden week, 1 week late August, late December-early January, Sunday and Bank Holiday Mondays

Open:
dinner 18:00-2:00 L.O.24:00

FRENCH CONTEMPORARY ꕥꕥ

Pierre Gagnaire

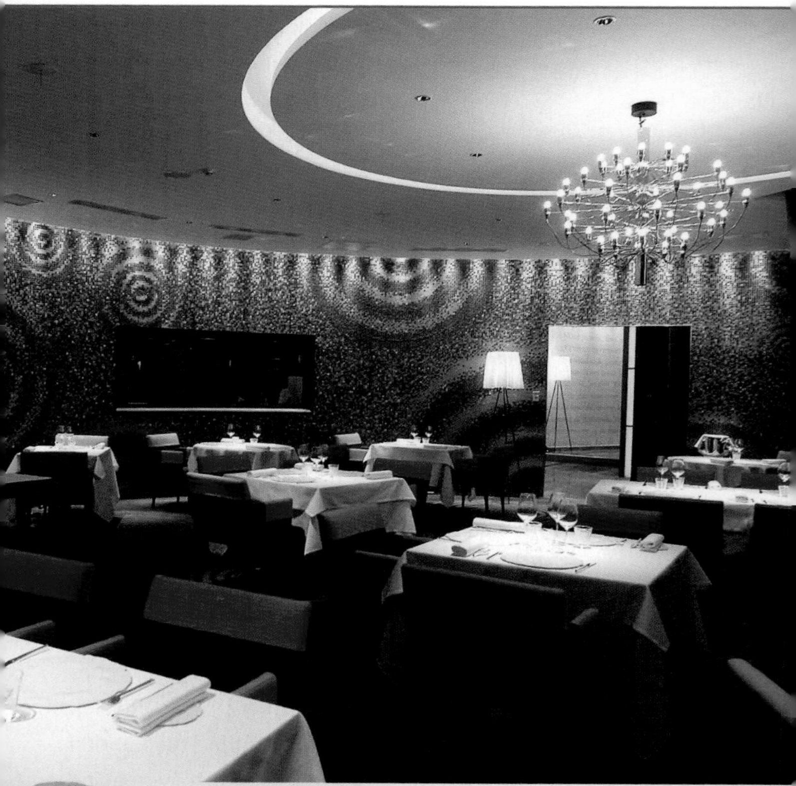

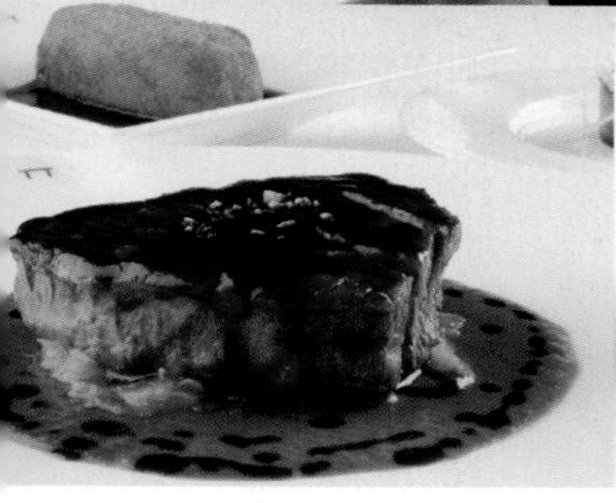

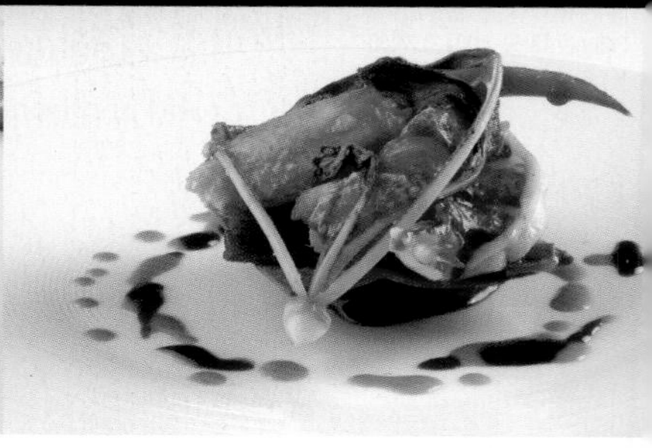

Pierre Gagnaire, Michelin

Lunch: menu ¥ 8,100
Dinner: menu ¥ 17,350

TEL 03–5791–3715
Barbizon 25 Building,
5-4-7 Shirokanedai, Minato-ku
www.quintessence.jp
8

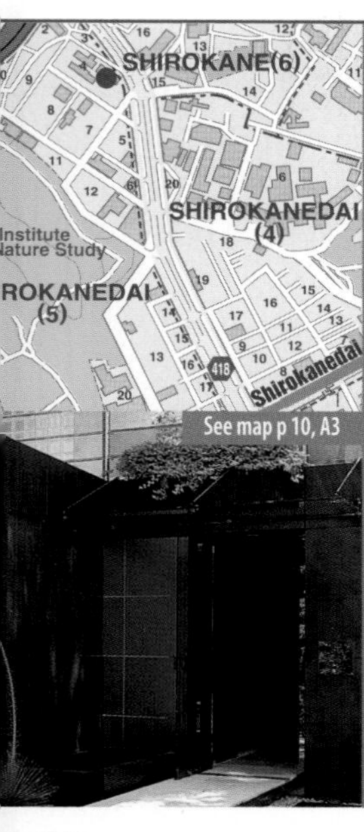

See map p 10, A3

This French restaurant opened in Shirokanedai in Spring 2006. The young chef found his calling because, as a child in Nagoya, his parents often dined out and took him along. After apprenticing in Japan, he honed his skills at some of France's finest establishments, culminating in a three-year stint at L'Astrance in Paris. At Quintessence, where he took the helm on returning to Japan, L'Astrance's influence shows in the single fixed price format. The "carte blanche" menu varies from table to table depending on the day's ingredients and inspirations. Lunch consists of seven dishes, dinner of thirteen. In each, the chef pays close attention to three essential elements: products, cooking, and seasoning. You can rest assured that his contemporary, stylishly crafted offerings will please your palate. The décor unobtrusively sets the scene for dining pleasure, hitting notes of modernity, elegance, and chic. The list of 500 wines focuses on French labels. There is a wine cellar near the entrance, and guests can admire the beauty of the bottles before enjoying the contents.

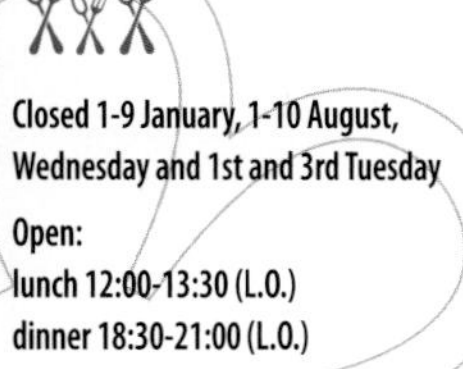

Closed 1-9 January, 1-10 August, Wednesday and 1st and 3rd Tuesday

Open:
lunch 12:00-13:30 (L.O.)
dinner 18:30-21:00 (L.O.)

Reikasai 厲家菜

Reikasai

Lunch: menu ¥ 9,240-51,975
Dinner: menu ¥ 17,325-51,975

TEL 03–5413–9561 / FAX 03–5413–9562
Residence B Roppongi Hills 3F,
6-12-2 Roppongi, Minato-ku
www.soho-s.co.jp
24

See map p 10, A4

A Chinese restaurant in Roppongi Hills. Inside there are just three private rooms decorated with Chinese furniture and ceramics. At first glance the food seems simple and unadorned, but don't be deceived: this is imperial Chinese cuisine that has been painstakingly prepared. The heart of Chinese cuisine is said to be the temperature at which it is cooked, and the skill with which the distinction between high and low heat is made here is marvelous. The owner's grandfather was a high-ranking courtier in the Qing Dynasty who supervised the meals of the imperial family and the Empress Cixi. The family's possession of the imperial recipes made it possible for the owner's parents to convert their home into the original Reikasai, a name meaning "Rei family cooking." There is only a set course (10-15 plates of appetizers followed by 4 to 7 main dishes). The flow of dishes one after another is reminiscent of the rules for composing Chinese poetry.

Open:
lunch 11:30-15:30 L.O.13:30
dinner 18:00-23:30 L.O.20:30

Ristorante Aso

Ristorante Aso

Lunch: menu ¥ 5,650-9,605
carte ¥ 4,520-10,170

Dinner: menu ¥ 11,300-22,600
carte ¥ 14,000-22,000

TEL 03–3770–3690 / FAX 03–3770–3554
29-3 Sarugakucho, Shibuya-ku
www.hiramatsu.co.jp

20

See map p 12, C3

If you follow Kyu Yamate-dori away from Daikanyama station you will come to a European-style outdoor café on the left-hand side of the street. Step into the café from the main entrance and walk towards the back, to this Tuscan mansion style restaurant opened in 1997. It has a classic but relaxed atmosphere, and a view of a courtyard garden that boasts a fine and vivid array of colorful flowers. The chef began his career in 1985, and has trained in restaurants in Japan and Paris. His cooking is filled with an aesthetic sensibility, and its arrangement and color harmonies are truly beautiful. The quality control of the ingredients is scrupulous. From June to August there is *madaka* abalone from Boshu and in winter, alfonsino from Inatori. Tilefish shipped directly from Hagi is wonderfully tender and robust in flavor. Miyazaki and Sendai beef is charcoal-grilled, and finished with a cream sauce wedding mascarpone with black sesame. Ristorante Aso's innovative, imaginative cuisine deserves the sobriquet "New Age Italian."

Closed mid-August, late December-early January, Monday and 1st Tuesday except Bank Holidays

Open:
lunch 12:00-15:30 L.O.13:30
dinner 18:00-24:00 L.O.21:00

Ristorante Hamasaki

Michelin

Lunch: menu ¥4,389-6,352
Dinner: menu ¥9,817-11,550
carte ¥8,500-10,500

TEL 03–5772–8520 / FAX 03–5772–8521
4-11-13 Minami-Aoyama, Minato-ku

6

See map p 9, A2

Closed Golden week, 2 weeks in August, late December-early January and Sunday

Open:
lunch only Thu. Fri. and Sat. 12:00-14:00 (L.O.)
dinner 18:00-21:30 (L.O.)

On a quiet residential street not far from Omotesando's name-brand boutiques, this *ristorante*'s leafy white façade has the fresh look of a highland inn. The interior is intimate and well-lit. The owner chef's ideal is to create "cooking which is so pleasurable, one is still savoring the memory of certain dishes the following morning." Flavors reflect his insistence on procuring choice items at their seasonal peak from all over the country—from Hokkaido veal, Sanriku sole and crab, and Ibaraki quail in the north, to saw-edged perch, grouper, and bream from the Genkai Sea in the south. The menu features seasonal concoctions such as baked risotto of freshwater trout in the spring, and seafood and mushroom ravioli in broth in the fall. "Expressing the seasons with pasta is a specialty of mine," says the chef. Grilling over Bincho charcoal adds savor to the impeccably selected Japanese and Western ingredients of various dishes. The attentive staff provide highly professional service.

Ristorante Honda

Michelin

Lunch: menu ¥ 2,887-7,507
Dinner: menu ¥ 7,507-9,817

TEL 03–5414–3723 / FAX 03–5414–3724
2-12-35 Kita-Aoyama, Minato-ku
www.ristorantehonda.jp

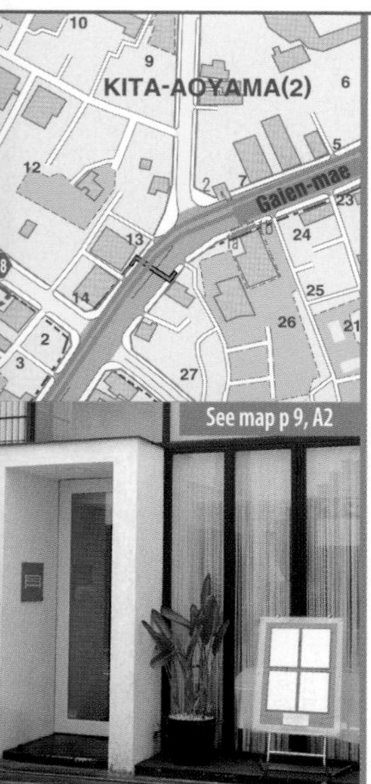

See map p 9, A2

An Italian restaurant in Kita Aoyama. After culinary school, the owner-chef first studied Italian cuisine, then trained in France; after a sojourn in Italy, he returned to Japan and opened his own place. The use of plates is distinctive, as are the preparation methods: Italian-based dishes are tweaked and accented with techniques from other cuisines, especially French. In spring, try the horse crab quiche and the tagliolini with sea urchin; in summer, the *gelée* of abalone and wax gourd, or the cold pasta with caviar; in autumn, the tagliatelle with porcini and the agnolotti of Pacific saury; in winter, the foie gras and truffle flan, and the roast Minami Izu wild boar or venison with raspberry sauce. The desserts include a Mont-Blanc *espuma* served in a clear glass, and a tea jelly with meringue. The menu is basically fixed price, but items can be ordered à la carte on request. The small dining room with white walls, black concrete floor and vermilion chairs is modern.

Closed mid-August, late December-early January and Monday

Open:
lunch 12:00-15:00 L.O.14:00
dinner 18:00-22:00 (L.O.)

JAPANESE CONTEMPORARY

Ryugin 龍吟

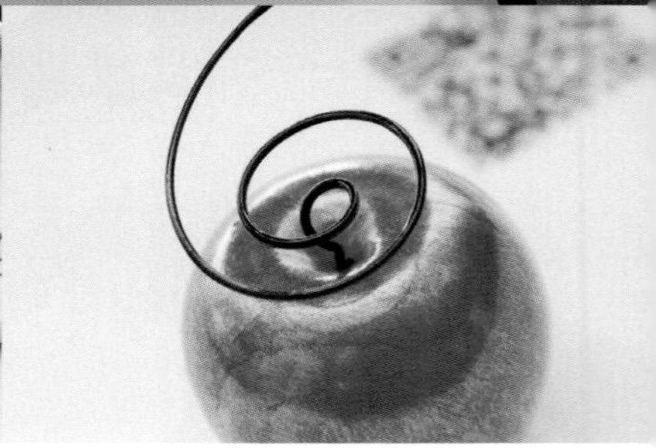

Michelin

Dinner: menu ¥ 17,330-28,880
carte ¥ 9,500-18,000

TEL 03–3423–8006 / FAX 03–3423–8003
7-17-24 Roppongi, Minato-ku
www.nihonryori-ryugin.com

8

Ryugin's owner-chef, Seiji Yamamoto, was turned on to cooking as a child, helping his mother at home. He prepared his first meal at the age of 11, handpicking every ingredient at the market. Today, while vastly more experienced, he retains the same passion for the best materials. At Ryugin, launched in 2003, he creates modern Japanese cuisine with an open-minded, inquiring spirit, personalizing the dishes to suit the customer's taste. Every year he takes part in an international chefs' congress in Spain, and he always brings back new ideas for his own menu. The set course consists of 13 original dishes, changed daily as they employ only the freshest seasonal products, locally grown. After 8:30 PM, there is an à la carte menu for those who want a less elaborate meal. Located on a Roppongi side street, the restaurant has an eye-catching red door. The white-walled, contemporary interior is pleasant, though not spacious. The wine list offers mostly French labels.

Closed 1-6 January, mid-August, Sunday and Bank Holidays

Open:
dinner 18:00-1:00 (L.O.)

✿

Sakuragaoka 桜ケ丘

Sakuragaoka, Michelin

Dinner: menu ¥ 13,860-17,325
carte ¥ 7,000-15,000

TEL 03–5770–5250 / FAX 03–5770–5250
6-8-21 Roppongi, Minato-ku
www.sakuraoka.com
8

Sakuragaoka's distinctive tastes have their basis in Kyoto kaiseki. The owner-chef trained in Kyoto's *haute cuisine,* and those skills form a basis that he has overlaid with Japanese home-style, Western, and Chinese elements. The menu gives prominence to seasonal products in the likes of shark's fin *chawanmushi*; croquettes of *matsutake* mushrooms or alfonsino with milt; oysters wrapped in bok choy; potage of Shogoin turnip; pilaf of assorted small fish; and an omelet filling of rice cooked with bamboo shoots and *tofu* skin. Assorted *sashimi* is presented on a large platter. The monthly-changing set menu features early, peak, and late-season ingredients. The dark-paneled building is decorated in the evocative old town house style. There is a counter as well as two private rooms; one has table seating and a small garden planted with flowers of the season.

Closed mid-August, late December-early January, Sunday and Bank Holidays

Open:
dinner 17:00-23:30 L.O.20:30

Sakuragawa 櫻川

Michelin

Lunch: menu ¥ 6,050
Dinner: menu ¥ 13,200

TEL 03–3279–0039 / FAX 03–3279–0040
Mitsui Tower 2F,
2-1-1 Nihonbashi-Muromachi, Chuo-ku
20

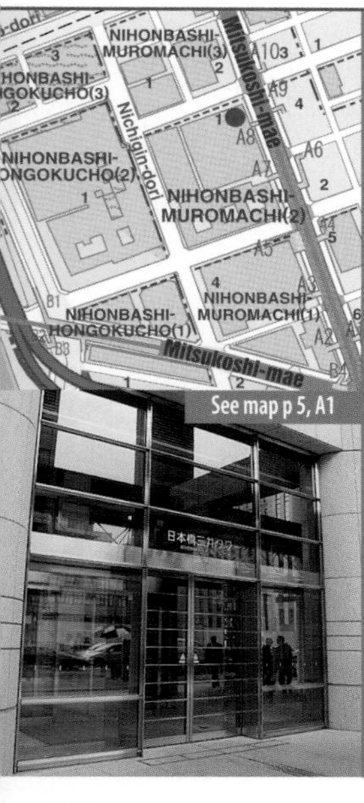

See map p 5, A1

A Japanese-style restaurant that reopened in 2005 in the Mitsui Tower in Nihonbashi after a move from Imoaraizaka in Roppongi. The name Sakuragawa is taken from the owner's birthplace, Osaka's Naniwa Ward. The general seating is at tables, and there are private rooms in different styles, including two in Japanese style and one in the modern style of the Taisho Period. The cuisine is old-school Japanese, respectful of traditional taste but friendly and accommodating. In addition to pressed sushi rolls and dishes using tilefish, Spanish mackerel, and pike eel, there are seasonal offerings such as *futomaki* rolls and dishes using cherry blossoms or leaves. A dish of shark's fin and bean curd skin over rice is served year-round. The course menu changes from month to month, and so does the tableware, with motifs depicting seasonal blossoms such as cherry, camellia, plum, iris, and hydrangea. Another special feature of this restaurant is the reasonable cost.

Closed mid-August
Open:
lunch 12:00-15:30 L.O.14:00
dinner 18:00-22:00 L.O.20:00

Sankame 三亀

Michelin

Lunch: menu ¥ 1,750
Dinner: menu ¥ 13,650
carte ¥ 8,000-12,000

TEL 03–3571–0573
6-4-13 Ginza, Chuo-ku
8

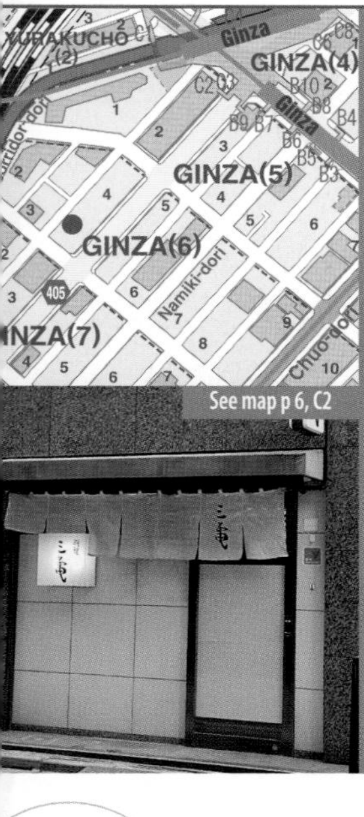

See map p 6, C2

A Japanese restaurant on Sukiyabashi-dori that has been in business since 1946. The present owner is a second-generation chef who carries on his father's tradition and serves Kansai-style cuisine which pays particular attention to the seasons. His suppliers are the same ones the restaurant has dealt with since his father's time. In spring there are bamboo shoots boiled in seasonal liquids and sea trout from Hokkaido; in summer fresh-water trout, conger eels and sea eels; in autumn *matsutake* mushrooms and ginkgo nuts; in winter *torafugu* from Usuki, Oita Prefecture. Sankame's *hirosu* uses chopped prawns steamed with *tofu* in the form of a dumpling. Customers who love the food at Sankame range from business people to famous novelists so the place is always full of regular customers. The owner is friendly with a wonderful personality and a keen sense of humor. In the evenings there is a set course but also a full selection of individual dishes. For lunch there is a set course only.

Closed mid-August, late December-early January, Saturday in July-August, Sunday and Bank Holidays

Open:
lunch 12:00-14:00 L.O.13:00
dinner 17:00-22:00 L.O.21:30

Sant Pau

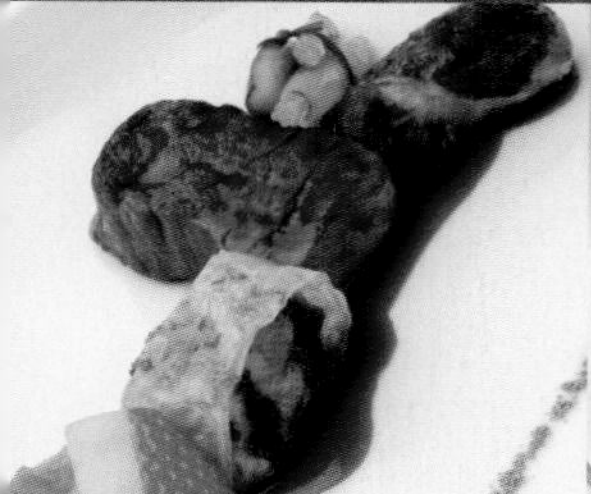

Sant Pau

Lunch: menu ¥ 6,050-24,200
carte ¥ 17,300-18,400

Dinner: menu ¥ 19,800-24,200
carte ¥ 17,300-18,400

TEL 03–3517–5700 / FAX 03–3517–5701
Coredo Nihonbashi Annex,
1-6-1 Nihonbashi, Chuo-ku
www.santpau.jp

8

See map p 5, B1

This Spanish restaurant in Nihonbashi is the offspring of Sant Pau in Sant Pol de Mar, near Barcelona, an establishment renowned for cuisine that reflects Catalan tradition and temperament. This branch adheres closely to its namesake's menu and culinary methods; in fact, it sets out to recreate the taste of the dishes using materials flown in from Catalonia. The large ground-floor kitchen has blue-tiled walls, like the original. Through the window, passers-by can watch cooks at work under the young chef's command. Imported products include Iberian pork, salt cod, olive oil, Majorcan salt, and dried green pimentos. The inspiration is traditional Catalan, creatively updated. The menus change with the season. A quick set lunch menu is available for business people. The contemporary interior features the work of Catalan artists such as Miró and Riera y Aragó. A large glass-encased wine cellar just inside the entrance houses some 400 wines; there are also a smokers' lounge and a cigar cellar.

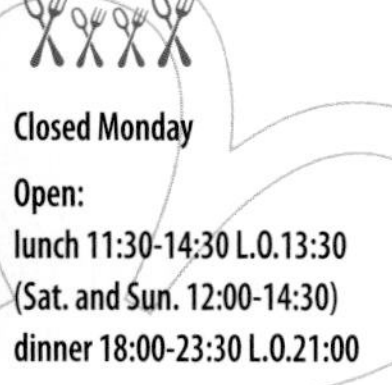

Closed Monday

Open:
lunch 11:30-14:30 L.O.13:30
(Sat. and Sun. 12:00-14:30)
dinner 18:00-23:30 L.O.21:00

Sasada 笹田

Michelin

Dinner: menu ¥ 10,500

TEL 03–3507–5501 / FAX 03–3507–5501
1-18-8 Nishi-Shinbashi, Minato-ku

See map p 9, C1

Sasada is a Japanese restaurant in Nishi-Shimbashi, run by the chef-owner and his wife. It has counter seating for just seven; the cozy space, with sliding doors right behind the chairs, makes for attentive and amiable service. The couple's aim is food that will tempt patrons to return over and over again. The chef handles every step himself, from daily buying at the Tsukiji market to the finishing touches. He makes the most of products with minimal fuss, stressing flavor over bravura. In spring, he uses bamboo shoots, *sansai* (edible wild plants), rock trout, ice goby; in summer, pike eel, scorpion fish, sweetfish, sea bass, Kamo eggplant, Fushimi peppers, wax gourd; in autumn, *matsutake* mushrooms, mackerel, barracuda, tilefish; in winter, crab, *shirako* (milt), sea cucumber, bluefish, oysters, and Shogoin radishes. The *omakase* course is the usual way to go, but you can also order the likes of clear soups, rice porridge in broth, pike eel or crab hotpot, or a sea bream medley. The prices are good value given the quality of the cuisine.

Closed mid-August, late December-early January, Sunday and Bank Holidays

Open:
dinner 18:00-21:30 (L.O.)

Sawada さわ田

Michelin

Dinner: menu ¥ 10,500

TEL 03–3507–5501 / FAX 03–3507–5501
1-18-8 Nishi-Shinbashi, Minato-ku

Sasada is a Japanese restaurant in Nishi-Shimbashi, run by the chef-owner and his wife. It has counter seating for just seven; the cozy space, with sliding doors right behind the chairs, makes for attentive and amiable service. The couple's aim is food that will tempt patrons to return over and over again. The chef handles every step himself, from daily buying at the Tsukiji market to the finishing touches. He makes the most of products with minimal fuss, stressing flavor over bravura. In spring, he uses bamboo shoots, *sansai* (edible wild plants), rock trout, ice goby; in summer, pike eel, scorpion fish, sweetfish, sea bass, Kamo eggplant, Fushimi peppers, wax gourd; in autumn, *matsutake* mushrooms, mackerel, barracuda, tilefish; in winter, crab, *shirako* (milt), sea cucumber, bluefish, oysters, and Shogoin radishes. The *omakase* course is the usual way to go, but you can also order the likes of clear soups, rice porridge in broth, pike eel or crab hotpot, or a sea bream medley. The prices are good value given the quality of the cuisine.

Closed mid-August, late December-early January, Sunday and Bank Holidays

Open:
dinner 18:00-21:30 (L.O.)

Sawada さわ田

Michelin

Lunch: menu ¥ 21,000
Dinner: menu ¥ 32,000

TEL 03–3571–4711 / FAX 03–3571–4711
MC Building 3F,
5-9-19 Ginza, Chuo-ku

See map p 6, D3

The owner of Sawada, which opened in 2004 on the third floor of a building in Ginza, has an unusual personal history: before setting up as an independent restaurateur, he worked for a shipping company. Nevertheless, he is a dedicated *sushi* craftsman. He uses only natural ingredients, which are ripened to just the right amount to bring it to a peak of delectability; the rice expertly seasoned with salt and vinegar to complement and enhance the flavors of the fish. It is original *sushi* fare, grounded in the traditional Edomae techniques but enhanced by his own sensibility and imagination. "I want people to be able to eat delicious food here in the same relaxed way they would enjoy a meal at home," says the chef. The bright interior, with a keynote of beige, is pure Japanese in style. The counter and chef's station are done in beautiful blonde wood. The upholstered red seats are a modern touch, giving the place more of an air of a *sushi* salon than a *sushi* shop.

Closed 1 week in August, 4-10 January and Monday

Open:
lunch 12:00-14:00 L.O.13:00
dinner 18:00-1:00 L.O.23:00 (Sat. and Sun. 17:00-20:00)

Sazanka さざんか

Sazanka, Okura Hotel

Lunch: menu ¥3,500-8,100
Dinner: menu ¥11,000-29,000

TEL 03–3505–6071 / FAX 03–3582–3707
Okura Hotel Main Building 11F,
2-10-4 Toranomon, Minato-ku
www.hotelokura.co.jp/tokyo/

11

See map p 9, B2

A *teppanyaki* restaurant on the 11th floor of the main building of the Hotel Okura Tokyo. The dining hall has a granite counter and general table seating, and there are four elegant private rooms that can each accommodate seven or eight people. The tables in both the main hall and private rooms are all equipped with *teppan* cooking surfaces. The interior of the restaurant is decorated with beautifully coordinated colors, and the leather chairs are very comfortable. Complementing the skill of the chefs is their attentiveness to the service overall. There are various themed courses (named Paulownia, Ginko,etc.), all featuring fillets of prime Kobe beef, as well as a "wagon service" in which the chef will cut the beef to order. In addition, there are lunch and dinner specials that can be enjoyed at somewhat more affordable prices. The customers are quite diverse, and the restaurant is popular with businesspeople and foreign visitors.

Open:
lunch 11:30-14:30 (L.O.)
dinner 17:30-21:30 (L.O.)

Sekihotei 赤芳亭

Michelin

Lunch: menu ¥ 5,775-16,170
Dinner: menu ¥ 12,705-16,170

TEL 03–5474–6889 / FAX 03–5474–6879
3-1-14 Jingumae, Shibuya-ku
10

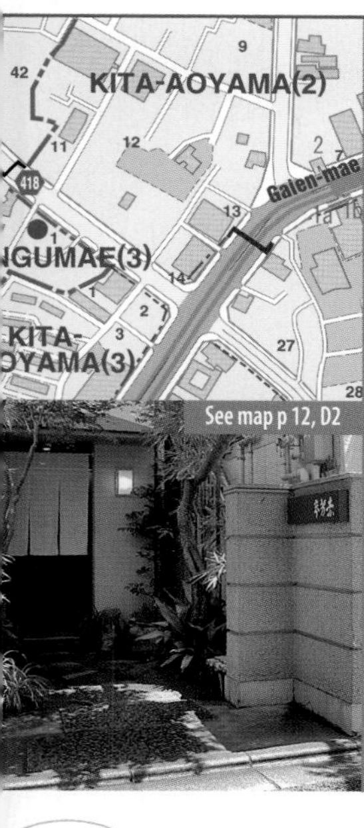

See map p 12, D2

A *kaiseki* restaurant around the corner from boutique-lined Killer-dori in Harajuku. There is no counter seating; on the first floor are four private rooms; on the second a *tatami* room and a main room with general seating at tables. The owner-chef, who worked in famous traditional-style restaurants in Akasaka and Shiga Prefecture, opened Sekihotei in 2004. He carefully selects the finest materials, and prepares them with techniques grounded in traditional cuisine. *Matsutake* mushrooms are charcoal-grilled whole on a ceramic ware. The chef is particularly fussy about his stock—the dried bonito used liberally as a main ingredient comes only from the bones and belly meat of the fish. The owner-chef has trained in the tea ceremony, and both its spirit of service and its overall flow inform his cooking. His tableware is for the most part elegantly simple; in summer he favors celadons and blue-and-white ware, and in winter polychrome ceramics in red and other warm colors. The courses offered change monthly, and reservations can be made for courses featuring *fugu*, *matsutake*, or pike eel.

Closed Golden week, mid-August, late December-early January and Sunday
Open:
lunch Wed.-Sat. 12:00-14:30 L.O.13:30
dinner 18:00-23:00 L.O.21:30

Shigeyoshi 重よし

Michelin

Lunch: menu ¥ 5,250-15,750
carte ¥ 10,000-16,000

Dinner: menu ¥ 18,900-31,500
carte ¥ 10,000-16,000

TEL 03–3400–4044
Co-op Olympia 1F,
6-35-3 Jingumae, Shibuya-ku

See map p 12, C2

In business since 1972, this restaurant is located below ground level of a building on Omote Sando. The simple interior is set up so that even a single guest can feel comfortable at the open counter, where it is easy to strike up a conversation with the cooks. The owner-chef is a Tokyoite, but trained in a traditional Japanese restaurant in Nagoya. He is unusually devoted to honing his craft: he spent a year of trial and error trying to figure out a way to cook Yoshino River snapping turtle without using fresh ginger before finally perfecting a soup. The menu is created each day by the owner. He keeps a large variety of ingredients at the ready, so that in addition to the chef's course, a wide range of à la carte choices are also available—Madaka abalone from Chiba, tilefish from Takeoka, bonito from the Boso Peninsula, conger eel and other white-meat fish from Naruto, small sardines from Kanazawa, and even the increasingly rare *satsuki* trout from the Nagara River.

Closed Golden week, 1 week in August, late December-early January, Sunday and Bank Holiday Mondays

Open:
lunch 12:00-13:30 (L.O.)
dinner 17:30-22:00 L.O.21:00

Shin 真

Michelin

Lunch: menu ¥3,150-8,400
Dinner: menu ¥15,750

TEL 03–5485–0031 / FAX 03–5485–0031
3F,
4-3-10 Nishi-Azabu, Minato-ku

See map p 9, A2

Shin is a *sushi* restaurant which respects the Edomae tradition. Dinnertime service is generally *omakase*. You begin with an appetizer: depending on the season, it might be plain-grilled conger eel flavored with salt and *yuzu*; *sake*-steamed abalone, octopus, and mantis shrimp; oysters; salmon roe; salted sea-cucumber entrails; and crab butter. The *nigiri* materials come from all over Japan: flounder from Chiba, marinated between sheets of kelp; yellow jack from Niijima; simmered Ibaraki clams; young sea bream from Kagoshima; shad from Kumamoto or Saga; surf clams from Hokkaido; prawns from Oita. The chef brings out the flavor and aroma of each one with a repertoire of traditional Edomae techniques, such as salting, marinating in vinegar, searing the skin, or half-smoking in a straw-burning oven. The rice is a blend of Niigata and Ibaraki varieties, cooked on the firm side so that the grains are distinct. The red rice vinegar is made with *sake* lees. The location is hard to find; look for the sign in front of the brown building.

Closed late December-early January, Monday and third Sunday
Open:
lunch 12:00-14:00 L.O.13:30
dinner 18:00-23:00 L.O.22:00

Shofukuro 招福楼

Michelin

Lunch: menu ¥ 6,930-19,635
Dinner: menu ¥ 13,860-25,410

TEL 03–3240–0003 / FAX 03–3240–1010
Marunouchi Building 36F,
2-4-1 Marunouchi, Chiyoda-ku
www.shofukuro.jp
14

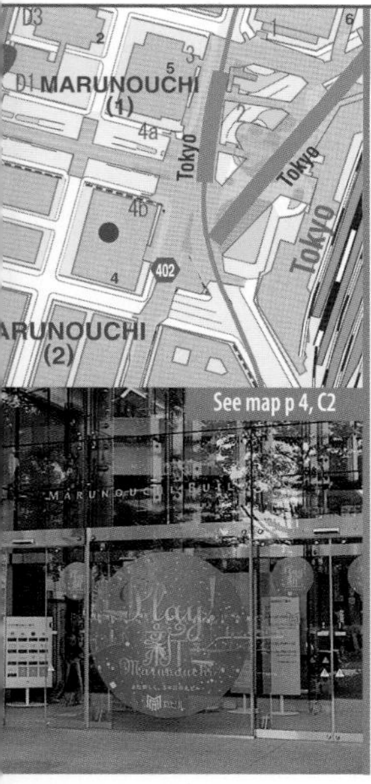

See map p 4, C2

The Tokyo branch of original Shofukuro, located in the city of Higashiomi in Shiga Prefecture, opened in 2002 in an outstanding location on the top floor of the Marunouchi Building. The owner believes that cuisine is one path along which to "pursue the beauty of Japan's traditional culture," and is putting this into practice in terms of the spirit of the host embodied here. The restaurant interior, which possesses a panoramic view of the Imperial Palace grounds and the northern part of the city, has one large 11-mat room designed to seat ten persons, and five smaller rooms with five seats each. The large main room takes its design cue of *kirei sabi*, or "elegant simplicity," from the Bosen teahouse of Kohoan, a sub temple of Daitokuji in Kyoto. The food is traditional *kaiseki* cuisine, which has refined the presentation of the sense and savor of the four seasons to an art.

Closed 1 January
Open:
lunch 11:30-15:00 L.O.14:00
dinner 17:00-23:00 L.O.22:00

Signature

Signature, Mandarin Oriental, Michelin

Lunch: menu ¥ 5,500-13,200
carte ¥ 13,000-21,000

Dinner: menu ¥ 15,400-22,000
carte ¥ 13,000-21,000

TEL 03–3270–8188 / FAX 03–3270–8886
Mandarin Oriental Hotel 37F,
2-1-1 Nihonbashi Muromachi, Chuo-ku
www.mandarinoriental.co.jp/tokyo

10

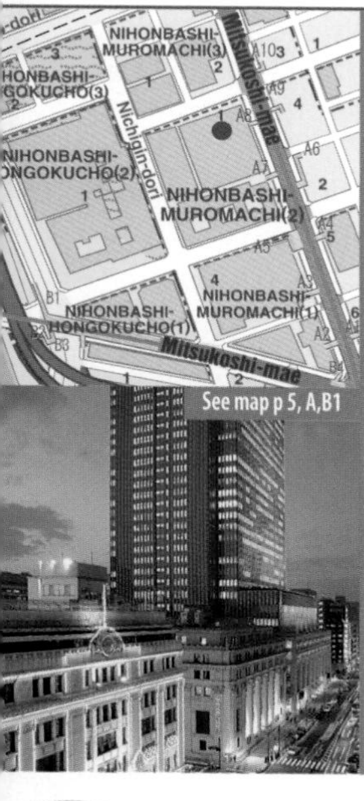

See map p 5, A,B1

Open:
lunch 11:30-14:30 (L.O.)
dinner 17:30-22:00 (L.O.)

A French restaurant opened in December 2005, on the 37th floor of the Mandarin Oriental Hotel in Nihonbashi Mitsui Tower. The dining room is blessed with one of the best views of any in the tower. Signature is divided into three areas. The entrance area opens onto the Mandarin Oriental Hotel's bar lounge and in the evenings you can listen to a live jazz trio there. Next is the main dining room, decorated in an imaginative contemporary style. The interior, with a keynote of silver, is bathed in modern illumination. From here, you can gaze out over the panorama of the city from comfortable armchairs and upholstered seats, and also have a partial view into the kitchen. The third area is semi-private, where you can settle into one of the lavender-colored chairs and enjoy a relaxed meal. No matter what area you choose, the cuisine is the same—refined, high-quality contemporary French. The menu changes seasonally. The wine list offers a selection of over 400 bins, centering on French wines.

Sugawara すがわら

Michelin

Dinner: menu ¥ 7,150

TEL 03–3793–0281 / FAX 03–3793–0281
2-19-12 Ebisu-Minami, Shibuya-ku

See map p 12, C3

This small Japanese restaurant, opened in 1992, is run by the Hakodate-born owner and his open-hearted wife. The owner has been working in kitchens as a cook for longtime. When young, he developed his own culinary aesthetics from his mother and then worked hard on his own at polishing his skills. Having long felt that the portions at Japanese restaurants are inadequate, the couple decided they wanted to serve meals that were substantial in both size and content, yet within a budget. The chef sets a high value on the natural flavor of fish, which he broils whole, sprinkling salt on grunt, rock cod and barracuda, then grilling them until they are fragrant. For seasonal tastes there is a salad that combines seafood and mountain greens with plum in spring. In summer he parboils conger eel and combines it with a soft-boiled egg, a slippery wild vegetable called water shield and *nameko* mushrooms. In winter, bonito broth is added to white radish, Japanese cabbage and fried *tofu* and served hot in an earthen pot.

Closed Golden week, 1 week in August, late December-early January, Sunday, 2nd and 4th Saturday and Bank Holidays

Open:
dinner 18:30-23:00 L.O.21:00

Sukiyabashi Jiro すきや橋 次郎

Michelin

Lunch: menu ¥ 27,000-32,000
Dinner: menu ¥ 27,000-32,000

TEL 03–3535–3600
Tsukamoto Sogyo Building B1F,
4-2-15 Ginza, Chuo-ku

See map p 6, C,D2

This restaurant located in the basement of a building, has become well known even outside of Japan. In the small interior there is a wide lacquered counter that seats ten and three tables for four. The owner is a skilled master who has been making *sushi* since 1965; he uncompromisingly purchases only the very finest fish at the Tsukiji fish market. While the owner and his oldest son make the *sushi*, two young assistants take out the fish, tidy up the *sushi* counter, pour tea, and deftly do other odd jobs. *Sushi* is a food in which the temperature is as important as the freshness of the ingredients. Here the temperature is controlled for each of the different fish used, and the sushi rice is always kept at body temperature. The cool and refreshing quality of the restaurant as a whole, the concern for the customer, the perfectionism in selecting the furnishings—the spirit shown here has much in common with the world of the tea ceremony. What has brought this restaurant to the level it is at today is probably the fact that it never stops experimenting to make the *sushi* even more delicious.

Closed mid-August, late December-early January, Saturday dinner, Sunday and Bank Holidays.

Open:
lunch 11:30-14:00
dinner 17:00-20:30

✿✿

Sushi Kanesaka 鮨 かねさか

Michelin

Lunch: menu ¥ 5,250-15,750
Dinner: menu ¥ 15,750-21,000

TEL 03–5568–4411 / FAX 03–5568–4412
Misuzu Building B1F,
8-10-3 Ginza, Chuo-ku

See map p 6, C3

Cherish the techniques of Edomae sushi yet give free play to the imagination in pursuit of delicious taste - this is what Kanesaka tries to do. In the world of Edomae sushi there has always been a strong tendency toward old-fashioned ideas and the craftsman's spirit, but the young owner of this restaurant has a thoroughly flexible attitude. For example, he believes it is not only the freshness of the neta (topping) that is important for sushi: "aging improves the taste," says the owner, who talks quietly and easily about sushi with his customers without any stiffness or awkwardness. Indeed, his genial personality pervades the entire restaurant. The shari rice, seasoned with a sprinkling of salt, is capped with superior toppings. The taste of the shrimp and cockles in particular is superb. The kimono-attired female wait staff also make a favorable impression, and the deft service matches the swift tempo of the sushi makers. In the evening sashimi is added before the base course; the drink menu also includes some 15 kinds of wine.

Closed Golden week, mid-August and late December-early January

Open:
lunch 11:30-14:00 L.O.13:00
dinner 17:00-22:00 L.O.21:00

✿✿✿

Sushi Mizutani 鮨 水谷

Michelin

Lunch: menu ¥ 15,000
Dinner: menu ¥ 15,000

TEL 03–3573–5258
Seiwa Silver Building B1F,
8-2-10 Ginza, Chuo-ku

See map p 6, C3

This famous *sushi* restaurant, hidden away in a basement opposite the Ginza Nikko Hotel, is run by one of the country's leading *sushi* chefs. The compact setup—10 counter seats in a plain interior—creates a pleasant bonhomie between customer and chef. Every move is masterly as he fashions the *sushi*, occasionally explaining a technique or a secret of the art. The chef visits chosen suppliers at the Tsukiji market every morning to obtain supremely high-quality seafood. Sushi Mizutani will have you relishing the full depth of flavor that Edomae *sushi* attains when made with the very best fish. The chef is also proud of the rice: a blend of several types, it is the product of a 40-year collaboration with his rice dealer. Salt and vinegar are added with a sure hand, complementing the intensity and the sublime flavors of the *nigiri*. Daytime and evening prices are the same, a sign perhaps of the owner-chef's uncompromising approach. It's better to go at lunch, when the place is less crowded, but be sure to make a reservation.

Closed Golden week, mid-August, late December-early January, Sunday and Bank Holidays

Open:
lunch 11:30-13:30
dinner 17:00-21:30

Sushi Nakamura 鮨 なかむら

Michelin

Dinner: menu ¥ 15,750

TEL 03–3746–0856 / FAX 03–3746–0856
7-17-16 Roppongi, Minato-ku

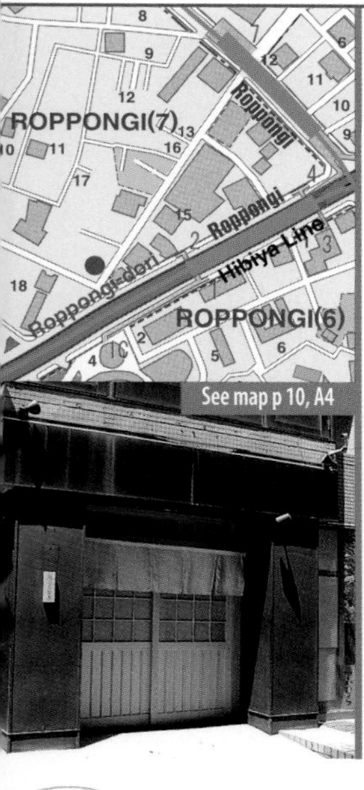

See map p 10, A4

The owner worked at many established Japanese restaurants, then apprenticed as a *sushi* chef before opening his own place. He entrusts the selection of ingredients to a reliable dealer in Tsukiji but also buys shellfish and white-fleshed fish directly from the Noto Peninsula in Ishikawa Prefecture. He makes *sashimi* from *akanishi*, a whelk found only on the Noto Peninsula, and toasts *kuchiko* (dried sea cucumber ovaries) for an accompaniment to *sake*. Live sea urchins from Amakusa in Kumamoto Prefecture are delivered packed in salt water; he serves them with a garnish of salt and *wasabi* that brings out their sweetness and natural taste. The owner has a strong predilection for tuna; he selects the top-grade from Sado in summer and from Oma in Aomori in winter. The *sushi* rice is specially seasoned to complement the tuna; aged Koshihikari rice is cooked the old-fashioned way in a heavy pot over high heat. The menu is simple, consisting mainly of *nigiri* and only a few appetizers. Another of the pleasures here is the full complement of *sakes* and *shochus*.

Closed Golden week, mid-August, late December-early January, Saturday, Sunday and Bank Holidays

Open:
dinner 19:00-1:00 L.O.23:30

Sushi Ohno すし おおの

Michelin

Dinner: menu ¥ 8,400-26,250

TEL 03–3572–0866 / FAX 03–3572–0866
7-2-17 Ginza, Chuo-ku

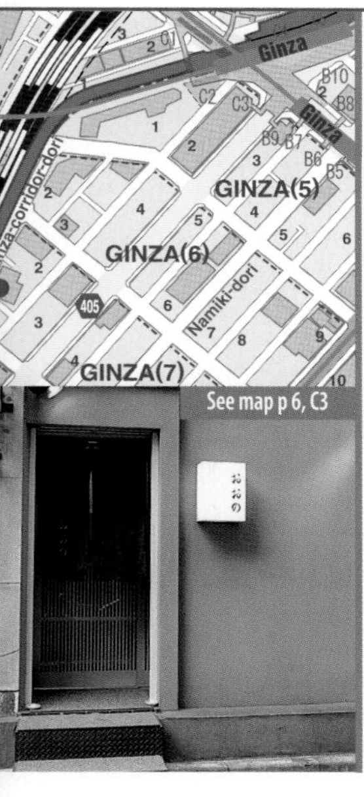

See map p 6, C3

Though just big enough for eight counter seats, Sushi Ohno stakes out its ground with serious craftsmanship. Regulars tend to start with an appetizer, then move on to *sushi*. Careful basic preparation and light seasoning are the keynotes. Versatility ensures that the flavors never pall: some products are served raw, others are steamed, seared, salted, or marinated between sheets of kelp, and each arrives at an optimum temperature. Abalone, tender and richly flavored, is *sake*-steamed after having been steeped for half a day in a *sake* and kelp marinade. Local conger eel, at its best from the rainy season to early summer, has a plumpness you can taste. In early autumn, firm-fleshed two-pound mackerel, caught off the Miura Peninsula, and dried salted mullet roe, a Nagasaki delicacy prepared in-house, are cooked rare. Fancy combinations are shunned; here, simplicity is the key to fine food. For the all-important rice, a contract grower in Akita supplies low-chemical Koshihikari, polished and shipped in a ten-day cycle to keep its fragrance.

Closed Golden week, mid-August, late December-early January, Sunday and Bank Holidays

Open:
dinner 17:30-22:00 (L.O.)

Sushi Saito 鮨 さいとう

Michelin

Lunch: menu ¥ 5,250-15,750
Dinner: menu ¥ 18,900-26,250

TEL 03–3589–4412
Nihon Jitensha Kaikan 1F,
1-9-15 Akasaka, Minato-ku

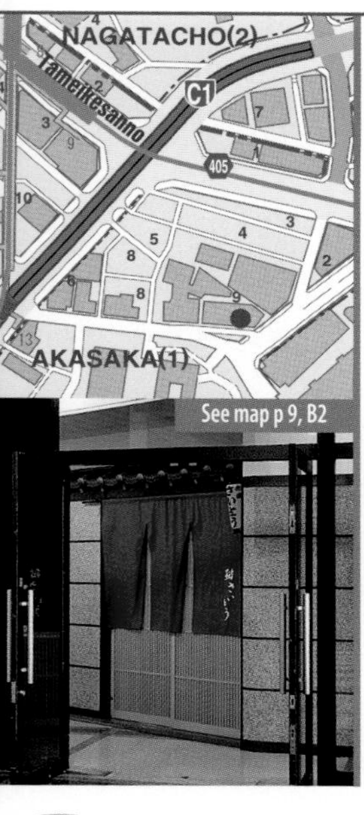

See map p 9, B2

This restaurant, which has no sign on the street in front, is located on the right as you enter the parking lot to the Nihon Jitensha Kaikan building opposite the American Embassy. The harmonious balance of *shari* (rice), *wasabi*, *neta* (ingredients), and soy sauce is respected here. This rice is especially suited to the tuna *nigiri*. The tuna itself is allowed to age for more than two weeks in the ice room; a sharp eye is kept on its condition, and adjustments are made to the thickness of the slice. The temperature is different depending on the fish used as *neta*. Tuna, for example, needs to wait "until the fat floats to the surface"; white-fleshed fish "shouldn't be too cold"; shiny silvery fish should be "somewhat on the low side." He uses *wasabi* from Umegashima in Izu and grates it on a copper-plated grater so it will not lose its pungent taste. The *nori* (laver) is from Ariake in Saga Prefecture. With only a counter seating six, this restaurant is filled both at lunchtime and in the evening with regular customers.

Closed mid-August, late December-early January, Saturday, Sunday and Bank Holidays

Open:
lunch 11:30-14:00 (L.O.)
dinner 17:00-22:00 (L.O.)

Sushisho Saito すし匠 齋藤

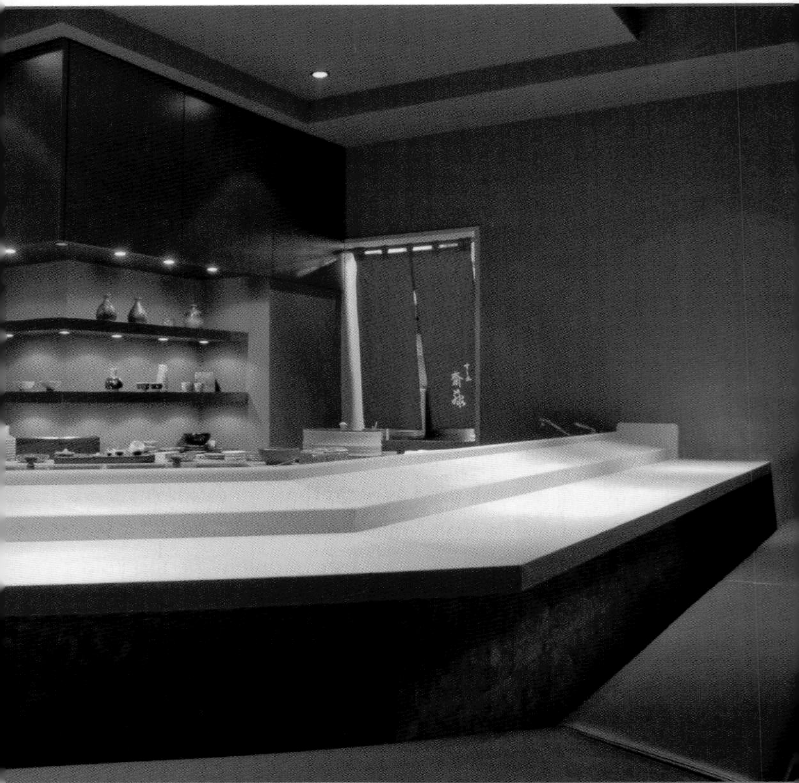

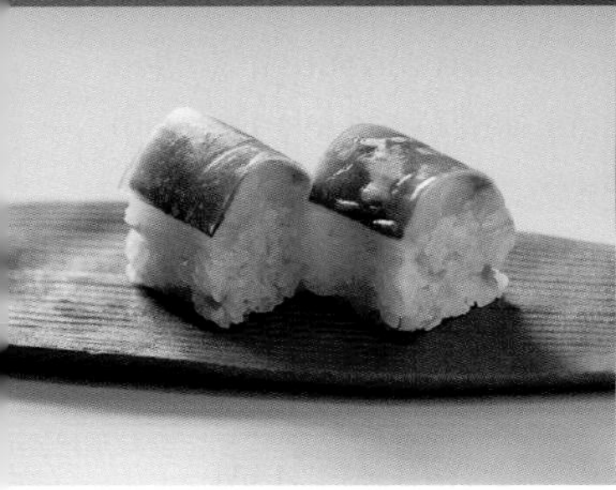

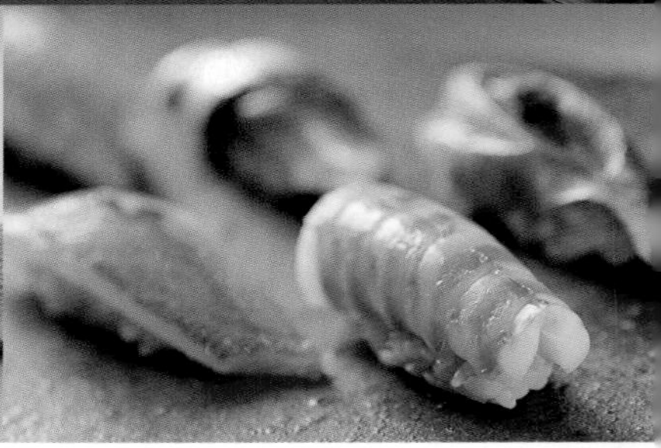

Michelin

Dinner: menu ¥ 20,000

TEL 03–3505–6380 / FAX 03–3505–6380
2F,
4-2-2 Akasaka, Minato-ku

See map p 9, B1

It's *omakase* all the way here; there is no à la carte menu. You start with a single *nigiri,* followed by a well-balanced sequence of *nigiri* and appetizers. Everything is prepared Edomae style: marinated in vinegar or between kelp sheets, brushed with a soy glaze, or sprinkled with salt or *yuzu* peel. *Sashimi* and other appetizers arrive on plates, *nigiri* on serving boards; the materials and preparation vary with the season. Products sourced directly include red sea urchin and razor clam from Karatsu in Saga, shrimp from the Amakusa Islands off Kumamoto, oysters from Moji in Fukuoka, abalone from Ohara in Chiba, and sandfish and blackthroat sea perch from Akita. The rice is cooked until a little firm, five or six hours before use, then seasoned with red vinegar for certain fish, with rice vinegar for others, and molded at body temperature. The course takes a leisurely two hours. Having worked in New York, the chef can give foreign customers explanations in English.

Closed Golden week, mid-August, late December-early January and Monday

Open:
dinner 18:00-23:30 (L.O.)

Suzuki すずき

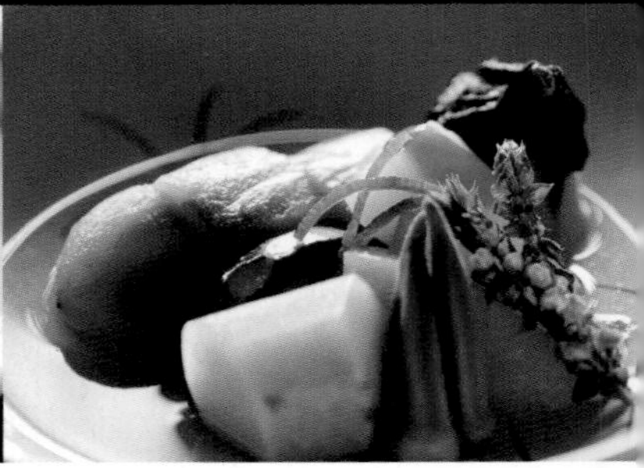

Michelin

Lunch: menu ¥ 6,300
Dinner: menu ¥ 10,500-15,750

TEL 03–3710–3696 / FAX 03–3710–3696
2-16-3 Takaban, Meguro-ku
www.kappou.jp

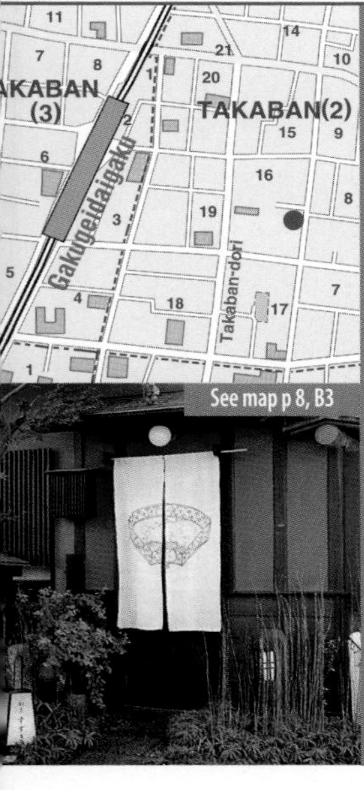

See map p 8, B3

Suzuki's proprietor, a self-taught cook who originally trained as a *sushi* chef, opened this Japanese restaurant in 1984. His creations owe their flair to a palate fine-tuned by sampling the menus at many other eateries. His forte is simple dishes that respect their fresh, flavorful ingredients. But he doesn't confine himself to Japanese fare: he also incorporates techniques and materials from Chinese and French cuisine. He plans the day's menu every morning while inspecting products at the Tsukiji market; choosing each ingredient by provenance, based on years of experience. The pale bamboo shoots that arrive in spring from Tamba in Kyoto have a limited run of just two weeks. Tilefish from Wakasa is soaked in brine, dried for a half-day, brushed with *sake* and then grilled with exquisite timing. The chef favors root vegetables, especially those from Kyoto's traditional *kyo yasai*, which he seasons lightly and then steams to delicate perfection. At lunchtime, the kitchen hosts a home-cooking class; lunch is served in the *tatami* room.

Closed Golden week, mid-August, late December-early January and Monday

Open:
lunch 12:00-14:00 L.O.12:30
dinner 18:00-22:00 L.O.21:00

Tahara 田はら

Michelin

Dinner: menu ¥8,000-10,000
carte ¥4,000-13,500

TEL 03–5410–0200 / FAX 03–5730–9647
3-5-4 Nishi-Azabu, Minato-ku

See map p 10, A4

This Japanese restaurant's Nishi-Azabu premises have a spare, clean look, with counter seating downstairs and tables upstairs. The spiral stairs suggest a hideaway loft but actually lead to a small private room (for up to eight). The owner-chef trained as a cook in an Ebisu eel restaurant before taking over his family's wholesale fish business. Drawing on the expertise that has won him high-class restaurateur clients, he opened Tahara with a fish specialty in 1992. The signature deep-fried saurel, for example, is fluffy, crisp-coated and fragrant, a far cry from most people's idea of the dish. The saurel (also available as *sashimi*) hails from Ehime's Okuchi Bay, whose catch is renowned for its fleshiness. Other offerings include clear soup with large clams direct from the Joban region in Ibaraki; black cod marinated in *sake* lees and Kyoto white *miso*; and, from late November on, Hamanako oysters, raw or fried. The techniques are very simple, but the premium products and attention to basics make this fare outstanding.

Closed Golden week, mid-August, late December-early January, Sunday and Bank Holidays

Open:
dinner 17:30-22:00 (L.O.) Saturday L.0.21:30

Takeyabu 竹やぶ

Michelin

Lunch: menu ¥ 5,250
carte ¥ 3,000-8,000
Dinner: menu ¥ 8,400
carte ¥ 3,000-8,000

TEL 03–5786–7500
Roppongi Hills Residence B 3F,
6-12-2 Roppongi, Minato-ku
10

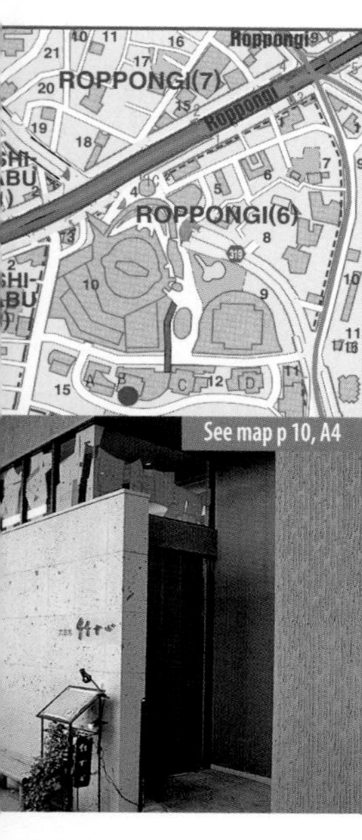

See map p 10, A4

The owner, who opened a restaurant called Takeyabu in Kashiwa, Chiba Prefecture in 1966 when he was 22 years old, opened the Roppongi Hills branch in 2003. Objets d'art handmade by the owner give the interior a unique atmosphere. The covers of the individual menus feature an original oil painting or collage, and among the tableware are pieces that the owner made and fired himself. Of course, a unique sensibility shines through in the *soba* dishes served here. The *soba* flour is all homemade from stone-ground whole-grain buckwheat. The water used in cooking comes from Hakojima Spring in Gunma, selected as one of Japan's top one hundred natural springs. Edo-style *soba*, which boasts a 400-year history, has numerous varieties with different characteristic flavors, but at Takeyabu, the owner characteristically goes his own way, providing the tastiest, most pleasing *soba* he knows how. The menu provides a rich selection of dishes, such as cold *sobagaki* (a dish normally served hot) and galettes, reminiscent of Brittany, made from *soba* flour.

Closed 1-3 January

Open:
lunch 11:30-15:30 (L.O.)
dinner 18:00-21:30 (L.O.)

✿✿

Taku 拓

Michelin

Dinner: menu ¥ 15,750-18,900

TEL 03–5774–4372 / FAX 03–5774–4373
2-11-5 Nishi-Azabu, Minato-ku

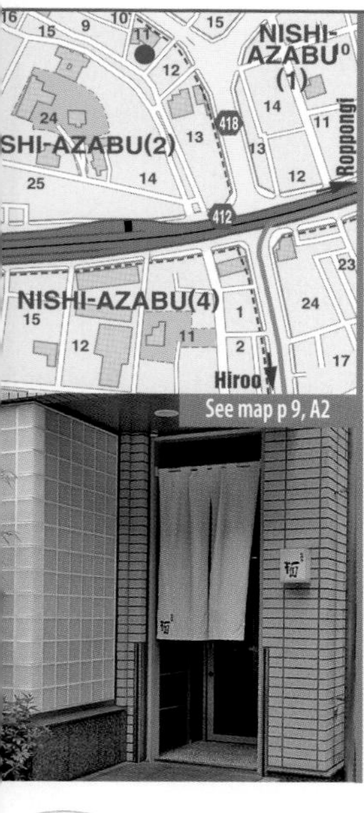

See map p 9, A2

Co-owned by a *sushi* chef and a female sommelier, Taku pulls off the tricky pairing of Edomae *sushi* and wine. But what's more obvious than this delicate balancing act is the attention they give to their guests: they want diners to have a good time. The venue, located in Nishi-Azabu, blends a Japanese interior with exposed concrete walls. It seats just nine at the counter and four in a private room, the latter with a leg well sunk into the *tatami* around a small *sushi* counter of its own. Working as he is with superbly fresh ingredients, the chef-owner considers it his duty to cut no corners in the routine preparation. His top priority is to give free play to the product's natural flavors by minimizing handling; his skill allows them to emerge delectably intact. There is an à la carte menu, but *omakase* is the way to go. Between rounds of *sushi*, the chefs will slip in another Japanese dish that complements your preference for wine or *sake*.

Closed mid-August, late December-early January, Sunday and Bank Holidays

Open:
dinner 18:00-1:00 (L.O.)

FRENCH CONTEMPORARY 

Tateru Yoshino

Tateru Yoshino, Michelin

Lunch: menu ¥ 4,050-17,330
carte ¥ 11,000-18,000

Dinner: menu ¥ 10,400-17,330
carte ¥ 11,000-18,000

TEL 03–5405–7800 / FAX 03–5405–7801
Shiba Park Hotel Annex 1F,
1-5-10 Shiba-Koen, Minato-ku
www.tateruyoshino.com

12

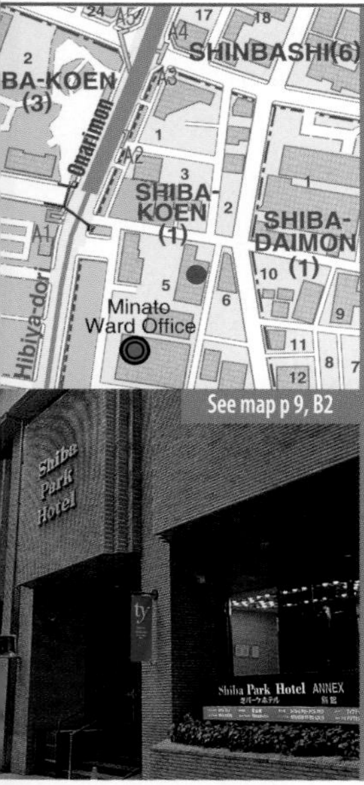

See map p 9, B2

This French restaurant, sister restaurant to "Gastronomie Française Tateru Yoshino" in Shiodome, opened in the annex of the Shiba Park Hotel in 2003. Chef Yoshino also manages the Stella Maris in Paris, and travels back and forth between them every two weeks. The main dining is comfortable and elegant with its wood-paneled walls and wooden floors, large tables, sleek vases, and paintings that are changed on a regular basis. The cuisine is French, expertly prepared with some contemporary touches; the fixed price menu changes every month. There is also a set course consisting mainly of organic vegetables grown by Matsuki Kazuhiro, who is well known among gourmets. There is also an impressive selection of French patisseries. The wine list runs to nearly 300 bins, almost all of them French, specially chosen by the enthusiastic sommelier. Whenever Chef Yoshino is in town, he comes out of the kitchen and greets guests toward the end of the meal.

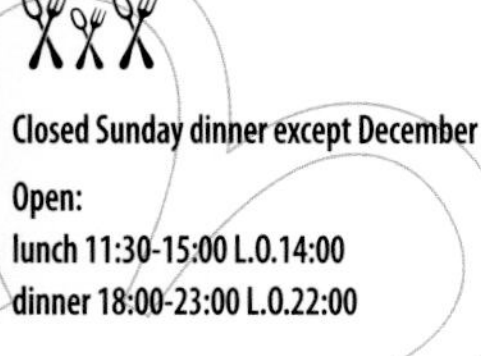

Closed Sunday dinner except December

Open:
lunch 11:30-15:00 L.O.14:00
dinner 18:00-23:00 L.O.22:00

Tatsumura たつむら

Michelin

Dinner: menu ¥ 13,860

TEL 03–3585–7285 / FAX 03–3585–7285
2F,
5-4-14 Akasaka, Minato-ku
8

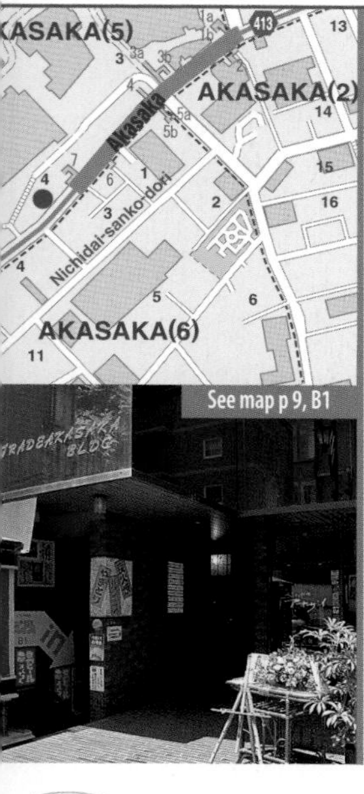

See map p 9, B1

A Japanese-style restaurant behind the TBS television station. The owner used to be the head chef of a famous Akasaka restaurant and in 2007 opened his own establishment. The menu consists of about ten *kaiseki* courses only. Ingredients normally quite difficult to find—*keiji* salmon from Hokkaido and *shiroshita* flounder from Oita, for example—are brought in from all over the country and prepared with the utmost simplicity. Even so, there is a variety to the flavorings that will keep you from being bored, such as the use of scallops and clams in making cooking stock, in addition to the usual dried bonito (*katsuobushi*). One of the specialties of the house is Mineoka *tofu*, and many of the patrons come specifically for this dish. The *taimeshi* (red sea bream and rice) is also exquisite. Seating is either at the counter, or in one of three private rooms. The private rooms are frequently used for business entertaining, while the counter tends to be occupied by people more concerned with savoring the food.

Closed mid-August, late December-early January, Sunday and Bank Holidays

Open:
dinner 17:30-21:00 (L.O.)

The Georgian Club

Michelin

Lunch: menu ¥ 7,000-10,000
carte ¥ 16,000-28,000

Dinner: menu ¥ 19,040-29,120
carte ¥ 16,000-28,000

TEL 03–5412–7177 / FAX 03–5411–0687
1-6-4 Nishi-Azabu, Minato-ku
www.georgian-club.com
P 12

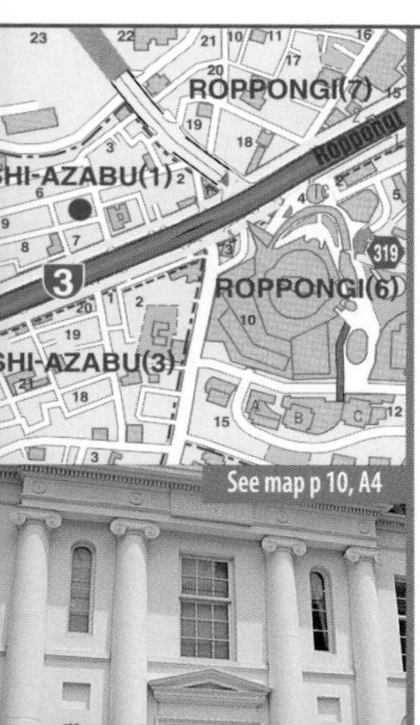

See map p 10, A4

A white, Western-style mansion on a residential street in Nishi-Azabu houses the French restaurant known as The Georgian Club. The British architect has faithfully recreated 18th-century Georgian splendor, and the imported English furnishings live up to the façade. As one descends a curving staircase to the basement-level dining room, the chandeliers are almost dazzling. Portraits of aristocratic English ladies grace the pale blue walls. The chef has worked in many of France's top restaurants. His esthetic is consistently Western: for one thing, he uses none of the signature Japanese vegetables, but regularly features novel Western items. This is also a healthy cuisine: with 40 spices and a dozen vinegars at his command, he does not rely on butter and cream. The house specialty salad, a composition of over 20 vegetables, is dressed with a faintly bitter coriander-infused olive oil called Hyblon. The likes of raw Breton oysters from Miyagi, Bresse pigeon, and wild bream from Sajima abound with flavor, aroma, and color. The wine list is also excellent.

Closed 1-10 January and August

Open:
lunch 12:00-13:30 (L.O.)
dinner 18:00-21:30 (L.O.)

Tofuya Ukai とうふ屋うかい

Tofuya Ukai

Lunch: menu ¥ 6,050-13,860
Dinner: menu ¥ 9,240-13,860

TEL 03–3436–1028 / FAX 03–3436–1029
4-4-13 Shiba-Koen, Minato-ku
70

See map p 9, B2

A traditional Japanese restaurant standing in almost 7,000 sq meters of land nestled in between Tokyo Tower and Shiba Park. The impressive setting is grandly and boldly Japanese: the restaurant is surrounded by trees more than a century old and natural stones. The building, in a simple *sukiyazukuri* style, is made up of 58 private rooms, decorated in a style that fuses Edo culture with Art Nouveau. The *tofu* served at Tofuya Ukai is prepared by veteran craftsmen with more than forty years of experience. They use top-quality Tsurunoko soybeans from Hokkaido not normally used for *tofu*, pure underground water from Owada, and natural brine from the Izu Peninsula. "With *tofu* it is the freshness and the aroma that are important," the chef says, and he is well aware of both the unexplained attraction of *tofu* and the difficulties involved in maintaining its consistent quality. In summer you can enjoy a refreshing dish of fresh chilled *tofu* floating in a *kombu* stock, accompanied by *junsai* (water shield) from Akita.

Closed 29 December-2 January

Open:
lunch 11:00-15:00 (L.O.)
dinner 15:00-22:00 L.O.20:00

Tomura と村

Michelin

Dinner: menu ¥ 23,100-46,200

TEL 03–3591–3303 / FAX 03–3591–3303
1-11-14 Toranomon, Minato-ku

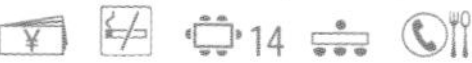

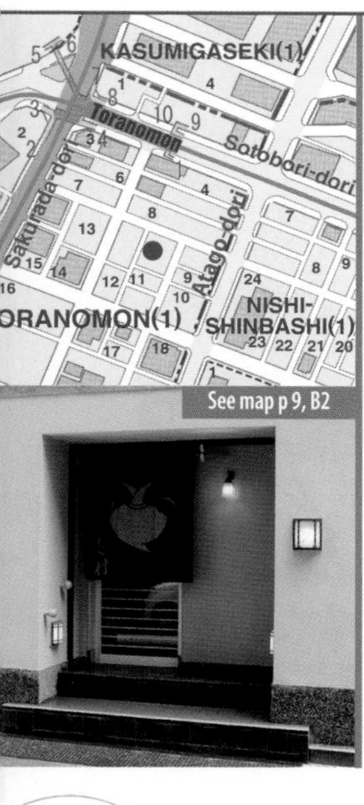

See map p 9, B2

Tomura, which moved in July 2007 from Akasaka to Toranomon, has a sign outside saying "Kyoto Cuisine," reflecting the 13 years the owner-chef spent cooking in the ancient capital. He has a keen sense of how to bring out the best flavor of his ingredients, with no unnecessary showboating. The menu offers only a chef's course, but that includes a variety of flavor combinations: heavy and light, cold and hot, hard and soft, sweet and sour, etc. The chef buys ingredients and materials at the Tsukiji market every day, but also directly orders items that cannot be found in Tokyo. In spring there is rice with fresh bamboo shoots from Higashi Muko in Kyoto; in summer, abalone from the eastern Boso Peninsula in Chiba is steamed, and pike eel from Awajishima is used for *sushi*. In autumn, there is *amadai* from Wakasa Bay and in winter we recommend a tasty dish using *ebi imo*, a wild root vegetable procured from Tondabayashi in Osaka, which are boiled and then deep-fried—pleasantly crunchy outside, soft and creamy inside.

Closed Golden week, mid-August, late December-early January, Sunday and Bank Holiday Mondays

Open:
dinner 18:00-21:30 (L.O.)

Toyoda とよだ

Michelin

Lunch: menu ¥ 5,775-11,550
Dinner: menu ¥ 11,550-23,100

TEL 03–5568–5822
2F,
7-5-4 Ginza, Chuo-ku

See map p 6, C3

This Japanese restaurant is located on the second floor of a small building on Ginza's Namiki-dori. The owner's previous venture, behind nearby Ginza Wako, specialized in pairing wines with Japanese food. Toyoda reopened here as a *kaiseki* restaurant in 2004. The cuisine has an unpretentious appeal with its emphasis on seasonal ingredients. The counterpoint of tastes and textures—sweet, sour, bitter, piquant, soft, chewy—is carefully orchestrated. The chef uses Yoshino *kuzu* starch and dark bonito flakes made to order—shaved to a specified thickness—by a supplier in Kansai. The presentation is imaginative and portions are ample. The interior was designed by the firm of the late Nakamura Sotoji, the 20th-century master of the *sukiyazukuri* style. The décor uses hemlock wood for the counter and Cameroonian bubinga wood for the table in the semi-private room. One could return here many times without tiring of the food, the décor, and the hospitality.

Closed mid-August, late December-early January, Sunday and Bank Holidays

Open:
lunch 11:30-14:30 L.O.13:30
dinner 17:30-22:00 L.O.20:30

Tsukiji Uemura つきじ 植むら

Michelin

Lunch: menu ¥ 7,000-20,000
Dinner: menu ¥ 7,000-25,000
carte ¥ 4,500-13,000

TEL 03–3541–1351 / FAX 03–3544–6722
1-13-10 Tsukiji, Chuo-ku
www.tukijiuemura.com
15

See map p 6, D3

This venerable Japanese restaurant, founded in 1928, was reborn in 2005 in a renovated building. The head chef trained at the Osaka branch, gained experience at a *ryotei*, then worked at Tsukiji Uemura's many branches for 12 years. He handpicks his suppliers, double-checks the products, and prepares them in classical style. From Kyoto come Kamo eggplant, Manganji chili, Shogoin turnips, dark-red carrots; from Nagasaki, tilefish, grunt, oval squid, and blackthroat sea perch; from Oita's Bungo Strait, the prized *Seki aji* and *Seki saba* mackerel; from Hokkaido, flounder and sea urchin. His special basic stock strikes a fine balance of tastes. While remaining within a Japanese ambit, he can be innovative: his outstanding "chilled soup featuring cherry tomatoes" are enhanced by *junsai* (water shield shoots) and chicken stock. The simple, understated Japanese décor, with its play of indirect lighting and its unvarnished, fine-grained counters, evokes the restaurant's motif of flowing water. Each floor provides options of counter seating, tables and private rooms.

Closed Golden week, mid-August, late December-early January, Sunday and Bank Holidays

Open:
lunch 11:30-15:00 L.O.14:00
dinner 17:00-22:00 L.O.20:00

Tsukiji Yamamoto つきじ やまもと

Tsukiji Yamamoto

Lunch: menu ¥ 11,500-40,250
Dinner: menu ¥ 40,250

TEL 03–3541–7730 / FAX 03–3541–7697
2-15-4 Tsukiji, Chuo-ku
www8.plala.or.jp/tsukijiyamamoto/

8

See map p 6, D3

Located near Tsukiji Honganji, Tsukiji Yamamoto is a third-generation restaurant that specializes in blowfish cuisine. The atmosphere in this lovely, old-fashioned house is homely and congenial. If you want to learn about the ingredients used in each dish as you savor it, sit at the counter with its sunken *kotatsu* and listen to the explanations made by the kind and friendly proprietor. For a more formal dining experience, request one of the private *tatami* rooms on the second floor. The set menu is a combination of traditional blowfish cuisine and original creations such as *nakaochi* (backbone fillet) marinated in whisky. The table accessories were selected by the proprietor himself in the blowfish off-season when the restaurant is closed. The tableware and copper pots with a fine patina of age acquired through many years of use reflect his careful attention to detail. From the moment you step though the door, the sincere, enthusiastic greetings will make you feel truly welcome. Prices are on the high side, but lunchtime prices are comparatively reasonable.

Closed April-September, Sunday and Bank Holidays

Open:
lunch 11:30-14:30
dinner 17:00-22:30

Twenty One

Twenty One, Hilton

Dinner: menu ¥ 9,820-18,200
carte ¥ 7,500-16,500

TEL 03–3344–5111 / FAX 03–3342–6094
Hilton Hotel Tokyo 2F,
6-6-2 Nishi-Shinjuku, Shinjuku-ku
www.hilton.co.jp

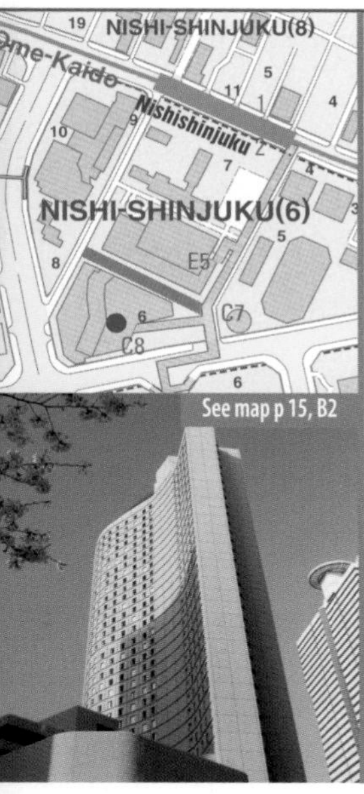

See map p 15, B2

On the second-floor of the Hilton, you will find Twenty One and its French cuisine. The elegant design is based on oval motifs, with a large oval table in the center of the room. The interior is bright, providing a lively contemporary atmosphere, with modern art work on the walls. A four-seat counter affords a prime view into the open kitchen, where you can see this team at work. The menu is comprised of orthodox French cuisine featuring natural ingredients direct from the farm and field, such as Maezawa beef from Iwate Prefecture and organic vegetables. Under the supervision of the executive chef, Stéphane Gaborieau (restaurant Le Pergolèse in Paris), who comes to Tokyo every season with a new menu, young but experienced French chef direct the team in the kitchen and provide evolving but consistently excellent cuisine. The wine list is interesting, giving you a chance to get acquainted with the wines from all over the world.

Closed Monday

Open:
dinner 17:30-23:00 L.O.22:00

Uchiyama うち山

Michelin

Lunch: menu ¥ 5,000-8,000
Dinner: menu ¥ 11,550-23,100

TEL 03–3541–6720 / FAX 03–3541–6720
B1F,
2-12-3 Ginza, Chuo-ku

16

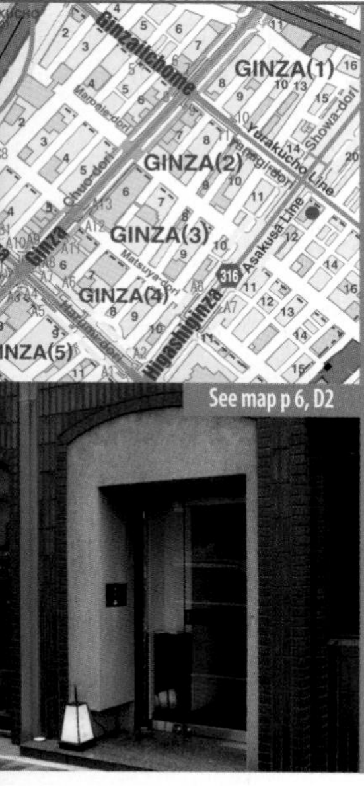

See map p 6, D2

A traditional Japanese restaurant that opened in 2002 in the first basement floor of a building off Showa Dori. With earthen walls and a stonework floor, the décor has a traditional Japanese bent. The private rooms are arranged in a contemporary manner, but with antique touches. The owner, who trained in a variety of Japanese restaurants, offers a rich palette of seasonal flavors based in the traditional *chakaiseki* cuisine. He is a craftsman who speaks of his desire to use authentic ingredients and master the art of truly Japanese cooking. Grilled sesame *tofu*, served as an appetizer, is creamy and flavorful, and is one of this restaurant's signature dishes. In autumn there is a single-serving hotpot of *hamo*, a sea eel from Mogi in Nagasaki Prefecture, with *matsutake* mushrooms and the leafy green *mizuna* from Nagano and Yamaguchi. Finish off your meal with a dessert of arrowroot jelly from the mountain village of Yoshino in Nara Prefecture sweetened with a caramel sauce made with brown sugar from Okinawa.

Closed Golden week, mid-August, late December-early January, Sunday and Bank Holidays

Open:
lunch 11:30-14:00 (L.O.)
dinner 17:00-21:00 (L.O.)

Ukai-Tei

Ukai

Lunch: menu ¥ 7,510-34,650
carte ¥ 15,000-45,000

Dinner: menu ¥ 13,860-34,650
carte ¥ 15,000-45,000

TEL 03–3544–5252 / FAX 03–3544–6868
Jiji-Tsushin Building,
5-15-8 Ginza, Chuo-ku
www.ukai.co.jp

9

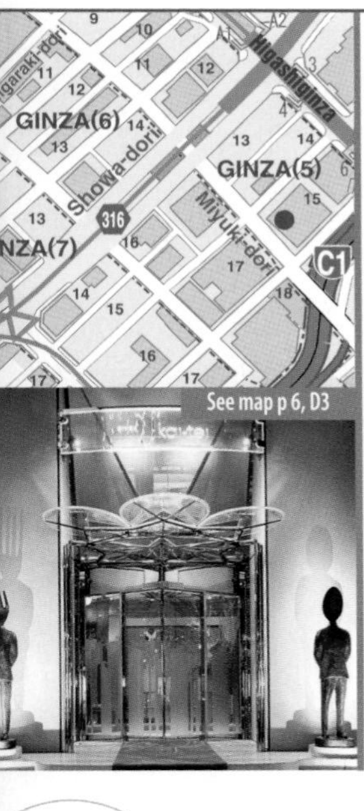

See map p 6, D3

This *teppanyaki* restaurant near Higashi-Ginza station was opened in 2003 by the Ukai group. The entrance is flanked by bronze figures of a fork and spoon that used to be owned by a famous restaurant in Paris. Ukai-tei has a noblewoman in the Art Nouveau style as its symbol, and the décor is reminiscent of La Belle Époque (late 19th and early 20th century France). The mosaic patterns scattered along the walls, Art Deco lamps by Daum Frères, a Müller Frères chandelier, Baccarat glassware, and other touches produce an atmosphere of 19th century aestheticism, but the stout post-and-beam construction of the interior provides an underlying feeling of sturdiness and weight. The specialty of the house is plump abalone from Sannohe in Aomori Prefecture, steamed in rock salt. The restaurant has established its own stock farm on the border between Tottori and Hyogo Prefectures, where it raises some 1,200 head of prime Kurobe beef cattle. After dinner you move to a lounge to relax and enjoy dessert.

Closed 29 December-2 January

Open:
lunch 12:00-15:00 (L.O.)
dinner 15:00-23:00 L.O.21:00

Umi 海味

Michelin

Dinner: menu ¥ 17,000

TEL 03-3401-3368
3-2-8 Minami-Aoyama, Minato-ku

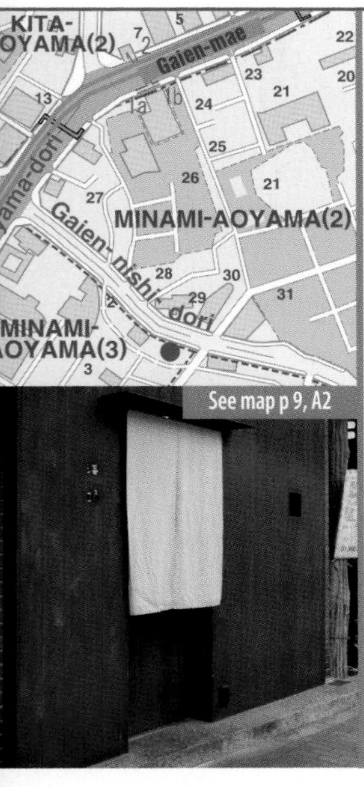

See map p 9, A2

The name means "Taste of the Sea," and is appropriate to this lively *sushi* restaurant, where you can indeed savor the ocean's bounty. The owner-chef was a practitioner of *kendo* and has the command of traditional etiquette you would expect from someone with such a background. When it comes to having his guests enjoy *sushi*, he begins with tuna, as a sort of greeting and introduction. "You can judge a *sushi* restaurant by the tuna it offers," he says. If you order the chef's course, you'll have the opportunity of tasting over 30 kinds of seafood. There are fish that are usually used in *sushi* only in Kyushu or Hokkaido. The rice is from Niigata, cooked al dente and given a liberal touch of salt. The vinegar is a blend of red vinegar aged for three years, which has a bouquet of *sake* lees, and thinner red vinegar. His dipping sauce uses hand-made soy sauce from Shodoshima, is left to "sleep" for three days. The *nori*, from the Ariake Sea, is fragrant and almost melts in the mouth. The *tamagoyaki* is juicy and flavorful, with a small portion of broth sealed inside.

Closed mid-August, late December-early January, Sunday and Bank Holidays

Open:
dinner 18:00-23:00 (L.O.)

Uotoku うを徳

Michelin

Lunch: menu ¥ 11,550-17,325
Dinner: menu ¥ 23,100-28,875

TEL 03–3269–0360 / FAX 03–3269–0373
3-1 Kagurazaka, Shinjuku-ku
www.uotoku.com
25

See map p 16, D1

A *ryotei* in Karukozaka, near Iidabashi Station. One of only four remaining *ryotei* restaurants in the Kagurazaka area, it dates back to the early Meiji era (1868-1912), when a fishmonger from Hatchobori set up shop here. The place became a *ryotei* in 1920, and the present proprietor is the fifth generation. Inside, there are two private *tatami* rooms and a large room upstairs. The culinary style is Edomae. Don't miss the *ebi shinjo* (shrimp dumplings). Salty-sweet vegetables simmered in *sake*, sugar, *mirin* and soy, and Shiba shrimp are both minced into balls, which retain the shrimp's consistency. The stock used for the broth changes with the composition of the dish. The tasty, aromatic fish dishes are also acclaimed. Guests can engage a *geisha* to grace a banquet with *samisen* playing, song and dance. In recent years, *ryotei* restaurants, with their particular atmosphere, have been attracting a growing clientele, and Uotoku often hosts special occasions such as betrothals and farewell parties.

Closed mid-August and late December-early January

Open:
lunch 11:30-14:30 L.O.13:00
dinner 17:00-23:00 L.O.21:00

Usukifugu Yamadaya 臼杵ふぐ山田屋

Michelin

Dinner: menu ¥ 23,100-34,650
carte ¥ 12,000-22,000

TEL 03–3499–5501 / FAX 03–3499–5502
Fleg Nishi-Azabu Vierge B1F,
4-11-14 Nishi-Azabu, Minato-ku
13

See map p 9, A2

A *fugu* restaurant that was opened in Nishi Azabu in 2006 by a restaurant that has been serving traditional Japanese cuisine at Usuki in Oita Prefecture since the end of the 19th century. Inside, the age-old beauty of Japanese architecture has been given a contemporary twist: careful attention has been lavished on every detail from the Cassina leather sofas down to the *kimonos* worn by the wait staff. During the season, wild *torafugu* and mackeral (*sekisaba* and *sekiaji*) are delivered daily from Oita. The chef prides himself on his *sashimi*, which is eaten with homemade *ponzu* sauce made of soy sauce from Usuki and *kabosu*, a citrus fruit native to Oita. No soy sauce at all is used in the *karaage*; instead, seasonings are added to the coating to bring out the flavor and give it its distinctive lightness. The hospitality of the wait staff exudes a sense of Japanese refinement and thoroughness, making this a restaurant that can also be recommended for business entertainment. You can enjoy fugu throughout the year if reserved in advance.

Closed Golden week, mid-August, late December-early January, Sunday and Bank Holidays

Open:
dinner 18:00-24:00 L.O.22:30

Waketokuyama 分とく山

Waketokuyama

Dinner: menu ¥ 17,325

TEL 03–5789–3838
5-1-5 Minami-Azabu, Minato-ku

8

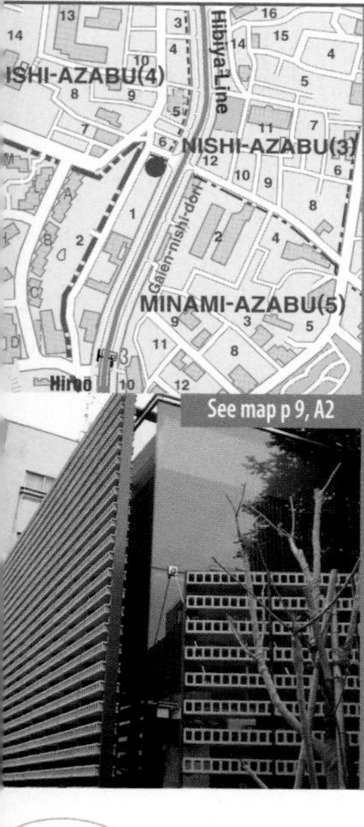

See map p 9, A2

This *kaiseki* restaurant Waketokuyama opened for business in 1987 and moved to its actual location in 2004 in an avant-garde concrete and glass building. The exterior design concept, created by a famous designer, is "lightness and nature." Step through the glass doors into the interior, and you find modern décor with a traditional Japanese accent. On each of the two floors, there is both counter and table seating, and there is a small annex with private rooms which have access to a small garden. The cuisine preserves Japanese tradition while adapting it to the times, with the emphasis less on deep flavors than on refreshing tastes which do not become cloying. The chef procures 80 to 100 different kinds of ingredients from suppliers all over the country. The food not only tastes good; it is good for you—the chef served as the head chef for the all-Japan baseball team at the Athens Olympics. Popular with the media, Waketokuyama has many celebrity patrons.

Closed 29 December-4 January and Sunday

Open:
dinner 17:00-23:00 L.O.21:00

Wako 和幸

Michelin

Lunch: menu ¥ 17,325-28,875
Dinner: menu ¥ 23,100-28,875

TEL 03–3982–2251 / FAX 03–3982–1533
2-16-3 Mejiro, Toshima-ku
8

See map p 17, B2

"We value human harmony and give thanks for the blessings and bounty of the sea and the mountains." This idea is incorporated into the name of the restaurant: wa means harmony, and ko means bounty. The owner already had this shop name in mind during his apprenticeship in the early '60s. He believes that true Japanese cuisine means drawing out all the delicious natural flavors from the food and devoting oneself wholeheartedly to the customer. Only the freshest natural ingredients are rigorously selected: tuna comes only from the Sea of Japan; sweetfish is caught in the Yoshida River at Gujo Hachiman on the days when the no-fishing ban is lifted; and bamboo sprouts in spring and *matsutake* mushrooms in autumn are from Tamba in Kyoto. The restaurant is located in a hidden street of a residential district in Mejiro. The dignified traditional *sukiya*-style interior is made up of three private rooms as well as a tearoom. While having an impeccable pedigree and being respectful of the traditions of Kyoto-style *kaiseki,* this is also a place that makes one feel the essence of warm hospitality.

Closed Golden week, mid-August, late December-early January, Sunday and Bank Holidays

Open:
lunch 11:30-13:30 (L.O.)
dinner 17:30-20:00 (L.O.)

Yamane やま祢

Yamane, Michelin

Dinner: menu ¥ 28,875-40,425

TEL 03–3541–1383 / FAX 03–3541–1384
7-15-7 Ginza, Chuo-ku
12

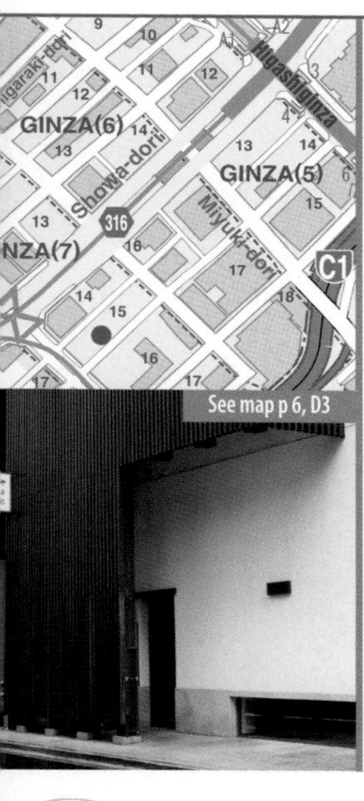

A long-established restaurant that has been serving *fugu* since 1954. The present chef is the founder's grandson who, after apprenticing in Osaka, succeeded his father to become the third in his family to pass down the founder's flavors to today's clientele. The restaurant was completely renovated in 2004. Inside, a gentle slope leads to individual rooms housed in a modern Japanese-style building. These high-ceilinged rooms made of fine-quality materials exude an atmosphere of dignity and grace, and the kimono-clad female staff provides attentive service. As for the *fugu* cuisine, it all comes down to the superior quality of the ingredients. The wild fish are flown in from Shimonoseki, *fugu*'s natural habitat. The *karaage* uses homemade *miso* to enhance the flavor, and white *miso* from Hiroshima is used in the *fugu* hotpot to lessen the fish's distinctive aroma. The red sea bream from Fukuoka is also very tasty; in summertime we recommend the fresh scorpion fish, flatfish, and conger eels.

Closed Golden week, mid-August, late December-early January and Sunday

Open:
dinner 17:30-19:30 (L.O.)

Yamasaki 山さき

Michelin

Dinner: menu ¥ 7,717-16,537

TEL 03–3267–2310
4-2-201 Kagurazaka, Shinjuku-ku

See map p 16, D1

Closed mid-August, late December-early January, Sunday and Bank Holidays

Open:
dinner 18:00-22:00 L.O.20:00

A Japanese-style restaurant in Kagurazaka. There is no shop sign, and the simple and unpretentious interior has only five tables. The lady owner-chef trained for eight years in *nabe ryori* (Japanese hotpots or stews) and other Japanese cuisines before she set up on her own in 2002. She serves simply and elegantly flavored *nabe ryori* using fresh seasonal ingredients, and says, "I want to be faithful to Edo cuisine." For summer *nabe* she uses a greenling from Joban, in a refreshing stock flavored with bonito flakes, *sake*, and salt-pickled Kishu plums. *Moryo nabe* features specially-bred Tokushima chickens. They are boiled whole, and then the meat is removed from the bones and incorporated in a stew with *daikon* radishes, *myoga* ginger, winter melon, and other vegetables. Beginning in October, there is an even more plentiful variety of *nabe* dishes, and the autumn *negima nabe* of leeks and tuna as well as the winter *miso nabe* are highly recommended. She also does not like to offer too many dishes as part of a course, so that she can concentrate on ensuring that each dish is truly satisfying.

Yebisu 惠比寿

Yebisu, Westin

Lunch: menu ¥ 2,430-23,100
carte ¥ 7,000-23,100

Dinner: menu ¥ 17,330-52,000
carte ¥ 7,000-23,100

TEL 03–5423–7790 / FAX 03–5423–1470
Westin Hotel 22F,
1-4-1 Mita, Meguro-ku
www.westin-tokyo.co.jp

10

See map p 7, C2

Located on the 22nd floor of The Westin in Meguro is Yebisu, a teppanyaki restaurant with a chic, subdued décor in tones of brown and beige and softly lit by indirect lighting from stylized lamps. The vases of artfully arranged flowers and fresco paintings on the walls display a modern yet subtle harmony. In addition to the counter, there are three large tables as well as three private dining rooms. Diners can savor the choice meat, seasonal vegetables and fresh seafood cooked on the grill plate right in front of their eyes. The chefs use a fusion of Japanese and Western culinary techniques, and are a pleasure to watch. Several courses are offered, including two steak courses (Miyazaki beef and Maezawa beef), a lobster course and a seafood course. In addition, Yebisu provides sweeping, panoramic views from its large windows. On a clear day the view of Mount Fuji is breathtaking. The service offered with a smile is thoroughly professional.

Open:
lunch 11:30-15:00 L.O.14:30
dinner 17:30-22:30 L.O.22:00

Yokota よこ田

Michelin

Dinner: menu ¥ 9,450

TEL 03–3408–4238
2F,
1-5-11 Azabu-Juban, Minato-ku

See map p 10, A4

The sign outside this Toriizaka restaurant says simply *"Tempura."* The cozy interior has black floor tiles, wattle-and-daub walls and cedar wainscots. The U-shaped bamboo-frame counter seats ten. The owner-chef worked at a famous Ginza *tempura* house before taking over Yokota from his father. He runs the place with his wife and son. He fries the *tempura*, while his son prepares food in the kitchen at the back. They visit the Tsukiji market together every morning. Yokota's consistently light touch with batter and oil gives full play to the ingredients' flavors, with no oily aftertaste. The oil is a blend of sesame and corn, their aromas in heady harmony. The *tempura* can be eaten with a dipping sauce, a touch of curry powder, lemon and salt. The menu is fixed price only. Goby and young sea bream are available in season. Here, Edomae ingredients and seasonal vegetables truly come into their own.

Closed Golden week, mid-August, late December-early January and Wednesday

Open:
dinner 17:30-20:00 (L.O.)

Yonemura よねむら

Michelin

Lunch: menu ¥ 6,000-12,000
Dinner: menu ¥ 14,000

TEL 03–5537–6699
Kojun Building 4F,
6-8-7 Ginza, Chuo-ku

See map p 6, C3

This restaurant, whose main branch is located in the Gion district of Kyoto, opened in Ginza in 2004. The cuisine here is so original that it can be said to be in a class by itself. Along with Japanese ingredients, it imaginatively uses Western ones such as foie gras to produce what might be called *kaiseki ryori* in which French culinary techniques are used to bring the seasonal flavors to life. Some ingredients are also brought in directly from Kyoto. The meal is well balanced with pairings of fried and light items so that diners can enjoy one dish after another. The interior consists of a long counter with 12 chairs, and tables and chairs separated from each other by a partition. There is an iron-barred gate at the entrance, and, a painting of some rice plants on the wall; a visual pun on the word "Yone" in the restaurant's name. The set course at lunchtime is both reasonable and ample.

Closed 31 December-1 January

Open:
lunch 12:00-15:30 L.O.14:00
dinner 17:30-23:00 L.O.21:00

Yoneyama よねやま

Michelin

Dinner: menu ¥ 10,500-15,750

TEL 03–3341–3117 / FAX 03–3341–3117
15 Arakicho, Shinjuku-ku

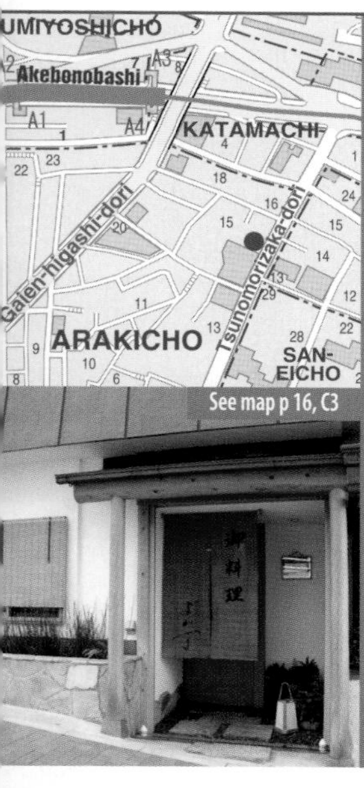

See map p 16, C3

At the counter kitchen in this quiet restaurant the chef and his assistant go about their business in silence. This is a small but quality Japanese restaurant with a counter that seats five, and two tables. Although the owner did not apprentice or work at any particularly famous restaurants, he is someone who has cultivated his own culinary esthetic and gives full play to the innate taste of good-quality ingredients and simple fare. The care lavished on the sea bream in particular is impressive, and he always serves sea bream *sashimi* when it is in season—three or four rather thickly cut slices of wild sea bream from Awaji. The blackthroat seaperch from Choshi is broiled with salt over a charcoal fire allowing excess fat to drip away. Abalone from Chiba is dipped and swirled in a hot bonito stock and garnished with a sauce made from its puréed liver. The food is served on blue and white Kyoyaki ceramics made more than 40 years ago. Selected Japanese *sakes* are offered at reasonable prices.

Closed mid-August, late December-early January and Sunday

Open:
dinner 18:00-21:30 (L.O.)

Yotaro 与太呂

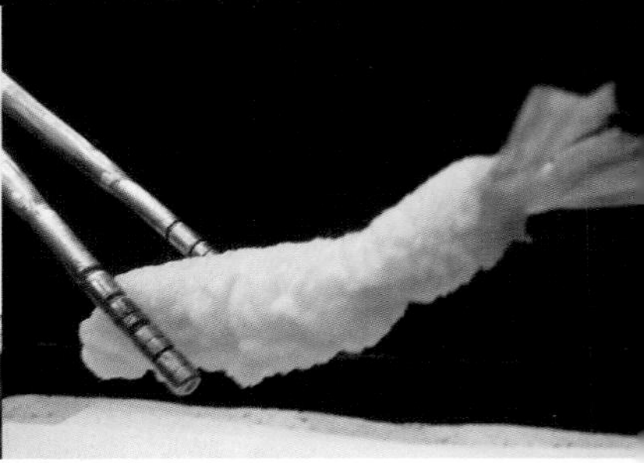

Yotaro, Michelin

Dinner: menu ¥ 13,650

TEL 03–3405–5866 / FAX 03–3746–2727
4-11-4 Roppongi, Minato-ku
www.roppongi-yotaro.com

See map p 9, B2

Closed Golden week, mid-August, late December-early January and Sunday

Open:
dinner 17:30-22:00 (L.O.)

The owner of this *tempura* restaurant opened Yotaro in 1981 and now operates it with his son, who trained as a chef in Kyoto. The interior is Japanese, its walls enhanced with black marble. The key to the cooking at Yotaro is, first and foremost, the careful selection of ingredients. Wild red sea bream (*tai*) is used for different dishes: *tai* from Matsuwa on the Miura Peninsula is served as *sashimi*, while *tai* from Tokushima in Shikoku is used for *taimeshi* (sea bream with rice). *Taimeshi* is one of Yotaro's signature dishes, and the Tokushima fish is used in it because its tender flesh and rich, concentrated flavor go well with rice, which the owner knows from many years of meticulously selecting ingredients. The light and airy coating of the *tempura* and the perfect timing of its cooking give it a quality you will find nowhere else. The way the dishes are prepared here, one after the other, by a father-son relay team, provides a happy atmosphere of familial warmth.

Yukicho 有季銚

Yukicho

Lunch: menu ¥ 4,180-38,500
Dinner: menu ¥ 17,600-38,500

TEL 03–3544–2700 / FAX 03–3541–6814
B1F,
7-13-10 Ginza, Chuo-ku
www.four-seeds.co.jp/brand/11_yukicho/
8

See map p 6, D3

During his apprenticeship years, the chef worked at the established Ginza *fugu* restaurant Santomo, and learned from its former owner that "*fugu* isn't *fugu* unless it feels firm to the bite." The chef still follows this precept and serves fugu as part of his winter kaiseki course. The *fugu* at Yukicho is wild *torafugu* delivered directly from Bungo, Oita Prefecture. In summer one can look forward to scorpion fish; what is unusual here is that, in addition to *sashimi*, they offer the head dipped briefly in hot water to be eaten with *ponzu* sauce. Red snapper and pike eel are flown in straight from Bungo. Oysters from the Noto peninsula in Ishikawa Prefecture are also first rate, toasted over a charcoal fire, and then grilled. Wild fresh-water trout is from Lake Biwa, the Shimanto River and Tochigi. All these foods are beautifully presented on a variety of exquisite serving ware including Kyoyaki ceramics, Wajima lacquer ware and Baccarat crystal. Customer service is also first class.

Closed Golden week, mid-August, late December-early January, Sunday and Bank Holidays

Open:
lunch 11:30-13:30 (L.O.)
dinner 17:30-21:00 (L.O.)

Yukimura 幸村

Michelin

Dinner: menu ¥ 25,410-34,650

TEL 03–5772–1610
3F,
1-5-5 Azabu-Juban, Minato-ku

See map p 10, A4

A Japanese restaurant in Azabu-Juban. There is no sign outside, just a small placard once you enter the building. At the center of the interior is a large framed calligraphy of the restaurant's name by the Kyoto traditional painter Kaho Akinobu. Behind the trapezoid-shaped counter is a massive cutting board made of ginko wood, beside which is a brazier for charcoal-grilling. The owner was born in Tokyo but spent 25 years working in a famous Kyoto restaurant, and from this experience now offers inspired Kyoto style cuisine to a Tokyo audience, employing a variety of ingredients commonly used there. There is no *sashimi* on the menu, as the owner prefers to create surprising dishes. Specialties of the house include steamed sea urchin with jellied lobster, *shabu-shabu* with beef and *sansho* flowers, *matsutake* mushrooms wrapped in pike eel and charcoal-grilled, and dishes using Matsuba crabs. The owner had the pots made specially to order, and they are known as "Yukimura nabe." Only full-course meals are offered.

Closed Golden week, mid-August and late December-early January

Open:
dinner 17:30-20:00 (L.O.)

Yûta ゆう田

Michelin

Dinner: menu ¥ 21,000

TEL 03–3423–2885 / FAX 03–3423–2885
3-13-1 Nishi-Azabu, Minato-ku
6

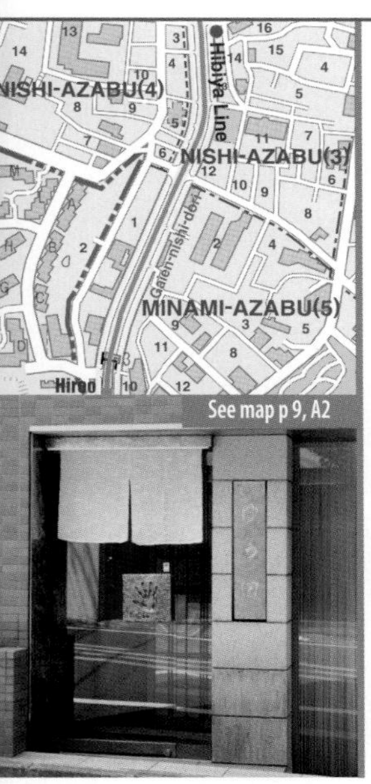

See map p 9, A2

Keep an eye out for the sculpture marking the entrance—a replica of the owner-chef's hand. The white interior, created by an architectural designer, is a modern interpretation of the traditional teahouse. This small *sushi* restaurant has six seats at the counter and a private room downstairs. The most attractive aspect of the cuisine is its simplicity, making full use of the natural flavor of its ingredients. The *sushi* rice is Koshihikari from prime harvest years, cooked just slightly al dente, seasoned only with red vinegar and salt. First and foremost among the seafood offerings is the finest quality *uni* (sea urchin). It is carefully selected by a specialist supplier in Hokkaido. *Sazae* (turban shells) from Ohara in Chiba Prefecture are plump and toothsome, and grilled in their shells–another of the specialties of the house. A summer seasonal treat is *mizunasu*, a unique variation of eggplant from the Senshu area of Osaka, lightly pickled with a touch of salt. In autumn, the *shimesaba* is delicious: fat mackerel from Matsuwa in Kanagawa Prefecture, lightly pickled in salt and vinegar.

Closed mid-August, late December-early January, Sunday and Bank Holidays

Open:
dinner 18:00-22:00 (L.O.)

Where to stay

Michelin

Hotels
by order of comfort

ANA Intercontinental

ANA Intercontinental

🚹	¥40,450-52,000
🚹🚹	¥40,450-52,000
Suite	¥75,100-323,400
☕	¥2,500

TEL 03–3505–1111 / FAX 03–3505–1155
1-12-33 Akasaka, Minato-ku
www.anaintercontinental-tokyo.jp

See map p 9, B2

Rooms: 835
Suites: 32
Restaurants: 8

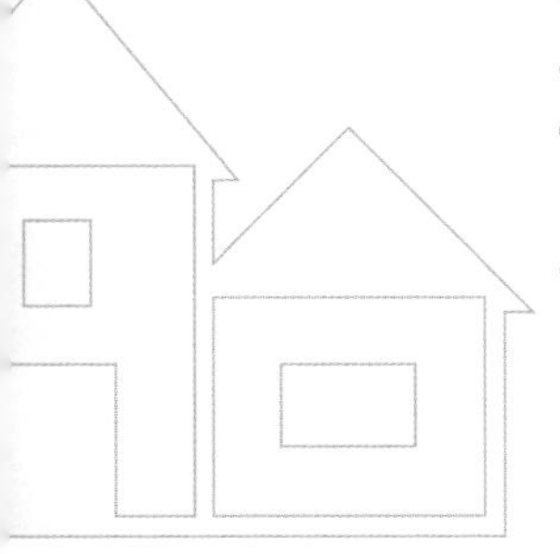

About midway to Roppongi from the central government office district, there is a 37-story hotel. In April 2007 it changed its name from the ANA Hotel to the ANA Intercontinental Hotel. Guest rooms occupy the 7th to the 35th floors. The Club Intercontinental Floors (32nd to 35th) are the executive floors where both the interiors and the views are better. Rooms and suites here include access to the club lounge and its exclusive services on the 34th floor. The guest rooms on the regular floors (7th to 31th) are not large (29-32 m^2) but the pleasant décor is attractive. The views differ depending on the room; there are three sides to choose from: facing either the Imperial Palace, the Tokyo Tower, or the southern part of Tokyo with Mount Fuji in the distance. The hotel has a wide range of facilities including many banquet rooms, an outside pool opened only during the summer, and a fitness room. There is a full complement of restaurants and bars offering a wide selection of cuisines. This is a hotel that offers guests a urban lifestyle and is also suited to foreign visitors.

Century Southern Tower

Century Southern Tower

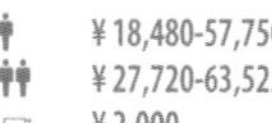

¥18,480-57,750
¥27,720-63,525
¥2,000

TEL 03–5354–0111 / FAX 03–5354–0100
2-2-1 Yoyogi, Shibuya-ku
www.southerntower.co.jp

See map p 12, C1

This hotel, a two-minute walk from Shinjuku Station, occupies the 19th to 35th floors of the Odakyu Southern Tower, a high-rise built in 1998. There are sweeping views of Tokyo from the main lobby on the 20th floor, particularly from the bar and lounge, where on clear days it is possible to see Mount Fuji. Guest rooms are suitable for both business travelers and tourists. Each has a compact bathroom equipped with all the amenities. Rooms range in size from 19 m^2 to 34 m^2; the more spacious executive rooms are 70 m^2 for a double and 80 m^2 for a twin. Located on the 22nd to the 35th floors, they are comfortable and quiet. Windows face out over either the western or the eastern part of Tokyo, and all rooms have stunning city views. In each room there is a panoramic map that lets you check the name and location of nearby buildings seen from the windows. The hotel also has a small fitness facility and three restaurants serving American, Japanese and Chinese cuisine.

Rooms: 375
Restaurants: 3

Cerulean Tower

Cerulean Tower

Single	¥31,500-78,000
Double	¥42,500-80,500
Suite	¥93,500-464,000
Breakfast	¥2,800

TEL 03–3476–3000 / FAX 03–3476–3001
26-1 Sakuragaokacho, Shibuya-ku
www.ceruleantower-hotel.com

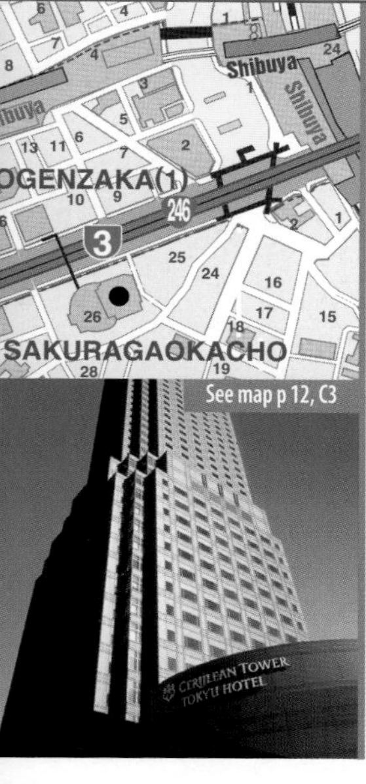

See map p 12, C3

The hotel occupies a 40-story building near Shibuya Station. A high-rise hotel with convenient access to transportation, it opened in 2001. The guest rooms are on the 19th to 37th floors and all of them have views looking out over metropolitan Tokyo. Although the hotel is located next to Route 246, the rooms are quiet, and the modern interior design exudes serenity. On the top floor guests can enjoy Provençal cuisine in the tower restaurant Coucagno or relax at the Bello Visto bar with its view of the night lights of northern Tokyo. There are also a number of restaurants and bars off the lobby on the first floor. To relieve stress and enhance one's health and appearance there is also an indoor pool, a fitness center, and a beauty salon. A beacon of traditional culture both domestically and internationally, the Cerulean Tower Noh Theater is used for public performances of Noh, Kyogen, and other traditional performing arts. This is a hotel that takes its guests' comfort fully into account, placing greater emphasis on functionality and style than on showy accoutrements.

Rooms: 405
Suites: 9
Restaurants: 5

Conrad

Conrad

🚹	¥60,000-75,000
🚹🚹	¥65,000-80,000
Suite	¥88,000-603,000
☕	¥3,200

TEL 03–6388–8000 / FAX 03–6388–8001
1-9-1 Higashi-Shinbashi, Minato-ku
www.conradtokyo.co.jp

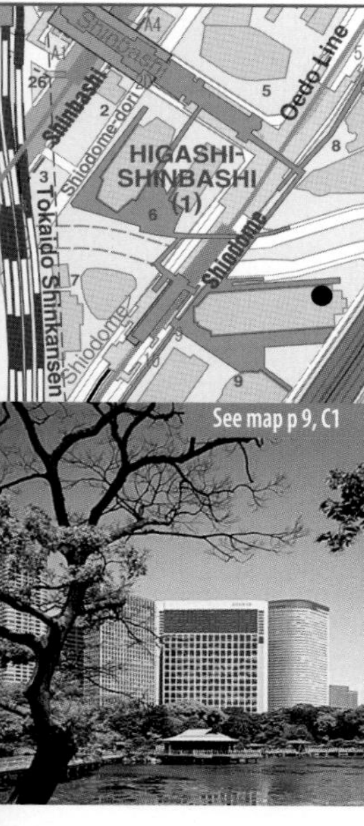

This hotel opened in 2005 in Shiodome, a district that has undergone a major facelift as a result of redevelopment. The reception area is located on the 28th floor of the Tokyo Shiodome Building; and guest rooms and other facilities occupy up to 37th floor, from which guests can enjoy panoramic views of the Hamarikyu Gardens, the Tsukiji market and Tokyo Bay. The hotel's concept is the blending of legendary Conrad elegance with modern Japanese design elements. Original sculptures are on display in the center of the first-floor lobby, while the spacious main lobby has high ceilings and is surrounded by huge glass windows that give it a feeling of openness. Here you will find the TwentyEight Bar and Lounge as well as three restaurants and a brasserie. In Mizuki Spa and Fitness one can look out the windows over the urban landscape of Shiodome from the stylish 25m swimming pool; it also offers a full spa menu. Modern Japanese design has been incorporated in every guestroom; stone and wood have been skillfully arranged to create a refined and elegant space.

Rooms: 222
Suites: 68
Restaurants: 4

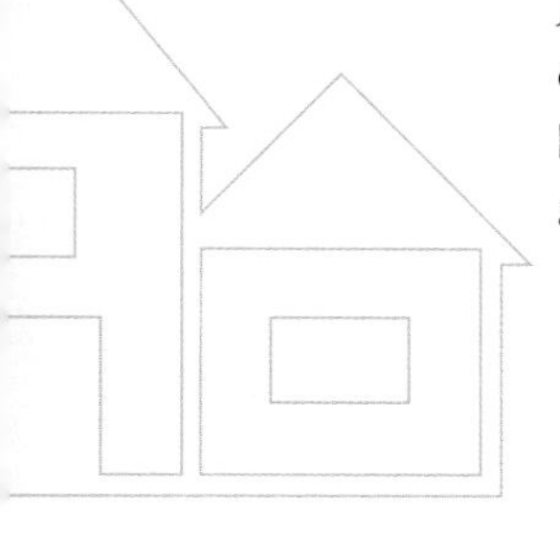

Four Seasons Chinzan-so

Four Seasons Chinzan-so

¥57,800-77,400
¥63,600-77,400
Suite ¥92,400-636,000
¥3,000

TEL 03–3943–2222 / FAX 03–3943–2300
2-10-8 Sekiguchi, Bunkyo-ku
www.fourseasons-tokyo.com

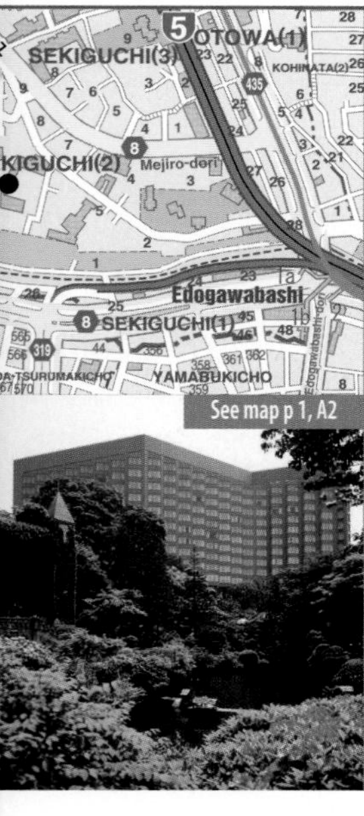

See map p 1, A2

Chinzan-so, which means "Mansion on Camellia Mountain", was the estate of Aritomo Yamagata, a noted military officer and statesman during the Meiji era. The Four Seasons Chinzan-so was built in 1992 on property that overlooks this magnificent garden, which features a natural stream and structures of historic interest such as a thirteen-storied pagoda and stone lanterns. The stylish lobby with its green marble floor and beautiful wooden walls is accented with Japanese screens, ornaments, vases and other works of art. The guest rooms décor mixes with elegance 19th century western style and Japanese style. Large windows offer a sweeping view of either the Chinzan-so garden or of the quiet neighborhood cityscape. The suites are particularly luxurious, with exquisite furnishings. In addition to a wide range of stores, Four Seasons offers a choice of restaurants including Le Jardin, a lounge with wall-to-wall windows overlooking the garden, and Il Teatro, an Italian restaurant. For the ultimate in relaxation, pamper yourself at the spa or health salon (Guerlain Paris) at Yu The Spa.

Rooms: 259
Suites: 24
Restaurants: 4

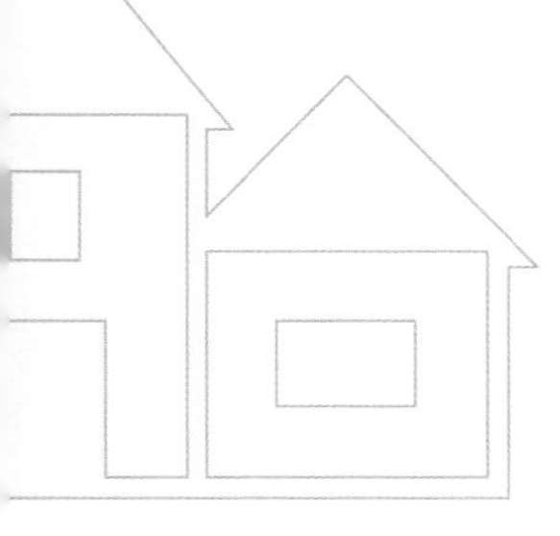

Four Seasons Marunouchi

Four Seasons Marunouchi

¥69,500-81,000
¥69,500-81,000
Suite ¥110,000-578,000
¥3,000

TEL 03–5222–7222 / FAX 03–5222–1255
Pacific Century Place Building,
1-11-1 Marunouchi, Chiyoda-ku
www.fourseasons.com/marunouchi

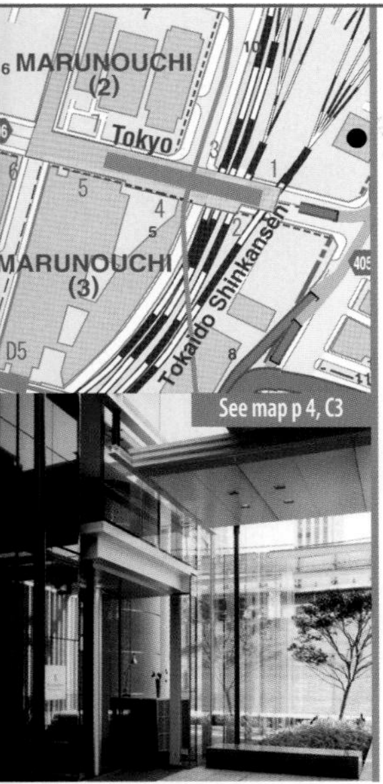

Opened in October 2002, this hotel is located from the third to seventh floors of the Pacific Century Place Marunouchi, a 31-story glass tower a three-minute walk from Tokyo Station and close to the Tokyo International Forum. Guests can easily use the Narita Express service to and from Narita Airport. Since all the exterior walls are glass, it is perfect for anyone wishing to enjoy urban views (railways on one side and boulevard on the other). The interiors are contemporary and elegant: floors and walls are coordinated in shades of beige and grey; there is a leather canopy above the bed; and the furnishings use sleek natural materials. There are only 57 rooms and suites, even the smallest of which is a spacious 44 m², and all are completely sound proof. The service is extremely solicitous. The restaurant and bar Ekki offers a New York contemporary cuisine served in an elegant brasserie-style dining room. Of course, the hotel also has well-equipped spa and fitness facilities. Small yet elegant and sophisticated, this is a place to which the term "boutique hotel" perfectly applies.

Rooms: 48
Suites: 9
Restaurants: 1

Grand Hyatt

Grand Hyatt

¥60,300-84,300
¥66,500-90,500
Suite ¥114,500-721,000
¥4,000

TEL 03–4333–1234 / FAX 03–4333–8123
6-10-3 Roppongi, Minato-ku
www.grandhyatttokyo.com

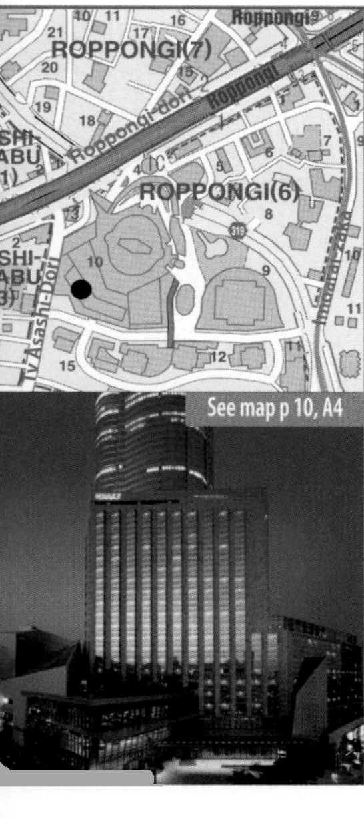

Rooms: 361
Suites: 28
Restaurants: 7

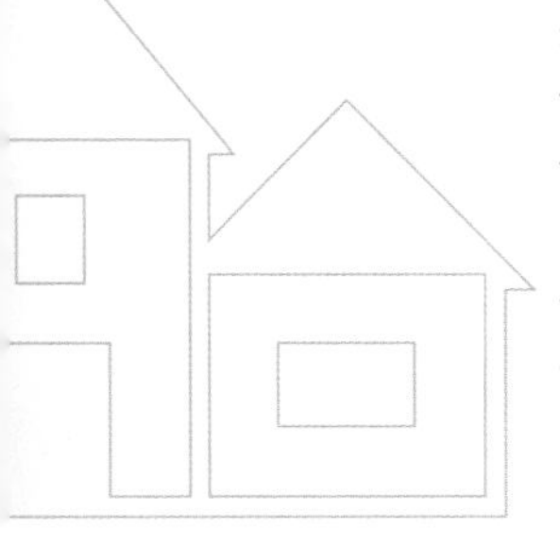

Opened in 2003, Tokyo hot spot Roppongi Hills is a multifunctional complex that integrates business, culture, shopping, dining and other urban functions. The Grand Hyatt is located next to the Mori Tower, the centerpiece of this complex. This ultra-modern hotel boasts an outstandingly original design. The team of designers that comprised Japan's Takashi Sugimoto, Fisher Marantz Stone from the U.S., and Hong Kong's Tony Chi & Associates lavishly incorporated Asian materials and design elements throughout the interior for a completely contemporary ambience. Grand Hyatt's wide variety of multinational restaurants appeals to local residents and visitors as well as to hotel guests. The Nagomi Spa and Fitness center, constructed from natural materials and with a magnificent red granite pool, is a wonderfully relaxing retreat. There are a total of 389 guest rooms including a selection of deluxe suites, each offering all the amenities that guests expect nowadays from a hotel room—exquisite furnishings, luxury bathroom facilities, leading-edge telecommunication services and a nice view.

Hilton

Hilton

🚹	¥22,900-48,900
🚹🚹	¥25,900-51,900
Suite	¥30,900-186,900
☕	¥3,360

TEL 03-3344-5111 / FAX 03-3342-6094
6-6-2 Nishi-Shinjuku, Shinjuku-ku
www.hilton.co.jp

See map p 15, B2

The first Hilton Tokyo opened in Nagatacho in 1963; founded by the worldwide hotel chain, Hilton International, it became the talk of the town as Japan's first foreign-owned hotel. In 1984 it moved to Nishi Shinjuku, the new multi-functional downtown area. The tall building with its distinctive S-shaped wave is thronged with guests every day; most of whom are here on business. The spacious lobby, together with the lounge area included, is always lively. The second floor is dedicated to restaurants, one of which is the French restaurant Twenty One. The hotel is well provided with banquet rooms for parties, weddings and seminars as well as a fitness center, outdoor tennis courts and other sports facilities. The deluxe rooms on the top floor are perfect for both business and pleasure; the suites and guest rooms offer upscale comfort and all the functions necessary to accommodate the needs of a business clientele. The outstanding features of these rooms also include the use of sliding doors as partitions, which bring a Japanese sensibility.

Rooms: 713
Suites: 103
Restaurants: 6

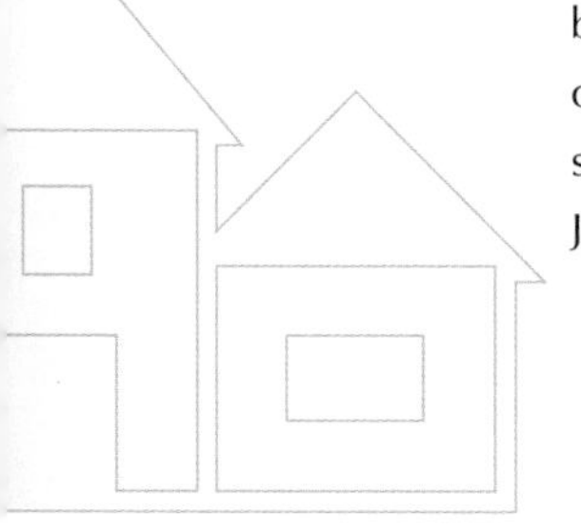

Imperial

Imperial

¥34,700-69,300	
¥40,500-75,100	
Suite	¥69,300-1,155,000
	¥3,200

TEL 03–3504–1111 / FAX 03–3581–9146
1-1-1 Uchisaiwaicho, Chiyoda-ku
www.imperialhotel.co.jp

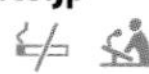

See map p 4, C3

Located right opposite Hibiya Park, in the vicinity of the Imperial Palace, the Imperial Hotel was opened in 1890. It was an establishment that was capable of providing Japanese-style hospitality even to overseas dignitaries, and undisputedly kept pace with Japan's modernization. The Wright building designed by the renowned architect Frank Lloyd Wright was opened in 1923 and the 31-floor Imperial Tower completed in 1983. Thousands of visitors pass through the hotel lobby every single day. The Old Imperial Bar that incorporates décor from the 1923 Wright building is a relaxing haven. The fine selection of restaurants includes the acclaimed French restaurant Les Saisons. 361 guest rooms are available in the Imperial Tower and 650 in the main building, including the magnificent 2300-square-foot Frank Lloyd Wright suite. The main building is currently undergoing renovations that will be completed in 2008. A guest room in the main building after renovations have been completed will be your best choice. The hotel also provides a full range of health/fitness and other guest facilities.

Rooms: 942
Suites: 69
Restaurants: 15

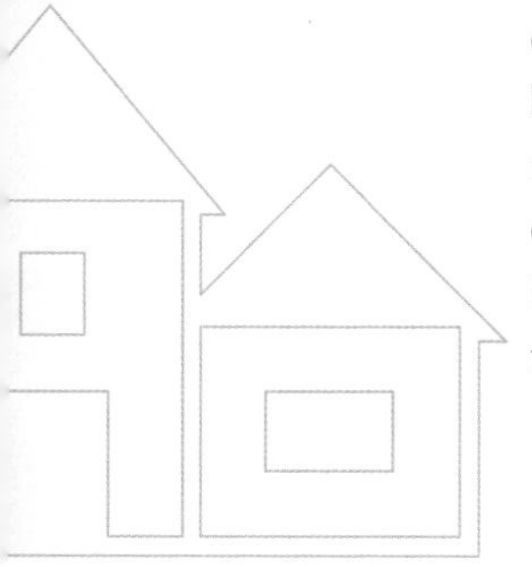

Intercontinental Tokyo Bay

Intercontinental Tokyo Bay

Single	¥42,000-72,000
Double	¥42,000-72,000
Suite	¥116,000-347,000
Breakfast	¥2,400

TEL 03–5404–2222 / FAX 03–5404–2111
1-16-2 Kaigan, Minato-ku
www.interconti-tokyo.com

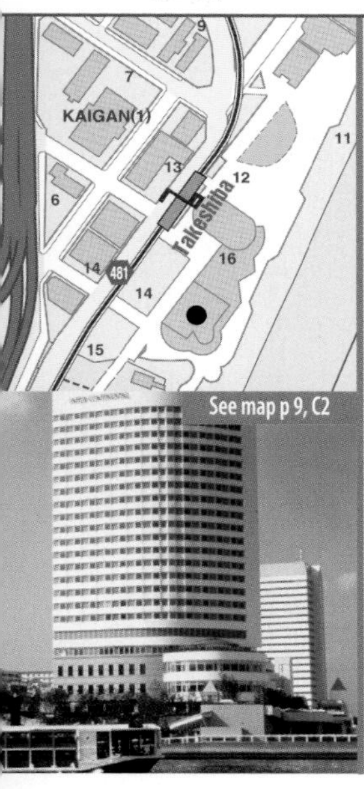

The InterContinental Tokyo Bay is connected by a walkway to Takeshiba Station on the fully-automated Yurikamome Line. Opened in 1995, the hotel offers spectacular views—Tokyo Bay on one side, and the Sumida River on the other. The 19th-century European-style lobby on the first floor features an arched ceiling decorated with gold leaf. Customers have a large choice of restaurants: The Blue Veranda for all-day dining, La Provence for French cuisine, Waketokuyama, a Japanese restaurant, and Asian Table, which specializes in Thai, Indonesian and Vietnamese cuisine. Other facilities include a fitness centre, a relaxation salon, and meeting and event rooms for international conferences, weddings, and other functions. The comfortable guest rooms are located from 8th to 24th floors; Club Inter Continental Floors are on the top five floors (dedicated reception desk on the 20th). However, as the rooms have not been redecorated since the hotel was opened, the overall design is somewhat outdated, but the good news is that large-scale renovations are planned from the start of 2008.

Rooms: 335
Suites: 4
Restaurants: 5

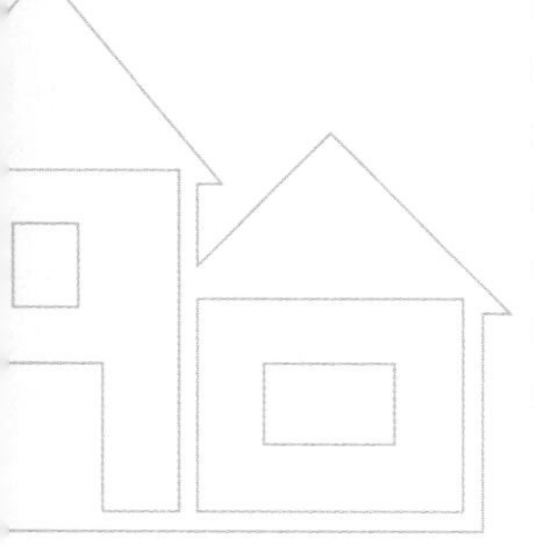

Keio Plaza

Keio Plaza

¥21,400-57,800
¥30,000-57,800
Suite ¥92,400-289,000
¥2,200

TEL 03–3344–0111 / FAX 03–3345–8269
2-2-1 Nishi-Shinjuku, Shinjuku-ku
www.keioplaza.com

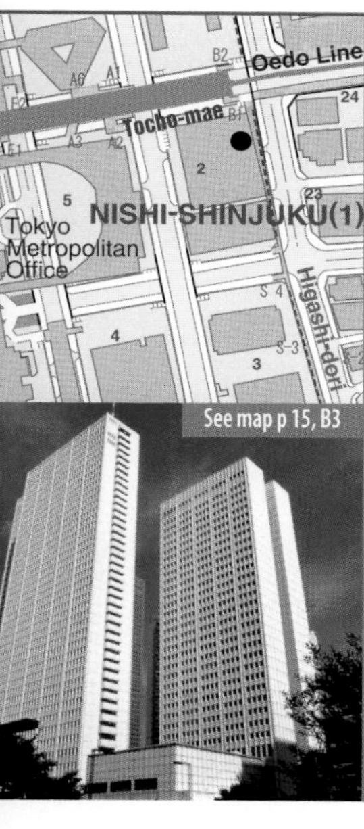

See map p 15, B3

Rooms: 1413
Suites: 27
Restaurants: 13

This hotel, opposite the Tokyo Metropolitan Government Office and close to Shinjuku Station, has 1,440 rooms in two wings. The 45-story Main Tower opened in 1971, the 34-story Southern Tower opened in 1980. The "Plaza Premier" category of rooms is especially recommended. These remodeled guestrooms, with pleasant modern décor, are more comfortable and are served by an exclusive check-in counter. About half the hotel's rooms have been upgraded in a renovation program that has been under way for several years; the rest are 1980s style. For overseas visitors who want a unique hotel experience, there are three suites with Japanese-style accommodation. 25 rooms have services and amenities for wheelchair users and the visually or hearing impaired. Naturally, every room commands a panoramic view. There are 13 restaurants, 8 bars, and numerous banquet and conference rooms. During the summer, an outdoor pool on the terrace is freely available to guests. The Keio Plaza's scale and facilities make it almost like a small town within the Tokyo metropolis.

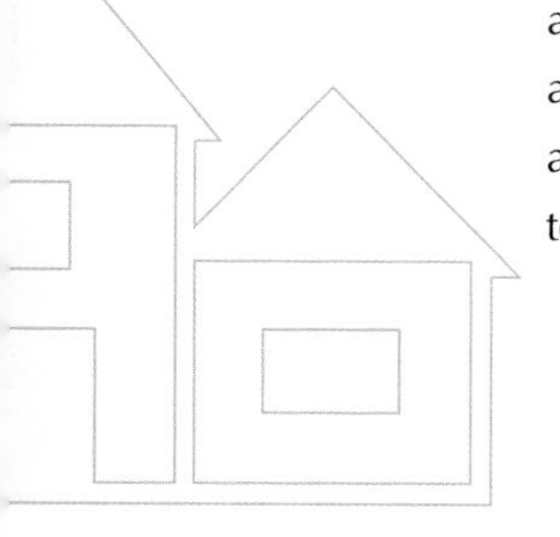

Le Meridien Grand Pacific

Le Meridien Grand Pacific

🚹	¥36,000-58,000
🚹🚹	¥36,000-58,000
Suite	¥90,000-460,000
☕	¥2,800

TEL 03–5500–6711 / FAX 03–5500–4507
2-6-1 Daiba, Minato-ku
www.meridien-grandpacific.com

  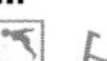

See map p 10, C4

In a highrise building that connects directly to Daiba Station on the Yurikamome line is Le Meridien Grand Pacific. This 30-story hotel, which opened in 1998, offers stunning views of the Rainbow Bridge and central Tokyo in one direction and Tokyo Bay and Haneda Airport in the other. In the middle of the spacious entrance and lobby on the first floor is an impressive dome. A French-style chandelier shines down on the sumptuous marble columns and floor. The hotel has rooms for banquets and parties as well as wedding facilities. It is also well supplied with restaurants that offer a wide range of options such as Japanese, Chinese, French and a buffet. A terrace pool, a fitness club, a beauty salon and other facilities are concentrated on the first to sixth floors; guest rooms are on the 6th to 28th floors. The rooms are decorated in an 18th-century European style and come in a variety of sizes. For those who desire even greater comfort, we recommend the Club President Floors.

Rooms: 860
Suites: 24
Restaurants: 7

Mandarin Oriental

Mandarin Oriental

¥75,500-83,500	
¥75,500-83,500	
Suite ¥139,000-924,000	
¥3,800	

TEL 03-3270-8800 / FAX 03-3270-8886
2-1-1 Nihonbashi-Muromachi, Chuo-ku
www.mandarinoriental.co.jp/tokyo

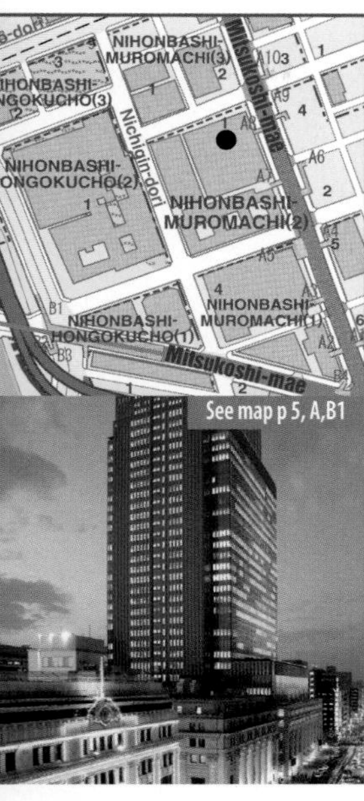

See map p 5, A,B1

Rooms: 157
Suites: 22
Restaurants: 5

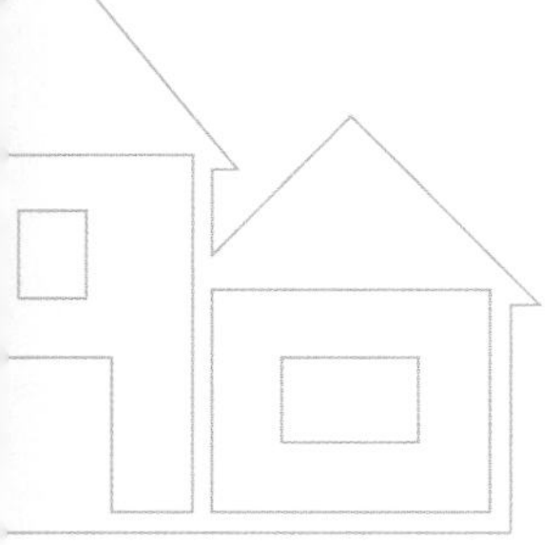

This hotel, which occupies the first four and top nine floors of the Nihonbashi Mitsui Tower, opened in 2005 in an ideal location; the heart of the business and financial district. Its design concept is wood and water. The entire building can be likened to a tree, and each guest room to one of its branches. From the windows one can look out to the east on the waters of Odaiba and the Sumida River and to the west on the woodlands of the Imperial Palace. Parts of the walls are decorated with bamboo, and there is also a natural motif in the floors and carpets. Decorations such as calligraphy, folding screens and ikebana introduce a Japanese sensibility that makes for a truly elegant interior. The reception area is on the 38th floor. On the floor below one can enjoy a panoramic view from the bar or one of the many restaurants. There is also a spa on the 37th and 38th floors, where one can enjoy ultimate relaxation in one of nine private rooms, all with stunning views. Like the well-laid-out interiors and the overall concept, the first-class service is also a major attraction.

Marunouchi

Marunouchi

¥23,300-52,175
¥31,385-52,375
Suite ¥115,700-115,900
¥2,310

TEL 03–3217–1111 / FAX 03–3217–1115
1-6-3 Marunouchi, Chiyoda-ku
www.marunouchi-hotel.co.jp

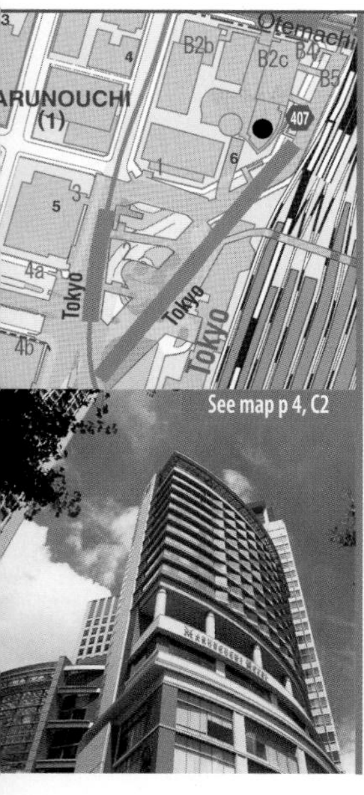

See map p 4, C2

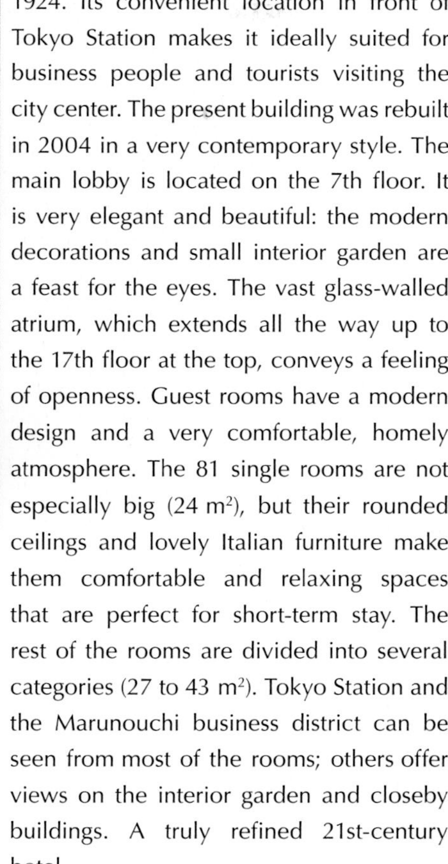
A hotel with a long history dating back to 1924. Its convenient location in front of Tokyo Station makes it ideally suited for business people and tourists visiting the city center. The present building was rebuilt in 2004 in a very contemporary style. The main lobby is located on the 7th floor. It is very elegant and beautiful: the modern decorations and small interior garden are a feast for the eyes. The vast glass-walled atrium, which extends all the way up to the 17th floor at the top, conveys a feeling of openness. Guest rooms have a modern design and a very comfortable, homely atmosphere. The 81 single rooms are not especially big (24 m^2), but their rounded ceilings and lovely Italian furniture make them comfortable and relaxing spaces that are perfect for short-term stay. The rest of the rooms are divided into several categories (27 to 43 m^2). Tokyo Station and the Marunouchi business district can be seen from most of the rooms; others offer views on the interior garden and closeby buildings. A truly refined 21st-century hotel.

Rooms: 204
Suites: 1
Restaurants: 3

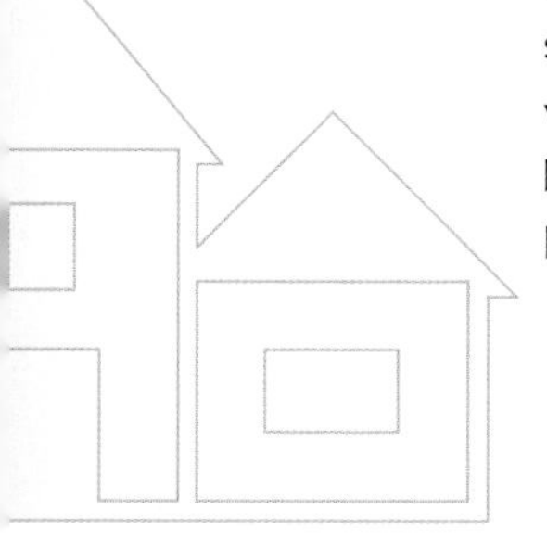

Mitsui Garden Ginza

Mitsui Garden Ginza

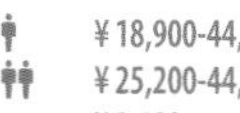

¥18,900-44,100
¥25,200-44,100
¥2,100

TEL 03–3543–1131 / FAX 03–3543–5531
8-13-1 Ginza, Chuo-ku
www.gardenhotels.co.jp

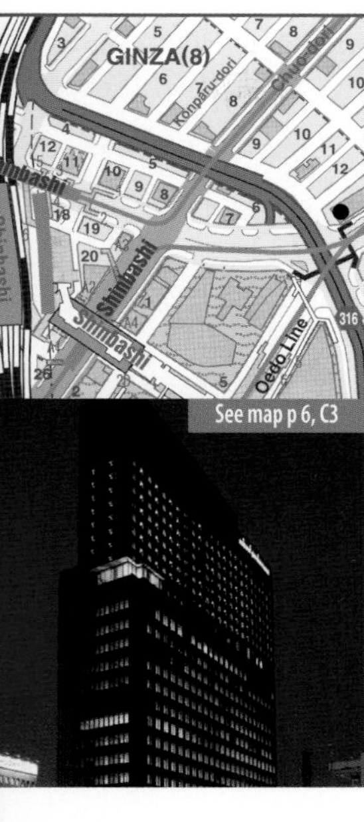

See map p 6, C3

This highrise hotel, which is located in the southern part of Ginza, opened in 2005. The reception area is on the 16th floor; guest rooms are on the 17th to 25th floors, and from every floor there are panoramic views of Ginza area or Tokyo Bay. On the lobby floor there are a modish salon bar and a restaurant where guests can savor contemporary Italian cuisine. Guest rooms are divided into categories according to size. Since most of the clientele are business people in town for a single night, there are 100 small rooms designated as Moderate (18.5 m²) and 122 as Superior (20.4 m²). Guests in the View Bath rooms can enjoy the luxury of looking out over the night skyline while lounging in the bath. The 25th floor is also an executive floor with rooms of 40 m². The functional design and refined interior decoration are by an Italian designer. The interiors in all the rooms are coordinated in earth and tree tones.

Rooms: 360
Restaurants: 1

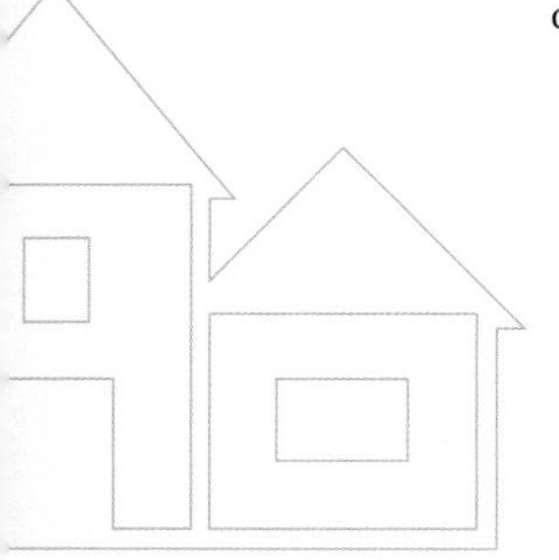

New Otani (Main Building)

New Otani

Single	¥44,000-75,000
Double	¥44,000-75,000
Suite	¥139,000-1,040,000
Breakfast	¥2,400

TEL 03-3265-1111 / FAX 03-3221-2619
4-1 Kioicho, Chiyoda-ku
www.newotani.co.jp

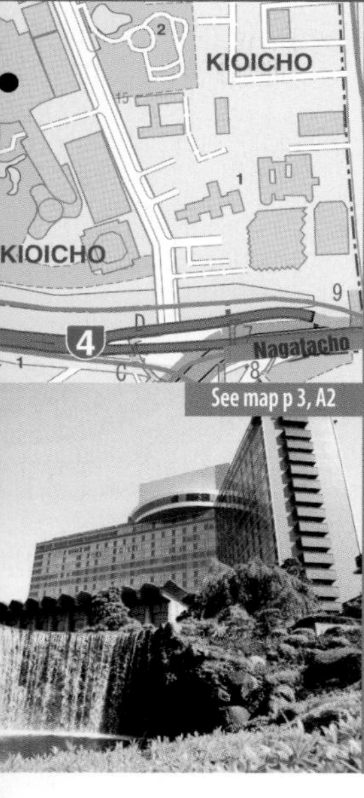

Rooms: 614
Suites: 29
Restaurants: 30

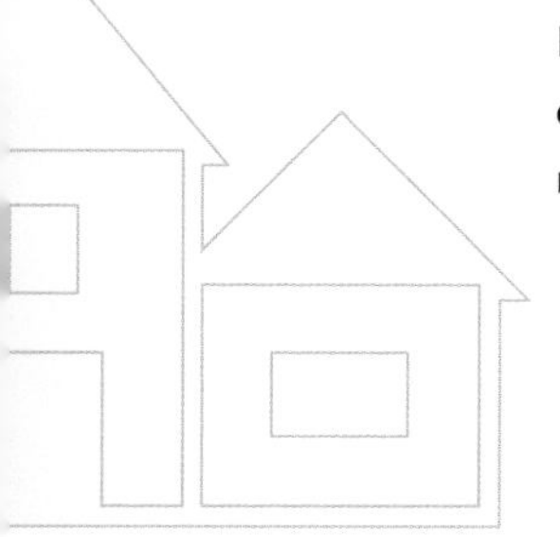

A hotel facing a vast and 400-year-old Japanese garden, the New Otani opened just before the Tokyo Olympics in 1964. It is comprised of two principal components: Main Building and Tower (not recommended). Renovation work on the Main Building had been in progress since the autumn of 2005 and was completed in October 2007. Called the hybrid hotel project, the plan is to reduce the hotel's environmental footprint. In the lobby of The Main building are some very large banquet halls, and there are boutiques of all kinds throughout the both buildings. The guest rooms have modern interiors predominantly in shades of gray, black and brown, Japanese-style paintings, calligraphy and paper-covered lamps. The standard room size is 36 m^2 though some are as large as 50 m^2. Rooms are completely equipped with all the amenities and are both comfortable and convenient. In addition to La Tour d'Argent and many other restaurants, there is even an art museum in the Garden Court.

Nikko

Nikko

🚹	¥34,000-54,000
🚹🚹	¥40,000-60,000
Suite	¥100,000-330,000
☕	¥3,300

TEL 03–5500–5500 / FAX 03–5500–2525
1-9-1 Daiba, Minato-ku
www.hnt.co.jp

Hotel Nikko has been operating at Odaiba, a new leisure-oriented city sub-center fronting Tokyo Bay, since 1996. The concept of the hotel is "Tokyo Balcony." Every guest room has a balcony, and you can gaze out over the towering cityscape of Tokyo. The best ones are located on the executive floors (from 13th to 15th) and have just been renovated in a cabin style. The second-floor lobby with its tall columns is adjacent to Veranda, a salon bar that overlooks the Rainbow Bridge. Clustered on the second and third floors are the restaurants, including Sakura, a charming Japanese restaurant, Toh-gu, a fashionable restaurant that serves Chinese food; and Terrace on the Bay, offering French cuisine. The Bayside Spa Zen relaxation space has an indoor pool looking out over the bay and a full menu of aromatherapy and massage treatments offering the "power of natural healing." There are also complete wedding reception facilities, including two chapels, one in a modern style made entirely of glass and with magnificent panoramic views of Tokyo Bay.

Rooms: 435
Suites: 18
Restaurants: 5

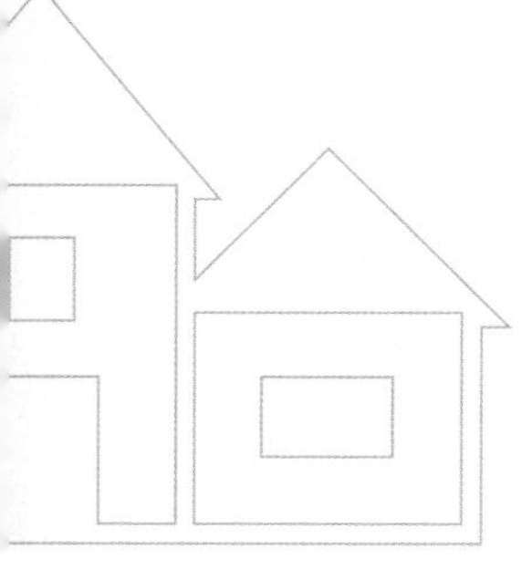

Okura

Okura

¥40,500-70,000
¥46,200-139,000
Suite ¥127,000-635,000
¥2,835

TEL 03–3582–0111 / FAX 03–3582–3707
2-10-4 Toranomon, Minato-ku
www.hotelokura.co.jp/tokyo

See map p 9, B2

The Hotel Okura opened in 1962, two years before the Tokyo Olympics, and still maintains a strong impression of the Japanese decorum and pride that were hallmarks of the 1960s. Visitors to the hotel are welcomed by the soft glow from the lantern-like lights suspended from the high ceiling in the lobby of the main building, which is beautifully decorated in different hues of wood. An annexe building was added in the 1970s, and a shopping arcade lined with exclusive boutiques connects the two buildings. While the guest rooms in the annexe building are a little small, all the rooms in both buildings offer a refined, calm ambience. The hotel also offers several spacious suites, including the Imperial Suite, which provide the ultimate in dignified luxury. Other facilities include convention and banquet rooms, an executive services salon, a fitness club, and the Relaxation Nature Court spa. The wide selection of Japanese, Western and Chinese restaurants will satisfy any taste. The Hotel Okura is the place for guests looking for a pleasant traditional atmosphere and scrupulous service.

Rooms: 773
Suites: 60
Restaurants: 8

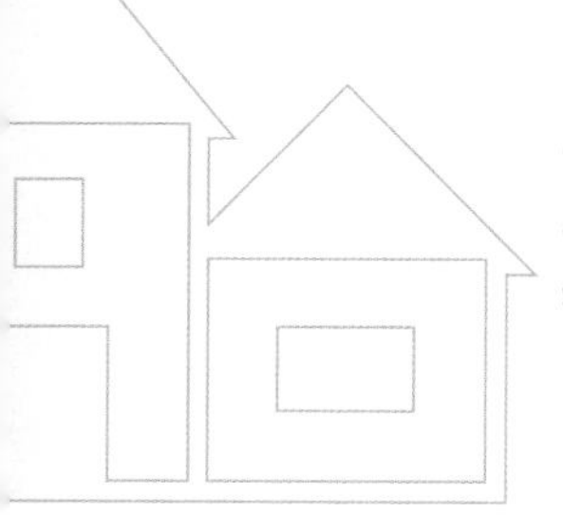

Park Hyatt

Park Hyatt

¥68,600-89,000
¥68,600-89,000
Suite ¥165,200-826,000
¥3,800

TEL 03–5322–1234 / FAX 03–5322–1288
3-7-1-2 Nishi-Shinjuku, Shinjuku-ku
www.parkhyatttokyo.com

See map p 15, A3

The Park Hyatt occupies the 41st to the 52nd floors of the Shinjuku Park Tower, a high-rise which opened in 1994; designed by the architect Tange Kenzo. Guest rooms are located above the 42nd floor, and the views from the windows are spectacular; Mount Fuji can be seen on clear days. The same magnificent views can be enjoyed in the Club on the Park spa & fitness center, one of this hotel's prime attractions. With a panorama of the city spreading out below, the pool and gym offer a sense of freedom and openness, while the atmosphere in the seven private treatment rooms of the spa is soothing and meditative. The hotel has a number of bars and restaurants, including the Kozue, New York Grill, Girandole and the Peak lounge. In the guest rooms, represented by the beige-themed wall, comfort takes priority over luxury. Throughout the hotel guests can enjoy drawings by the master of Italian cinema, Federico Fellini, as well as works by contemporary artists. On the subject of movies, most of Sofia Coppola's Lost in Translation takes place here. A shuttle service is provided to Shinjuku station.

Rooms: 154
Suites: 23
Restaurants: 5

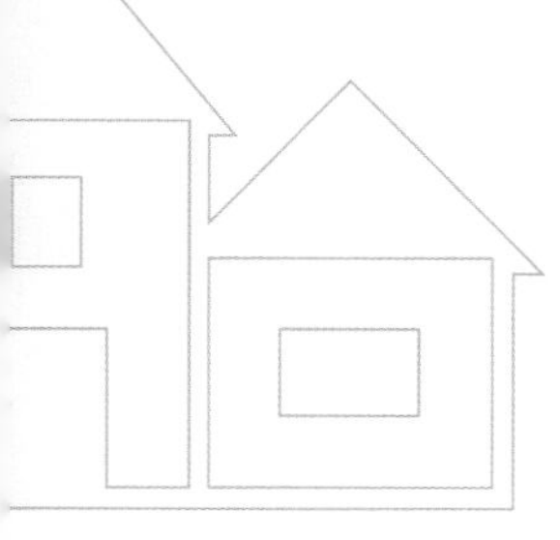

Royal Park

Royal Park

🚹	¥30,000-58,900
🚹🚹	¥39,300-63,600
Suite	¥52,000-289,000
☕	¥2,700

TEL 03–3667–1111 / FAX 03–3667–1115
2-1-1 Nihonbashi Kakigara-cho, Chuo-ku
www.rph.co.jp

See map p 5, B1

The Royal Park Hotel, which opened in 1989, is next to the Tokyo City Air Terminal for buses traveling to and from Narita and Haneda airports. The spacious lobby with its marble floors and gorgeous "Milky Way" chandelier has the usual reception area but also a "female traveler's check-in," which provides female guests with privacy, personalized information, reservations and other services. Guest rooms on the 6th to 18th floors have been completely renovated. They come in various sizes ranging and have chic, contemporary décor with walls in warm color tones, panoramic views, and all the amenities including a computer. Guests staying on the executive floors have free access to the private salon, the pool, the fitness center and the conference rooms. The hotel has many styles of restaurants serving French, Japanese and Chinese cuisine as well as bars like the Lobby Lounge and the Sky Lounge. If one has time, the beautiful garden on the fifth floor is worth a visit.

Rooms: 397
Suites: 11
Restaurants: 7

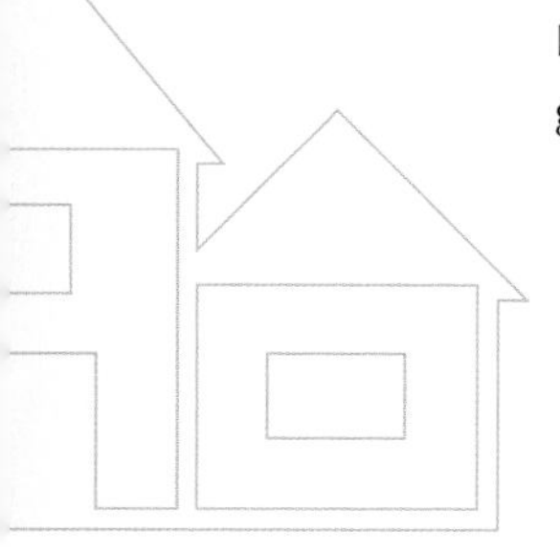

Royal Park Shiodome Tower

Royal Park Shiodome Tower

¥22,000-39,300
¥25,500-63,600
Suite ¥98,200
¥2,300

TEL 03–6253–1111 / FAX 03–6253–1115
1-6-3 Higashi-Shinbashi, Minato-ku
www.rps-tower.co.jp

See map p 9, C1

A high-rise hotel in a 38-story building that opened in 2003 in the business, information and cultural district of Shiodome. Although also suited for tourists, the amenities of this hotel make it perfect for business guests. All the guest rooms come equipped with high-speed internet access as well as a personal computer that doubles as a television set. The computer also functions as a cyber-concierge providing information about the hotel's facilities and dealing with requests for delivery services, etc. Rooms come in many sizes ranging from 20 m² to the 57 m² corner deluxe double. All have modern interiors that invite guests to relax and make themselves comfortable. The views are also stunning, overlooking Hama Rikyu, the Tsukiji market and the Sumida River. For further relaxation, the Mandara Spa in the second basement brings a touch of Bali to Tokyo and offers a diverse spa menu. There are also few restaurants, including one open until one in the morning.

Rooms: 488
Suites: 2
Restaurants: 3

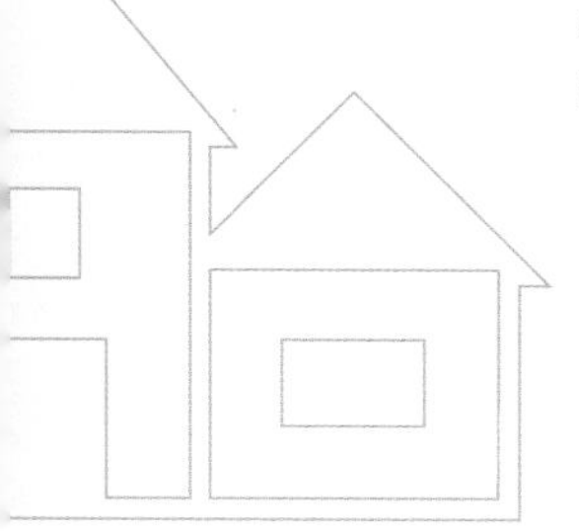

Seiyo Ginza

Seiyo Ginza

¥61,215-75,075
¥61,215-75,075
Suite ¥103,950-254,100
¥2,550

TEL 03–3535–1111 / FAX 03–3535–1110
1-11-2 Ginza, Chuo-ku
www.seiyo-ginza.co.jp

See map p 6, D2

This 12-floor hotel opened in the Ginza area in 1987. Located on bustling Chuo Dori, Hotel Seiyo Ginza nonetheless maintains an aura of quiet elegance. Although it is a small hotel with only 77 guest rooms and suites on the top five floors, it offers 60 room types, each with a different layout. The hotel's concept is to provide the ambience of a private residence for the ultimate in rest and relaxation. To achieve this end, a butler is assigned to each room to attend to all the guest's needs. This personal butler service, along with the concierge service, is available 24 hours a day, a first for a Tokyo hotel. The guest rooms were redecorated in 2001 in an 18th-century European style, and the beige walls and light brown carpet create a chic, elegant atmosphere. Unusually spacious, the well-appointed bathrooms are decorated in white marble and provide separate shower and bath areas. The variety of restaurants and bars includes Repertoire for French cuisine, Kitcho for Japanese, Attore for Italian, and the salon bar Prelude.

Rooms: 51
Suites: 26
Restaurants: 4

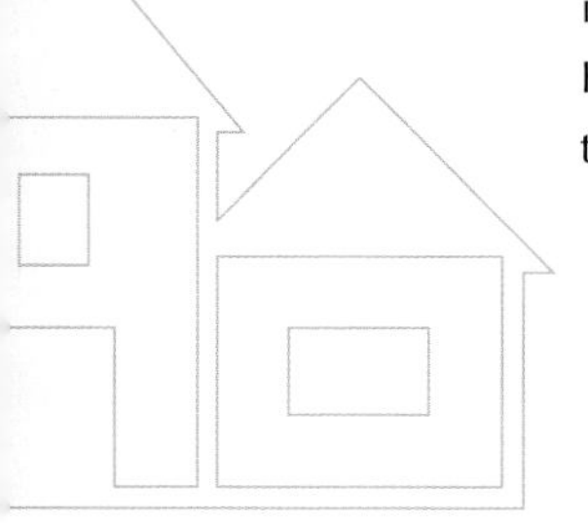

The Agnes

The Agnes

🚹	¥23,000-30,000
🚹🚹	¥29,000-42,000
Suite	¥50,000-80,000

TEL 03–3267–5505 / FAX 03–3267–5513
2-20-1 Kagurazaka, Shinjuku-ku
www.agneshotel.com

See map p 16, D1

A hotel which opened in 2000 off Sotobori-dori; its nearest station is Iidabashi. Because the number of guest rooms is small, the many staff can be attentive to the needs of each and every guest. The hotel offers comfortable and restful lodgings in serene shades of beige, ideal for someone who likes peace and quiet and wants to relax. Each room has a small jacuzzi bath and a separate shower booth and some rooms come with small balconies. There are also apartments equipped with a kitchen (a refrigerator and microwave) and a washing machine. Since there is a long-term rate for guests who plan to stay for a month or more, it is advisable to make inquiries in advance. The restaurant serves classical French cuisine featuring carefully selected fish. There is also a bar that can be used to meet friends or in which to just relax. This hotel has many repeat visitors, so be sure to make reservations well in advance.

Rooms: 51
Suites: 5
Restaurants: 1

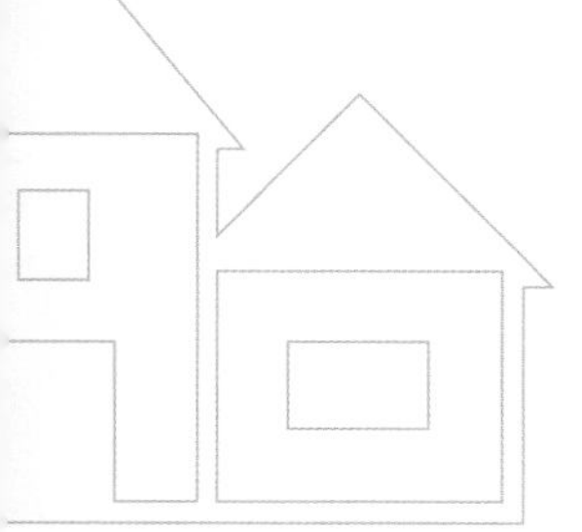

The Peninsula

The Peninsula, Michelin

¥69,300-92,400
¥69,300-92,400
Suite ¥115,500-981,750
¥2,800

TEL 03–6270–2888 / FAX 03–6270–2000
1-8-1 Yurakucho, Chiyoda-ku
www.peninsula.com

 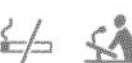  

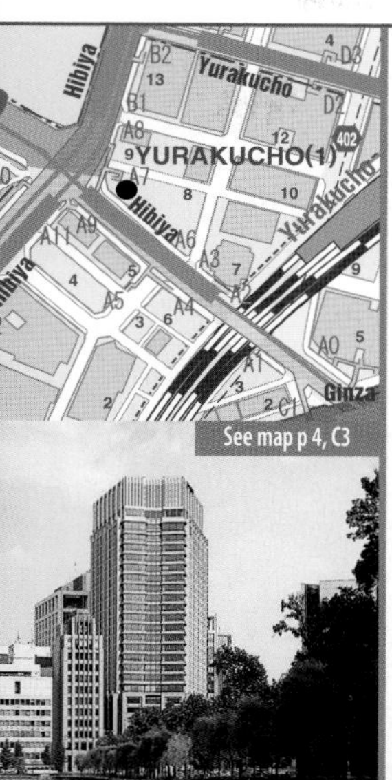

See map p 4, C3

In September 2007 the Hong Kong-based hotel group opened a branch in Tokyo. Very well located in Yurakucho, The Peninsula, whose architecture is inspired by the form of a traditional stone lantern, occupies its entire building. Overall the concept is "modern Japanese", and the rooms, while equipped with the latest conveniences, show great attention to the details of design: doors of horse-chestnut, vermillion-lacquered counters, ceilings of woven cedar strips. The spacious lobby also functions as a dining area where breakfast and afternoon tea are served. On the second-floor Hei Fung Terrace serves Chinese cuisine in an exotically romantic atmosphere, and on the basement level Tsuruya serves traditional Japanese cuisine. On the top floor you'll find The Rooftop Restaurant & Bar, with bold interior design and a splendid vista of Tokyo. The hotel is chock full of other amenities including a swimming pool and a modern Asian-style spa. Even more noteworthy is the heliport on the top floor, accompanied by The Seven Seas Pacific Aviation Lounge with airplane-inspired design and interior.

Rooms: 267
Suites: 47
Restaurants: 4

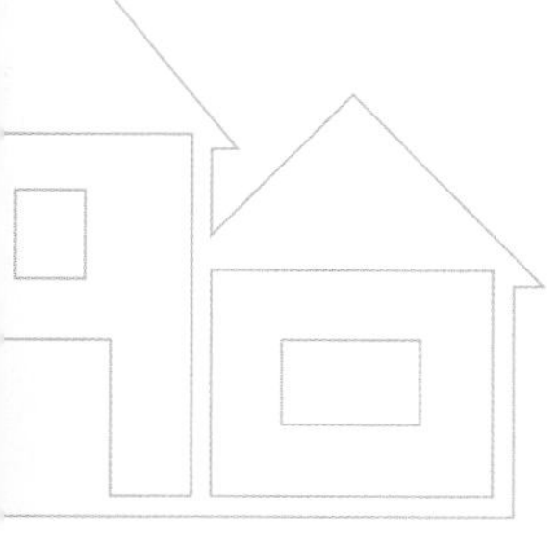

The Prince Park Tower

The Prince Park Tower

¥34,000-65,000
¥34,000-65,000
Suite ¥104,000-980,000
¥3,000

TEL 03–5400–1111 / FAX 03–5400–1110
4-8-1 Shibakoen, Minato-ku
www.princehotels.co.jp/parktower

See map p 9, B2

This hotel opened in 2005 amid the greenery of Shiba Park; designed for relaxation, with ample amenities, it truly has the feel of a downtown oasis. The 33-story tower is divided between the Park Floors (3 through 18) and the Executive Floors (2, and 19 through 31, with Executive Premium Floors). The Royal Floor on the 32nd story provides butler service and four Royal Suites, in English, French, Italian, and Japanese styles. The modern, pastel-toned guestrooms are hung with artwork by the French painter Paul Guiramand. Every care has been taken in order to provide for guests' well-being. In-house restaurants offer a wide choice, including Japanese and Chinese cuisine, *sushi, tempura, yakitori,* a steakhouse, and a café-restaurant. The top floor has a lounge bar, with a view of Tokyo Tower, and a French restaurant. A wine-tasting corner is located on the first basement floor. The luxurious amenities include a spa and fitness center, and banquet rooms with wedding facilities.

Rooms: 640
Suites: 33
Restaurants: 13

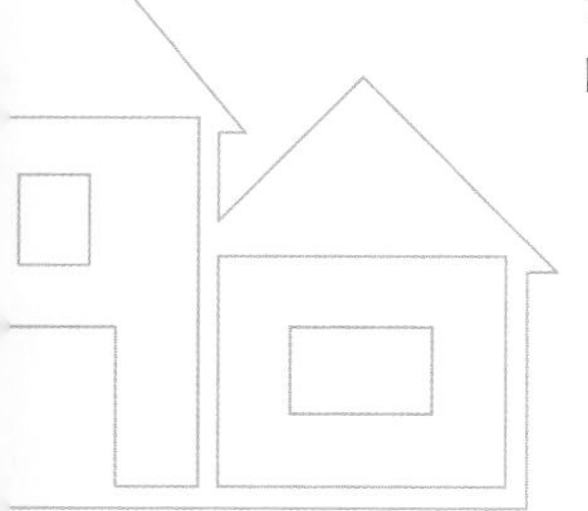

The Ritz-Carlton

The Ritz-Carlton

¥75,000-92,400
¥75,000-92,400
Suite ¥115,500-2,310,000
¥3,500

TEL 03–3423–8000 / FAX 03–3423–8001
Tokyo Midtown,
9-7-1 Akasaka, Minato-ku
www.ritzcarlton.co.jp

See map p 9, B2

Soaring over the vast commercial area of Tokyo Midtown, which opened in March 2007, is a 53-story building. The Ritz-Carlton occupies the upper floors from the 45th. The lobby lounge, beneath the eight-meter-high ceiling, is surrounded by contemporary paintings; guests can relax and listen to a live performance of piano and violin. The view from the bar is one of the most beautiful panoramas in all of Tokyo. On the same floor you will find Forty Five, an international restaurant and the Japanese restaurant Hinokizaka. All guest rooms are a spacious 52 m^2. Each has serene and elegant art deco style furnishings with Asian touches, either a city view or a Tokyo Bay view, all the amenities including a large-screen television, and a bathroom in which not even the smallest detail has been overlooked. The huge indoor pool, the fully equipped fitness facilities and the spa, offering the ultimate in relaxation, also leave nothing to be desired. This is a deluxe hotel that will make one's stay in Tokyo truly unforgettable.

Rooms: 210
Suites: 38
Restaurants: 4

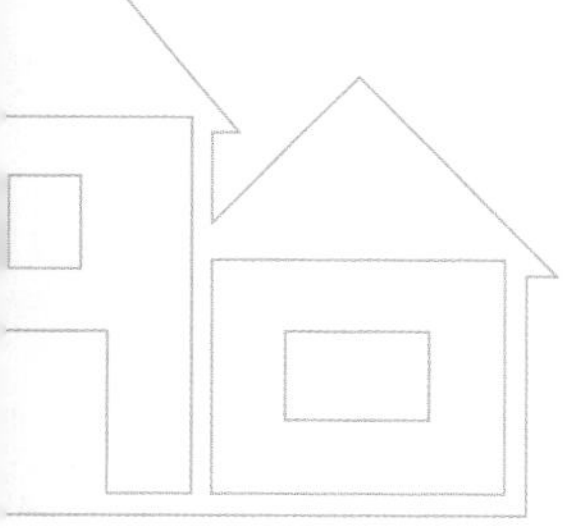

The Strings by Intercontinental

The Strings by Intercontinental

1 person	¥37,000-56,000
2 persons	¥48,000-62,000
Suite	¥140,000-206,000
Breakfast	¥3,200

TEL 03–5783–1111 / FAX 03–5783–1112
Shinagawa East One Tower,
2-16-1 Konan, Minato-ku
www.intercontinental-strings.jp

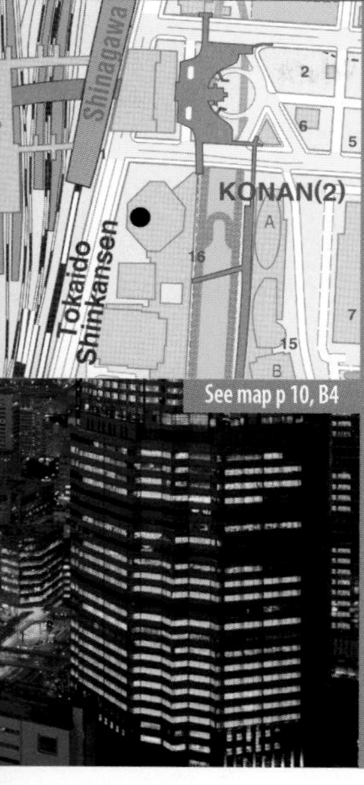

A hotel in a 32-story high-rise which opened in 2003; its location within two minutes' walk of Shinagawa Station makes it perfect for tourists and business guests using the station. The light-filled lobby on the 26th floor exudes an air of tranquility. The soaring atrium and the water feature spanned by a glass bridge are particularly impressive. After crossing the bridge, one proceeds to the French fusion restaurant and bar and a Chinese restaurant. Guest rooms are located on the 27th to 32nd floors; all have contemporary furniture and elegant modern décor conducive to thorough relaxation. Rooms are divided into categories depending on size and range from 30 m² to 42 m². All have panoramic views of Tokyo from the wide windows. Bathroom interiors are beautiful, especially the marble flooring. There is a fitness room, which has the same breathtaking views as the guest rooms. Rooms for the Club InterContinental offer a higher level of amenities and include breakfast and a free minibar.

Rooms: 200
Suites: 6
Restaurants: 2

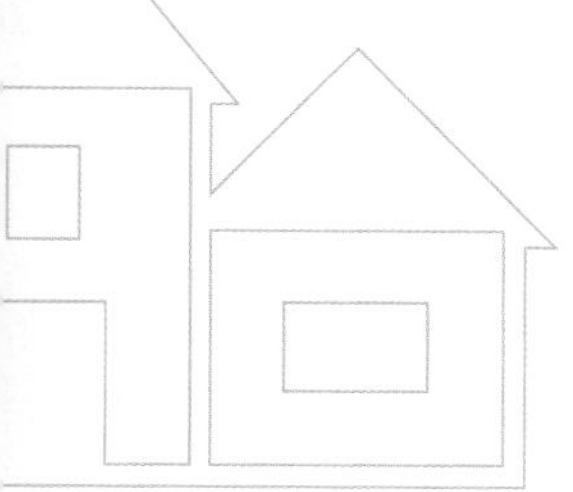

Westin

Westin

Single	¥65,000-87,000
Double	¥65,000-87,000
Suite	¥141,000-523,000
Breakfast	¥3,600

TEL 03–5423–7000 / FAX 03–5423–7600
1-4-1 Mita, Meguro-ku
www.westin-tokyo.co.jp

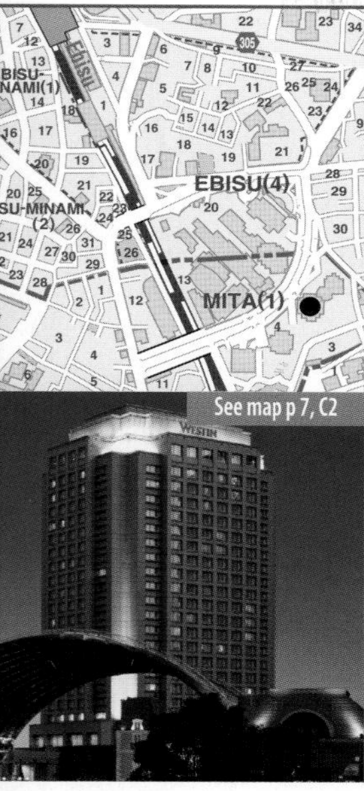

See map p 7, C2

A 22-story hotel in Yebisu Garden Place opened in 1994. The décor is a fusion of early 19th-century European (particularly French Empire) styles with Japanese decorative touches (flower decorations, woodblock prints, folding screens, etc.), giving it an overall atmosphere of graceful elegance. The spacious ground-floor main lobby leads into The Lounge, and a casual modern buffet restaurant The Terrace. On the second floor are Ryutenmon, a Chinese restaurant and bar, and Mai, a traditional Japanese restaurant featuring an indoor garden for your appreciation. On the top floor, 22 stories above the city, there are a sky lounge, Compass Rose, and a *teppanyaki* restaurant, Yebisu. The guest rooms, like the public spaces, are decorated in a fusion of 19th-century European and traditional Japanese styles, and have excellent views and amenities. From the 16th to the 21st floors are a variety of suites for members of the Westin Executive Club. The entire 5th floor is for women only. Le Spa Parisien, for total relaxation, newly opened in July 2007.

Rooms: 398
Suites: 40
Restaurants: 5

渋谷駅前
Shibuya Sta.

Maps

Tips/Photononstop

Tokyo in 18 maps

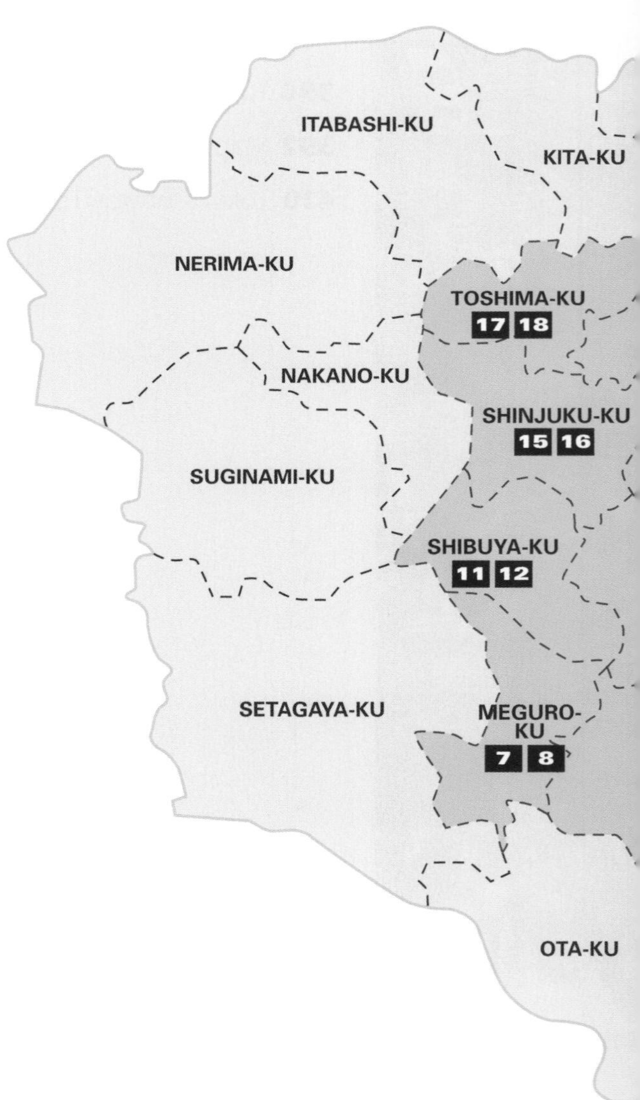

ADASHI-KU
KATSUSHIKA-KU
ARAKAWA-KU
BUNKYO-KU
1 2
TAITO-KU
SUMIDA-KU
EDOGAWA-KU
CHIYODA-KU
3 4
CHUO-KU
5 6
KOTO-KU
MINATO-KU
9 10
SHINAGAWA-KU
13 14

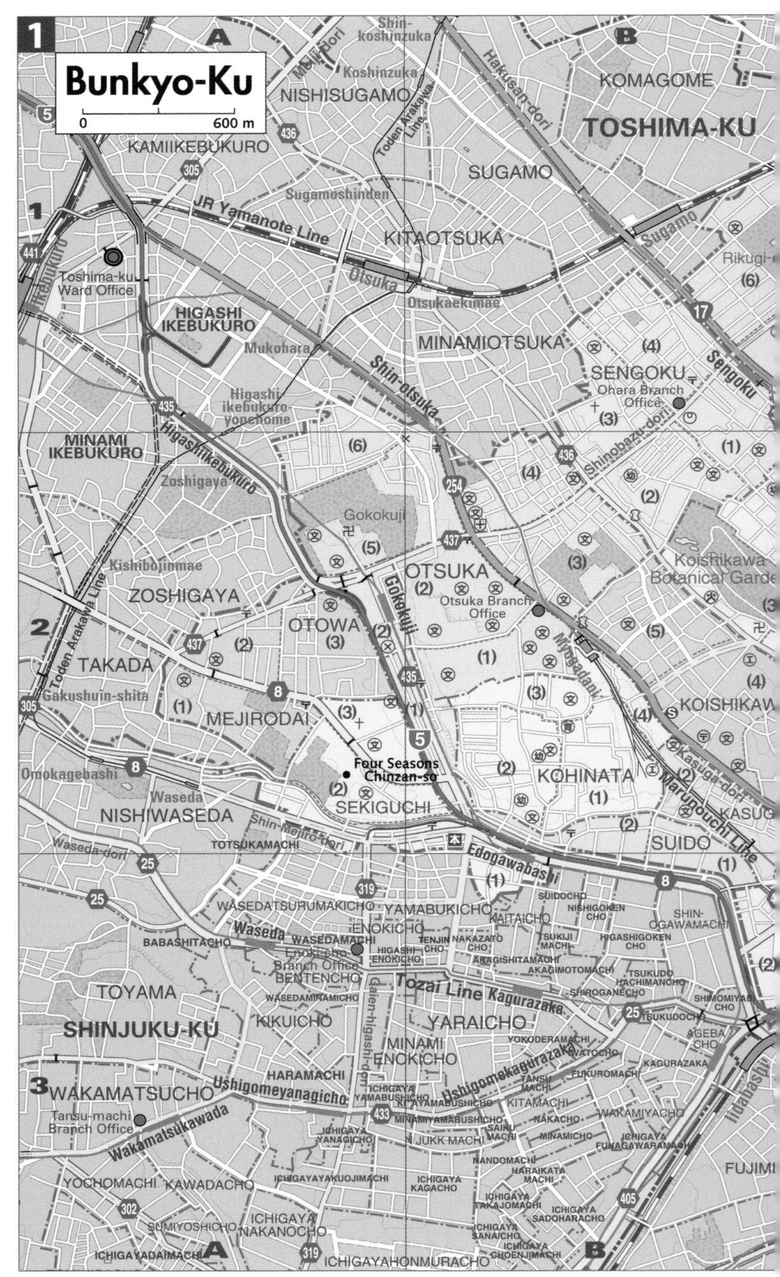
1
Bunkyo-Ku
0
600 m
A
B
NISHISUGAMO
KOMAGOME
TOSHIMA-KU
KAMIIKEBUKURO
SUGAMO
JR Yamanote Line
KITAOTSUKA
Toshima-ku Ward Office
HIGASHI IKEBUKURO
MINAMIOTSUKA
SENGOKU
Ohara Branch Office
MINAMI IKEBUKURO
Gokokuji
Koishikawa Botanical Garden
ZOSHIGAYA
OTSUKA
Otsuka Branch Office
OTOWA
TAKADA
MEJIRODAI
KOISHIKAWA
Four Seasons Chinzan-so
KOHINATA
NISHIWASEDA
SEKIGUCHI
SUIDO
TOTSUKAMACHI
Edogawabashi
WASEDATSURUMAKICHO
YAMABUKICHO
ENOKICHO
BABASHITACHO
WASEDAMACHI
Enoki-cho Branch Office
BENTENCHO
Tozai Line
TOYAMA
KIKUICHO
YARAICHO
SHINJUKU-KU
MINAMI ENOKICHO
WAKAMATSUCHO
Tansu-machi Branch Office
Wakamatsukawada
Ushigomeyanagicho
Ushigomekagurazaka
KAGURAZAKA
YOCHOMACHI
KAWADACHO
ICHIGAYA NAKANOCHO
SUMIYOSHICHO
ICHIGAYADAIMACHI
ICHIGAYAHONMURACHO
FUJIMI
Iidabashi
3
2

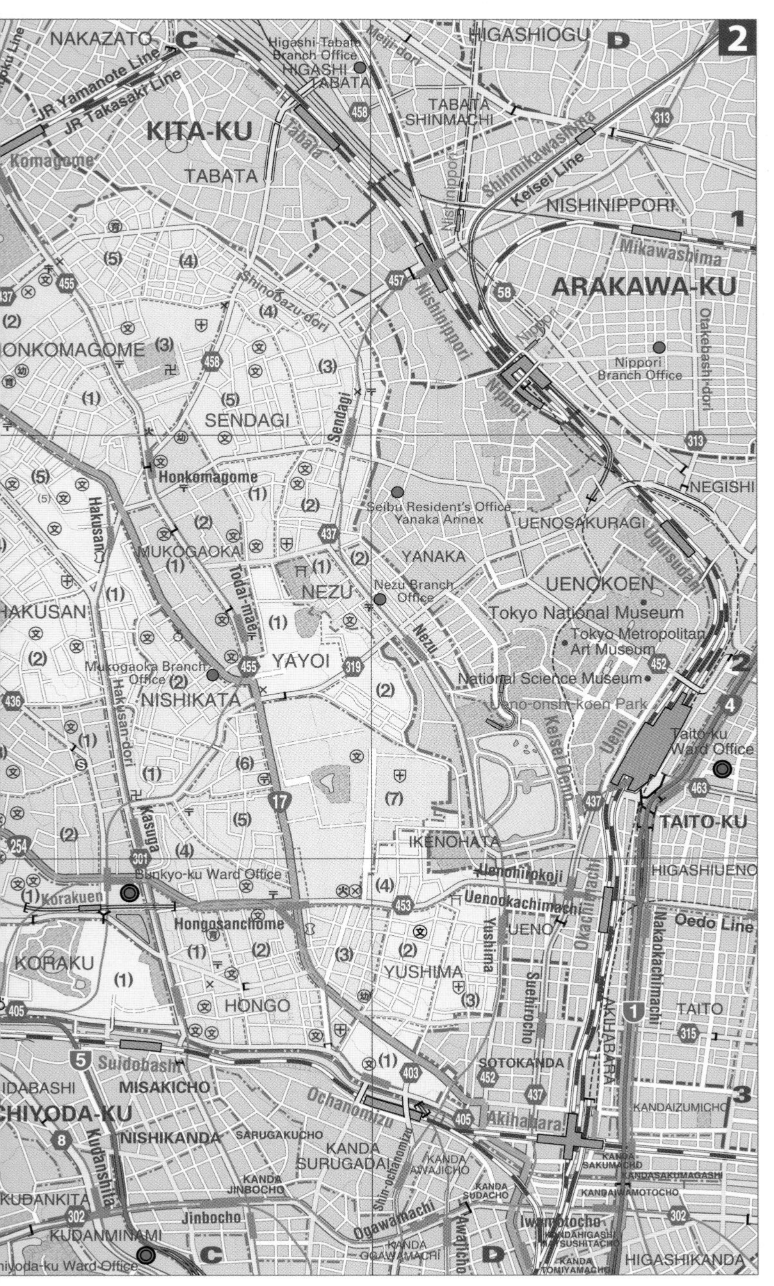

KITA-KU
ARAKAWA-KU
TAITO-KU
CHIYODA-KU
NAKAZATO
HIGASHIOGU
TABATA
TABATA SHINMACHI
NISHINIPPORI
SENDAGI
HONKOMAGOME
MUKOGAOKA
HAKUSAN
NISHIKATA
NEZU
YAYOI
YANAKA
UENOSAKURAGI
UENOKOEN
NEGISHI
IKENOHATA
KORAKU
HONGO
YUSHIMA
UENO
TAITO
HIGASHIUENO
SOTOKANDA
KANDAIZUMICHO
MISAKICHO
NISHIKANDA
SARUGAKUCHO
KANDA SURUGADAI
KANDA AWAJICHO
KANDA SUDACHO
KANDA JINBOCHO
KUDANKITA
KUDANMINAMI
HIGASHIKANDA
Higashi-Tabata Branch Office
Nippori Branch Office
Seibu Resident's Office Yanaka Annex
Nezu Branch Office
Mukogaoka Branch Office
Bunkyo-ku Ward Office
Taito-ku Ward Office
Chiyoda-ku Ward Office
Tokyo National Museum
Tokyo Metropolitan Art Museum
National Science Museum
Ueno-onshi-koen Park
JR Yamanote Line
JR Takasaki Line
Keisei Line
Oedo Line
Shinobazu-dori
Hakusan-dori
Meiji-dori
Otakebashi-dori

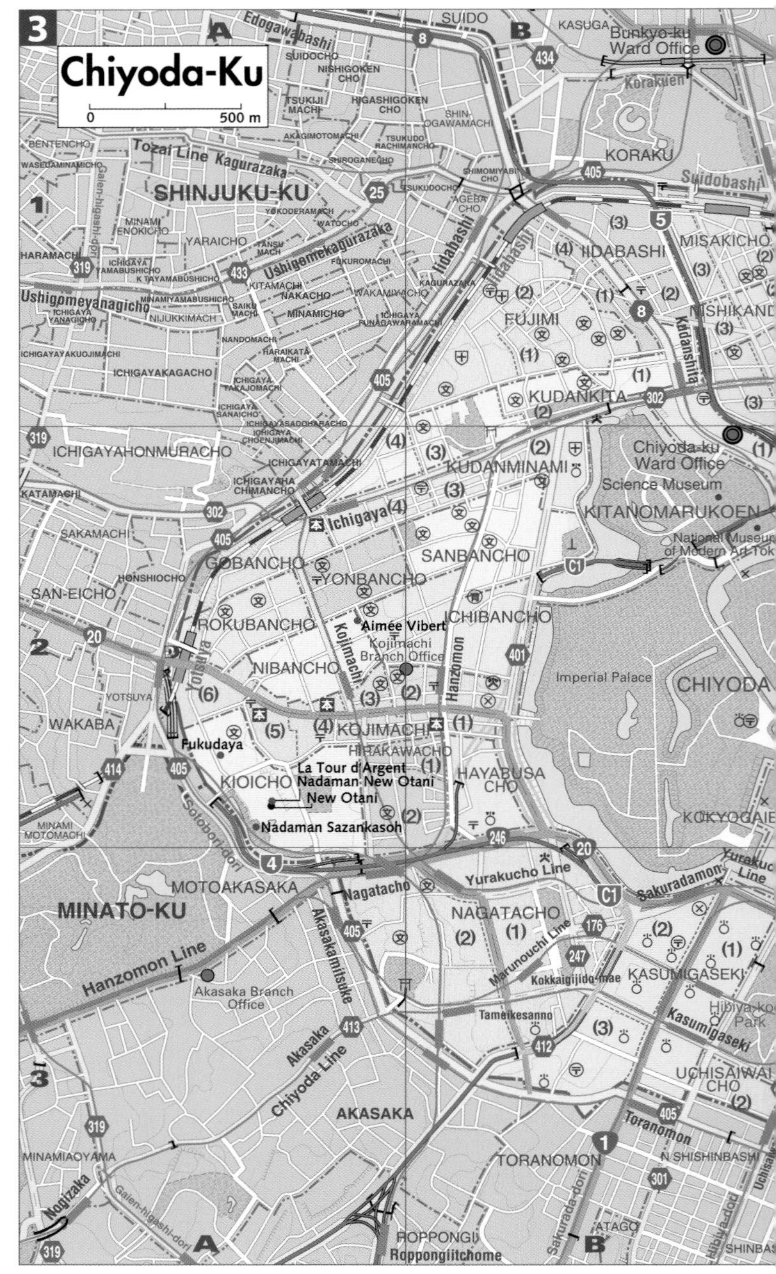
3
Chiyoda-Ku
0
500 m
A
B
1
2
3
SHINJUKU-KU
MINATO-KU
Tozai Line Kagurazaka
Edogawabashi
Ushigomekagurazaka
Ushigomeyanagicho
Iidabashi
Ichigaya
Yotsuya
Kojimachi
Hanzomon
Nagatacho
Akasakamitsuke
Akasaka
Chiyoda Line
Hanzomon Line
Yurakucho Line
Marunouchi Line
Kokkaigijido-mae
Tameikesanno
Kasumigaseki
Sakuradamon
Toranomon
Roppongiitchome
Nogizaka
Suidobashi
Korakuen
Kudanshita
Bunkyo-ku Ward Office
Chiyoda-ku Ward Office
Science Museum
National Museum of Modern Art Tokyo
Imperial Palace
Aimée Vibert
Kojimachi Branch Office
Fukudaya
La Tour d'Argent
Nadaman New Otani
New Otani
Nadaman Sazankasoh
Akasaka Branch Office
Gaien-higashi-dori
Sotobori-dori
Sakurada-dori
Hibiya-dori
KORAKU
IIDABASHI
FUJIMI
KUDANKITA
KUDANMINAMI
KITANOMARUKOEN
SANBANCHO
YONBANCHO
GOBANCHO
ROKUBANCHO
NIBANCHO
ICHIBANCHO
KOJIMACHI
HIRAKAWACHO
HAYABUSA CHO
KIOICHO
CHIYODA
KOKYOGAIEN
NAGATACHO
KASUMIGASEKI
UCHISAIWAI CHO
MISAKICHO
NISHIKANDA
TORANOMON
AKASAKA
MOTOAKASAKA
ROPPONGI
ATAGO
YOTSUYA
WAKABA
SAN-EICHO
SAKAMACHI
ICHIGAYAHONMURACHO
ICHIGAYATAMACHI
ICHIGAYAKAGACHO
YARAICHO
MINAMI ENOKICHO
BENTENCHO
WASEDAMINAMICHO
HARAMACHI
SUIDO
KASUGA
SUIDOCHO
NISHIGOKEN CHO
HIGASHIGOKEN CHO
SHIN-OGAWAMACHI
KAGURAZAKA
MINAMIAOYAMA
MINAMI MOTOMACHI
N SHISHINBASHI
SHINBASHI
Hibiya-koen Park

BUNKYO-KU
TAITO-KU
CHUO-KU
Gout du Jour Nouvelle Ere
Marunouchi
Monnalisa Shofukuro
Four Seasons Marunouchi
The Peninsula
Imperial Les Saisons
Chuo-ku Ward Office

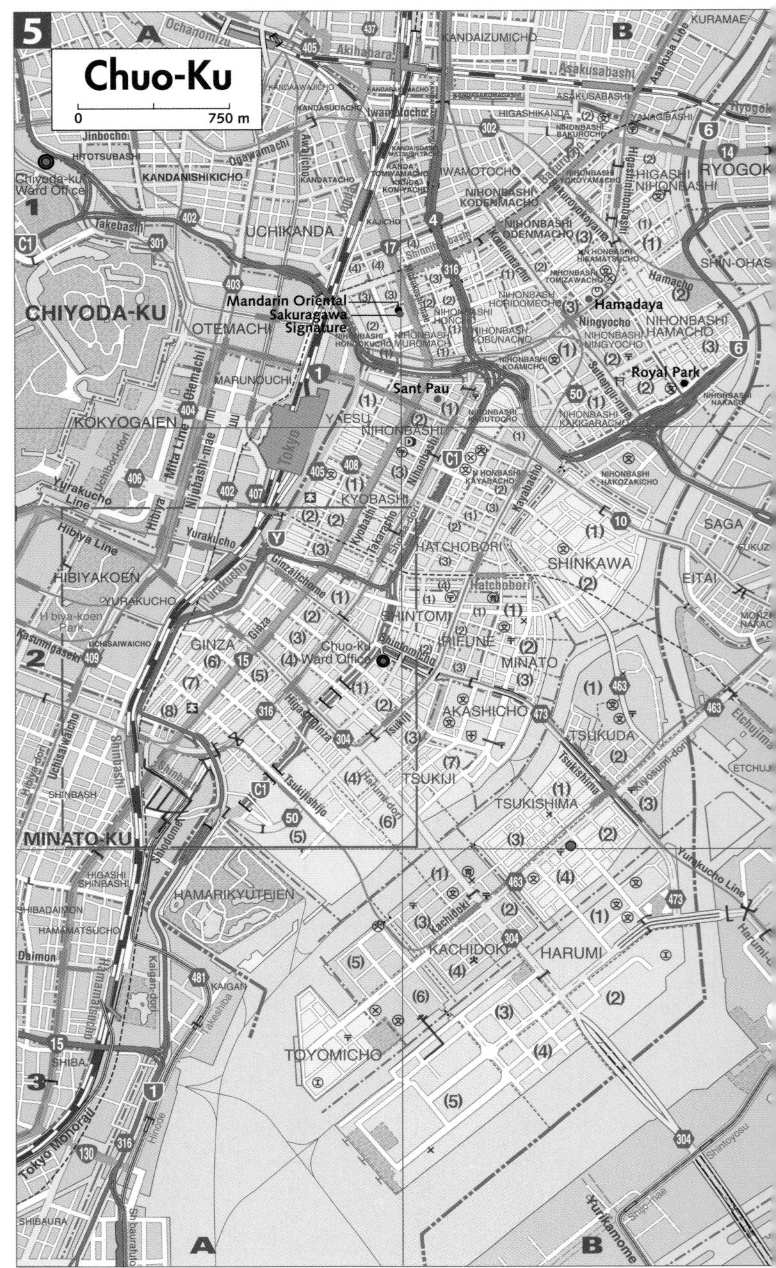
5
Chuo-Ku
0
750 m
CHIYODA-KU
MINATO-KU
Mandarin Oriental
Sakuragawa
Signature
Hamadaya
Royal Park
Sant Pau
Chuo-Ku Ward Office
Chiyoda-ku Ward Office
NIHONBASHI
GINZA
TSUKIJI
TSUKISHIMA
KACHIDOKI
HARUMI
TOYOMICHO
SHINKAWA
HATCHOBORI
KYOBASHI
YAESU
MARUNOUCHI
OTEMACHI
KOKYOGAIEN
HIBIYAKOEN
AKASHICHO
MINATO
IRIFUNE
SHINTOMI
TSUKUDA
HAMARIKYUTEIEN
UCHIKANDA
RYOGOKU

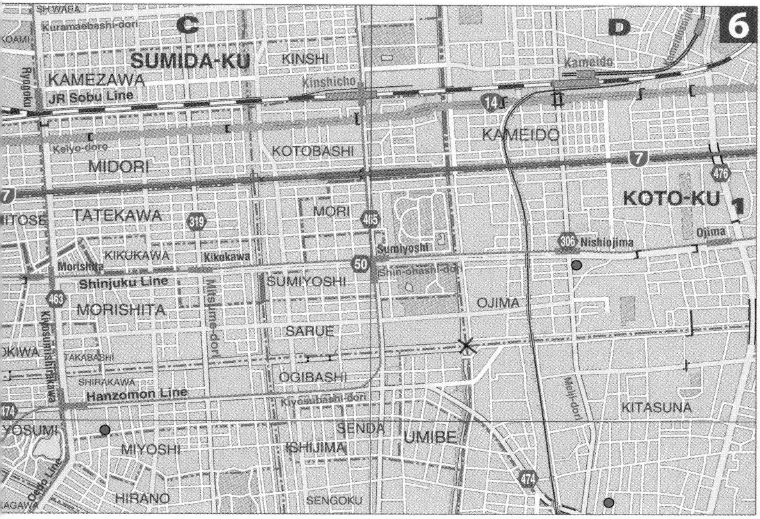

C
D
6
SUMIDA-KU
KAMEZAWA
JR Sobu Line
KINSHI
Kinshicho
Kameido
KAMEIDO
KOTOBASHI
MIDORI
TATEKAWA
MORI
KOTO-KU
1
KIKUKAWA
Kikukawa
Morishita
Shinjuku Line
SUMIYOSHI
Sumiyoshi
Shin-ohashi-dori
Nishiojima
Ojima
MORISHITA
Mitsume-dori
SARUE
OJIMA
TAKABASHI
SHIRAKAWA
Hanzomon Line
OGIBASHI
Kiyosubashi-dori
Meiji-dori
KITASUNA
SENDA
UMIBE
ISHIJIMA
MIYOSHI
HIRANO
SENGOKU
Oedo Line
Kiyosumishirakawa
Ryogoku
Keiyo-doro

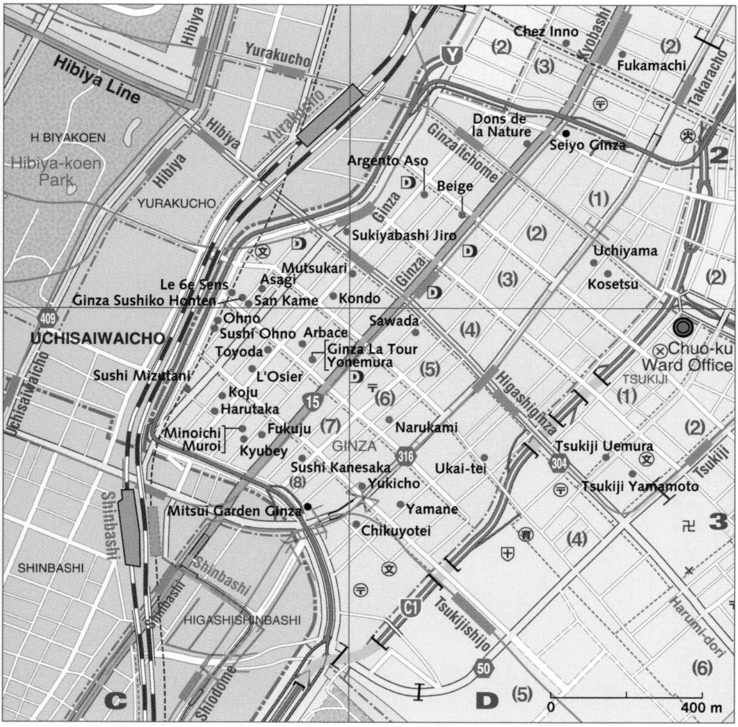

Hibiya Line
Hibiya
Yurakucho
H BIYAKOEN
Hibiya-koen Park
YURAKUCHO
Chez Inno
Kyobashi
Fukamachi
Takaracho
Dons de la Nature
Seiyo Ginza
Ginzaitchome
Argento Aso
Beige
Ginza
Sukiyabashi Jiro
Uchiyama
Kosetsu
Mutsukari
Asagi
Le 6e Sens
Ginza Sushiko Honten
San Kame
Kondo
Ohno
Sushi Ohno
Arbace
Sawada
UCHISAIWAICHO
Toyoda
Ginza La Tour Yonemura
Chuo-ku Ward Office
TSUKIJI
Sushi Mizutani
L'Osier
Koju
Harutaka
Higashiginza
Minoichi
Muroi
Fukuju
Narukami
Kyubey
GINZA
Tsukiji Uemura
Sushi Kanesaka
Ukai-tei
Tsukiji Yamamoto
Yukicho
Mitsui Garden Ginza
Yamane
Chikuyotei
Shinbashi
SHINBASHI
HIGASHISHINBASHI
Tsukijishijo
Harumi-dori
Tsukiji
Shiodome
Uchisaiwaicho
C
D
0
400 m

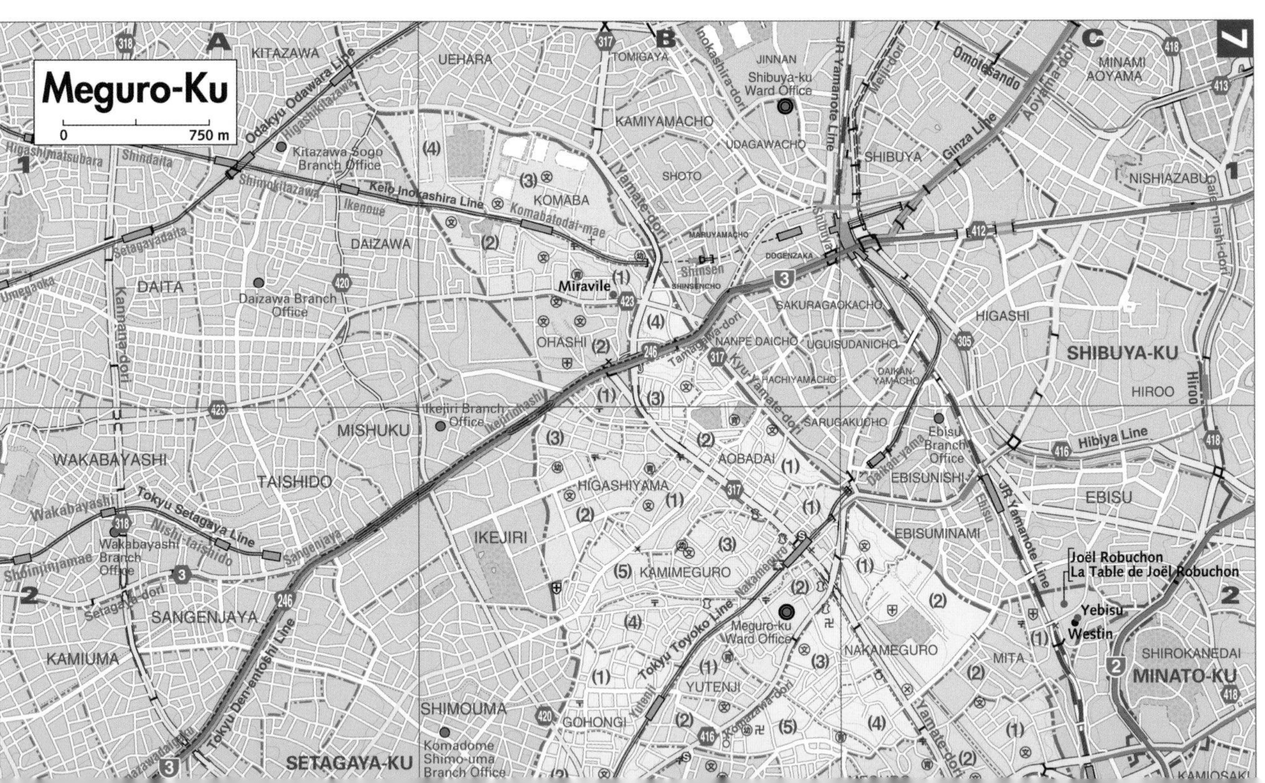
7
Meguro-Ku
0
750 m
SHIBUYA-KU
MINATO-KU
SETAGAYA-KU
Shibuya
Ebisu
Hiroo
Omotesando
Miravile
Joël Robuchon
La Table de Joël Robuchon
Yebisu
Westin
Shibuya-ku Ward Office
Meguro-ku Ward Office
JR Yamanote Line
Tokyu Toyoko Line
Tokyu Den-entoshi Line
Tokyu Setagaya Line
Keio Inokashira Line
Odakyu Odawara Line
Hibiya Line
Ginza Line
Yamate-dori
Kyu-Yamate-dori
Kannana-dori
Inokashira-dori
Aoyama-dori
Meiji-dori
Gaien-nishi-dori
KOMABA
OHASHI
AOBADAI
HIGASHIYAMA
KAMIMEGURO
NAKAMEGURO
YUTENJI
IKEJIRI
MISHUKU
TAISHIDO
SANGENJAYA
DAIZAWA
DAITA
KITAZAWA
UEHARA
SHOTO
TOMIGAYA
KAMIYAMACHO
JINNAN
UDAGAWACHO
SHIBUYA
HIGASHI
HIROO
EBISU
EBISUNISHI
EBISUMINAMI
MITA
SHIROKANEDAI
NISHIAZABU
MINAMI AOYAMA
SHIMOUMA
GOHONGI
WAKABAYASHI
KAMIUMA
Ebisu Branch Office
Ikejiri Branch Office
Komadome Shimo-uma Branch Office
Kitazawa Sogo Branch Office
Daizawa Branch Office
Wakabayashi Branch Office

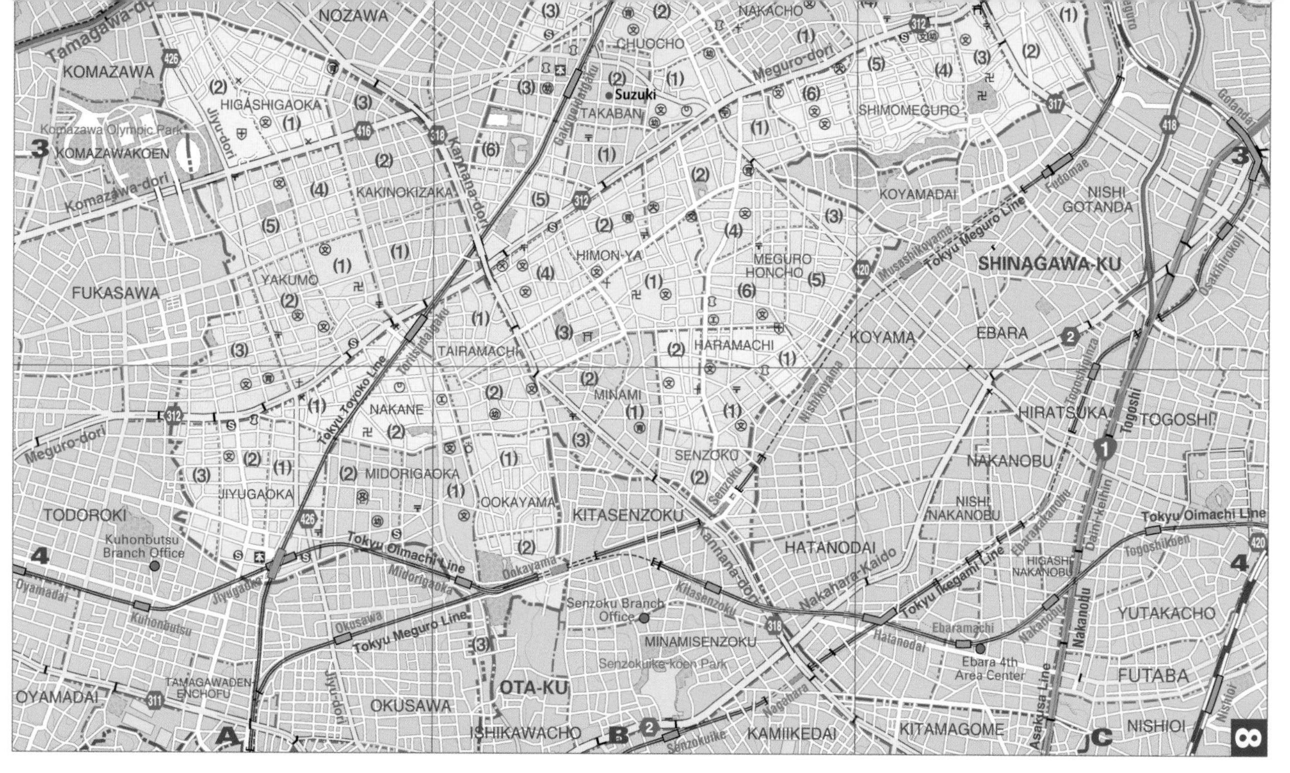
NOZAWA
KOMAZAWA
HIGASHIGAOKA
Komazawa Olympic Park
KOMAZAWAKOEN
Jiyu-dori
Komazawa-dori
Tamagawa-dori
KAKINOKIZAKA
Kannana-dori
CHUOCHO
NAKACHO
Suzuki
TAKABAN
Gakugeidaigaku
Meguro-dori
SHIMOMEGURO
KOYAMADAI
Fudomae
NISHI GOTANDA
Gotanda
Tokyu Meguro Line
Musashikoyama
SHINAGAWA-KU
Osakihirokoji
HIMON-YA
MEGURO HONCHO
YAKUMO
FUKASAWA
TAIRAMACHI
Toritsudaigaku
Tokyu Toyoko Line
HARAMACHI
KOYAMA
EBARA
Togoshiginza
MINAMI
NAKANE
Nishikoyama
HIRATSUKA
TOGOSHI
Togoshi
SENZOKU
Senzoku
NAKANOBU
Dai-ni-keihin
MIDORIGAOKA
JIYUGAOKA
OOKAYAMA
KITASENZOKU
NISHI NAKANOBU
Ebaranakanobu
TODOROKI
Kuhonbutsu Branch Office
Tokyu Oimachi Line
Ookayama
HATANODAI
Nakahara-Kaido
Tokyu Ikegami Line
HIGASHI NAKANOBU
Togoshikoen
Oyamadai
Jiyugaoka
Midorigaoka
Kuhonbutsu
Okusawa
Tokyu Meguro Line
Senzoku Branch Office
Kitasenzoku
MINAMISENZOKU
Senzokuike-koen Park
Hatanodai
Ebaramachi
Ebara 4th Area Center
Nakanobu
YUTAKACHO
FUTABA
Asakusa Line
TAMAGAWADEN-ENCHOFU
OYAMADAI
OKUSAWA
OTA-KU
ISHIKAWACHO
Nagahara
Senzokuike
KAMIIKEDAI
KITAMAGOME
NISHIOI
Nishioi
8

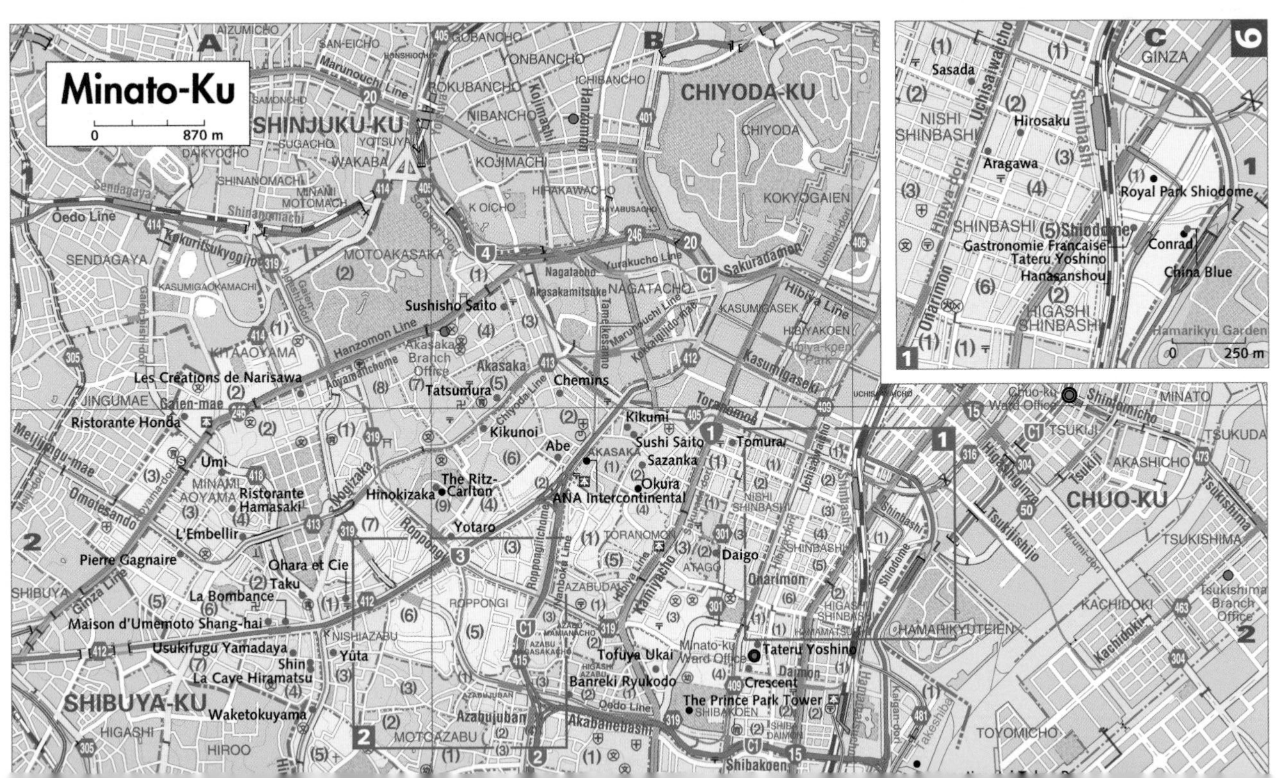

Minato-Ku
0
870 m
9
1
2
0
250 m
CHIYODA-KU
SHINJUKU-KU
SHIBUYA-KU
CHUO-KU
Royal Park Shiodome
Conrad
China Blue
Gastronomie Française
Tateru Yoshino
Hanasanshou
Sasada
Hirosaku
Aragawa
Ristorante Honda
Les Créations de Narisawa
Umi
Ristorante Hamasaki
L'Embellir
Pierre Gagnaire
Ohara et Cie
Taku
La Bombance
Maison d'Umemoto Shang-hai
Usukifugu Yamadaya
Shin
La Cave Hiramatsu
Waketokuyama
Yûta
Hinokizaka
The Ritz-Carlton
Yotaro
Sushisho Saito
Tatsumura
Kikunoi
Abe
Chemins
Kikumi
Sushi Saito
Sazanka
Okura
ANA Intercontinental
Tomura
Daigo
Tofuya Ukai
Banreki Ryukodo
The Prince Park Tower
Crescent
Tateru Yoshino
Minato-ku Ward Office
Chuo-ku Ward Office

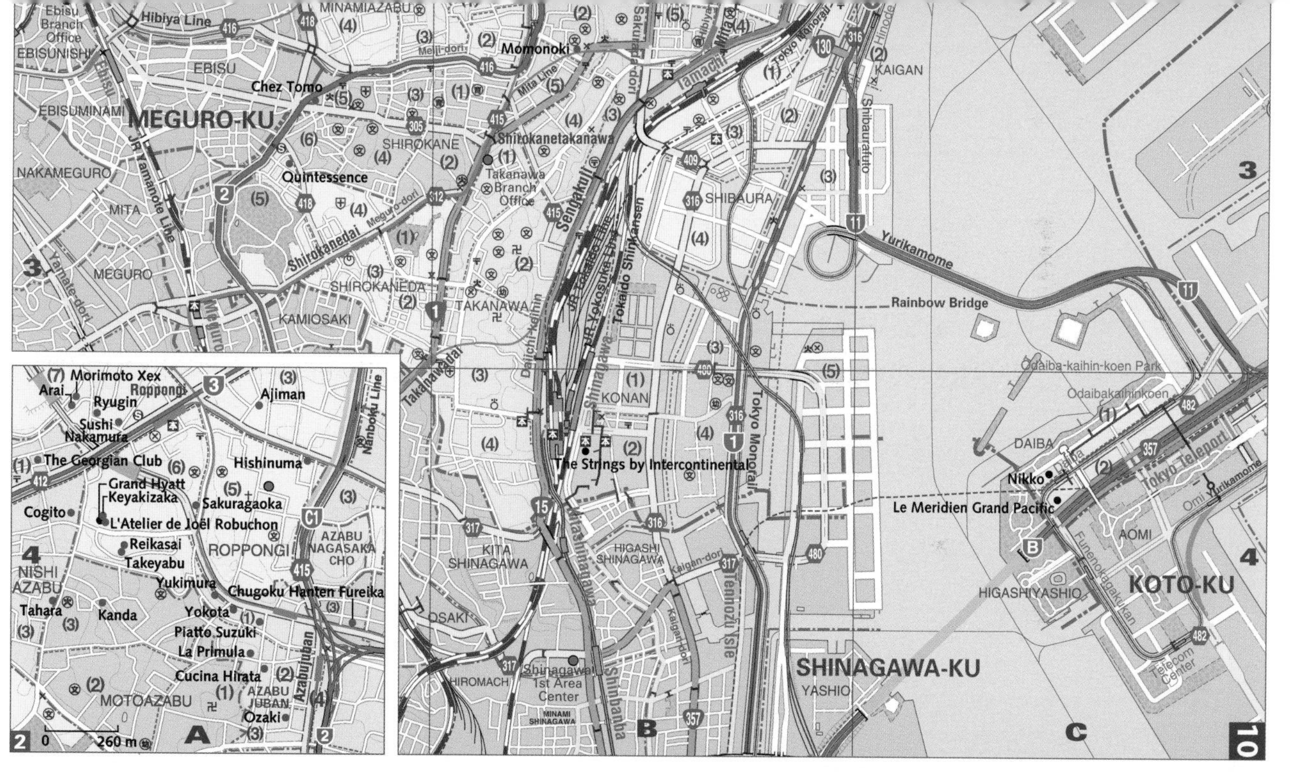
MEGURO-KU
Ebisu Branch Office
EBISUNISHI
Hibiya Line
EBISU
Ebisu
EBISUMINAMI
MINAMIAZABU
Meiji-dori
Momonoki
Chez Tomo
SHIROKANE
Shirokanetakanawa
Quintessence
Takanawa Branch Office
NAKAMEGURO
JR Yamanote Line
MITA
MEGURO
Yamate-dori
Meguro
Meguro-dori
Shirokanedai
SHIROKANEDA
KAMIOSAKI
TAKANAWA
Takanawadai
Daiichi-keihin
Sengakuji
Sakurada-dori
Mita Line
Tamachi
Mita
Tokyo Monorail
KAIGAN
Hinode
Shibaurafuto
SHIBAURA
JR Tokaido Line
JR Yokosuka Line
Tokaido Shinkansen
Shinagawa
KONAN
Yurikamome
Rainbow Bridge
Odaiba-kaihin-koen Park
Odaibakaihinkoen
DAIBA
Daiba
Nikko
Le Meridien Grand Pacific
Tokyo Teleport
Omi
AOMI
HIGASHIYASHIO
Funenokagakukan
KOTO-KU
Telecom Center
The Strings by Intercontinental
KITA SHINAGAWA
HIGASHI SHINAGAWA
Kitashinagawa
Kaigan-dori
Tennozu Isle
OSAKI
HIROMACH
Shinagawa 1st Area Center
MINAMI SHINAGAWA
Shinbanba
SHINAGAWA-KU
YASHIO
Morimoto Xex
Arai
Roppongi
Ryugin
Sushi Nakamura
Ajiman
The Georgian Club
Hishinuma
Grand Hyatt
Keyakizaka
Sakuragaoka
Cogito
L'Atelier de Joël Robuchon
Nanboku Line
AZABU NAGASAKA CHO
Reikasai
Takeyabu
ROPPONGI
NISHI AZABU
Yukimura
Chugoku Hanten Fureika
Tahara
Kanda
Yokota
Piatto Suzuki
La Primula
Cucina Hirata
Azabujuban
AZABU JUBAN
MOTOAZABU
Ozaki
0
260 m
A
B
C
2
3
4
10

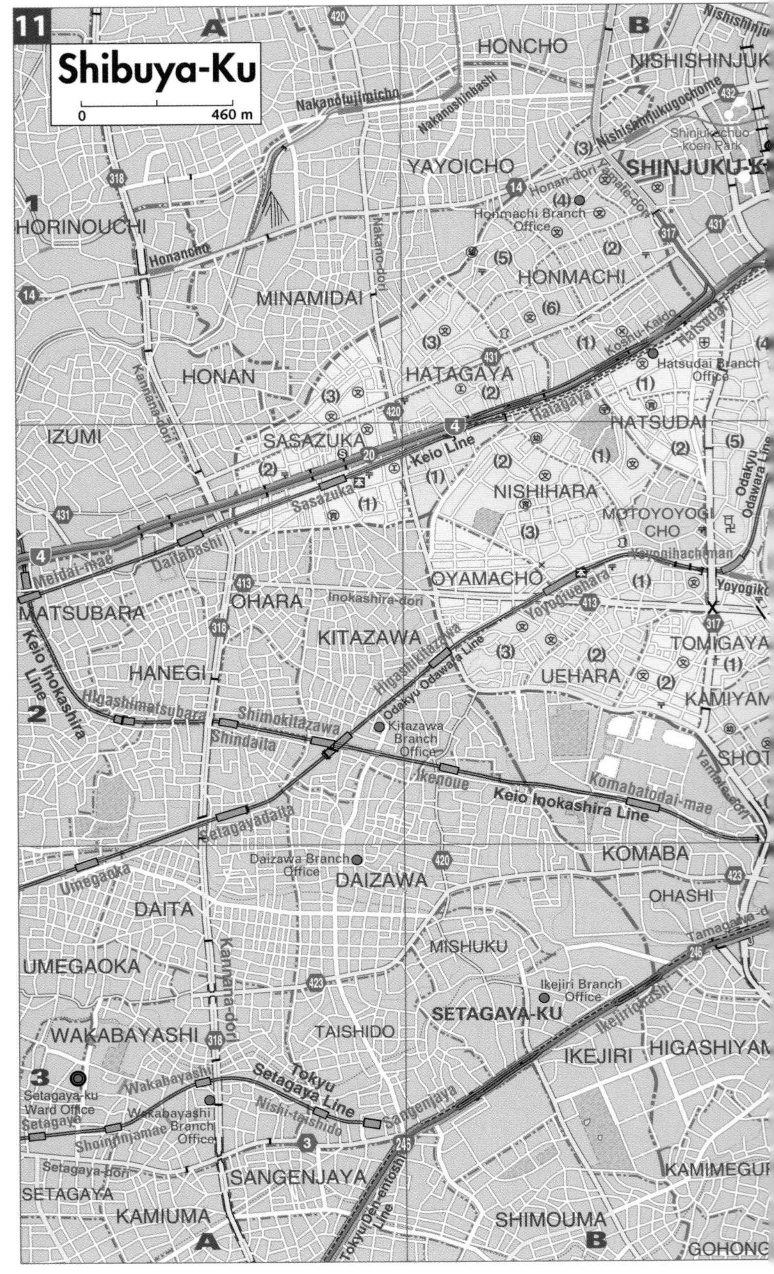
11
Shibuya-Ku
0
460 m
A
B
1
2
3
HONCHO
NISHISHINJUKU
Nakanofujimicho
Nakanoshinbashi
Nishishinjukugochome
Shinjukuchuo-koen Park
SHINJUKU-KU
YAYOICHO
Honan-dori
Yamate-dori
Honmachi Branch Office
HORINOUCHI
Honancho
Nakano-dori
HONMACHI
MINAMIDAI
Koshu-Kaido
Hatsudai
Hatsudai Branch Office
HONAN
HATAGAYA
Kannana-dori
Hatagaya
HATSUDAI
IZUMI
SASAZUKA
Keio Line
NISHIHARA
Sasazuka
Odakyu Odawara Line
MOTOYOYOGI CHO
Daitabashi
Meidai-mae
Yoyogihachiman
OYAMACHO
Yoyogiuehara
Yoyogiko
OHARA
Inokashira-dori
MATSUBARA
KITAZAWA
TOMIGAYA
Keio Inokashira Line
HANEGI
Higashikitazawa
UEHARA
KAMIYAMA
Higashimatsubara
Shimokitazawa
Shindaita
Kitazawa Branch Office
SHOTO
Yamate-dori
Ikenoue
Komabatodai-mae
Keio Inokashira Line
Setagayadaita
Daizawa Branch Office
KOMABA
DAIZAWA
Umegaoka
OHASHI
DAITA
Tamagawa-dori
MISHUKU
UMEGAOKA
Kannana-dori
Ikejiri Branch Office
SETAGAYA-KU
Ikejiriohashi
TAISHIDO
WAKABAYASHI
IKEJIRI
HIGASHIYAMA
Tokyu Setagaya Line
Wakabayashi
Setagaya-ku Ward Office
Wakabayashi Branch Office
Nishi-taishido
Sangenjaya
Setagaya
Shoinjinjamae
Setagaya-dori
SANGENJAYA
KAMIMEGURO
SETAGAYA
Tokyu Den-entoshi Line
KAMIUMA
SHIMOUMA
GOHONGI

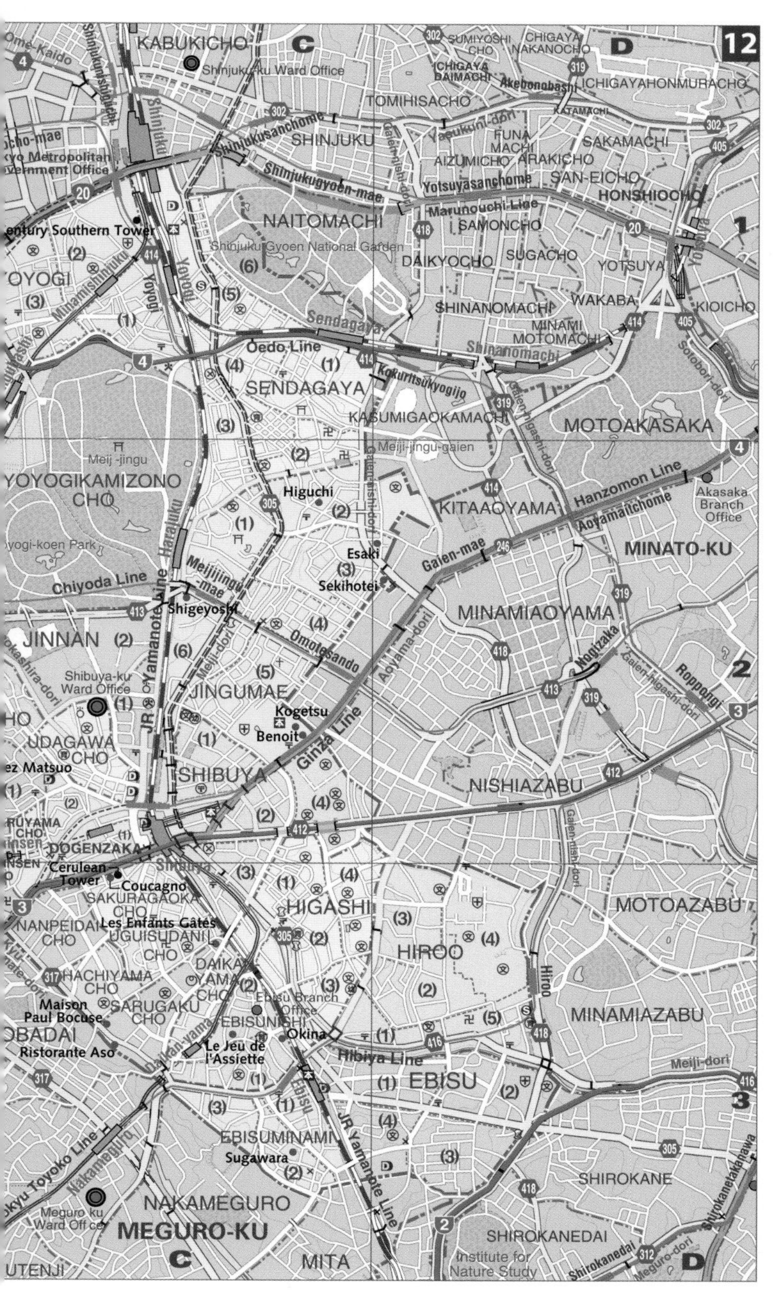
12
KABUKICHO
Shinjuku-ku Ward Office
SHINJUKU
NAITOMACHI
Shinjuku Gyoen National Garden
SENDAGAYA
KASUMIGAOKAMACHI
Meiji-jingu-gaien
YOYOGIKAMIZONO CHO
Higuchi
Esaki
Sekihotei
Shigeyoshi
JINNAN
Shibuya-ku Ward Office
JINGUMAE
Kogetsu
Benoit
UDAGAWA CHO
SHIBUYA
DOGENZAKA
Cerulean Tower
Coucagno
SAKURAGAOKA CHO
Les Enfants Gâtés
UGUISUDANI CHO
HACHIYAMA CHO
Maison Paul Bocuse
SARUGAKU CHO
Ristorante Aso
Le Jeu de l'Assiette
Ebisu Branch Office
EBISUNISHI
Okina
HIGASHI
HIROO
EBISU
EBISUMINAMI
Sugawara
NAKAMEGURO
MEGURO-KU
Meguro-ku Ward Office
MITA
TOMIHISACHO
SUMIYOSHI CHO
CHIGAYA NAKANOCHO
ICHIGAYA DAIMACHI
ICHIGAYAHONMURACHO
FUNA MACHI
SAKAMACHI
AIZUMICHO
ARAKICHO
SAN-EICHO
HONSHIOCHO
SAMONCHO
DAIKYOCHO
SUGACHO
YOTSUYA
SHINANOMACHI
WAKABA
MINAMI MOTOMACHI
KIOICHO
MOTOAKASAKA
KITAAOYAMA
Akasaka Branch Office
MINATO-KU
MINAMIAOYAMA
NISHIAZABU
MOTOAZABU
MINAMIAZABU
SHIROKANE
SHIROKANEDAI
Institute for Nature Study
Hanzomon Line
Chiyoda Line
Ginza Line
Hibiya Line
Oedo Line
Marunouchi Line
JR Yamanote Line
Omotesando
Meiji-dori
Aoyama-dori
Gaien-higashi-dori
Gaien-nishi-dori
Roppongi
Nogizaka
Meguro-dori
C
D
1
2
3

13
Shinagawa-Ku
0
750 m
YUTENJI
A
B
SHIROKANE
MITA
SHIROKANEDAI
Meguro-dori
Shirokanedai
MINATO-KU
NAKAMEGURO
Komazawa-dori
Yamate-dori
KAMIOSAKI
1
NAKACHO
MEGURO
HIGASHI GOTANDA
Sakurada-dori
Takanawadai
Asakusa Line
Meguro-dori
SHIMOMEGURO
Gotanda
MEGURO-KU
JR Yamanote Line
KOYAMADAI
Fudomae
NISHI GOTANDA
Tokyu Meguro Line
Ohara's
MEGURO HONCHO
Musashikoyama
OSAKI
Osakihirokoji
Osaki
Osaki 2nd Area Center
KOYAMA
HARAMACHI
Togoshiginza
Togoshi
NISHI SHINAGAWA
SENZOKU
EBARA
HIRATSUKA
TOGOSHI
Nishikoyama
2
NAKANOBU
Ebara nakanobu
Senzoku
Rinkai
NISHI NAKANOBU
HIGASHI NAKANOBU
Daini-keihin
Togoshikoen
Shinagawa-ku Ward Office
HATANODAI
Kaido
Oimachi Line
Shimoshinmei
Line
Ikegami Line
Tokyu
YUTAKACHO
Kitasenzoku
Nakahara
Sangen-dori
OI
Ebaramachi
Nakanobu
FUTABA
MINAMISENZOKU
Hatanodai
Tokyu
Ebara 4th Area Center
Nagahara
Nishioi
KITAMAGOME
Asakusa Line
NISHIOI
KAMIIKEDAI
Magome
HIGASHIMAGOME
NAKAMAGOME
3
Tokaido Shinkansen
JR Yokosuka Line
Ikegami-dori
JR Tokaido Line
OTA-KU
SANNO
Kannana-dori
Makimur
NISHIMAGOME
NAKAIKEGAMI
MINAMIMAGOME
Nishimagome
Omori
OMORIKIT
A
B

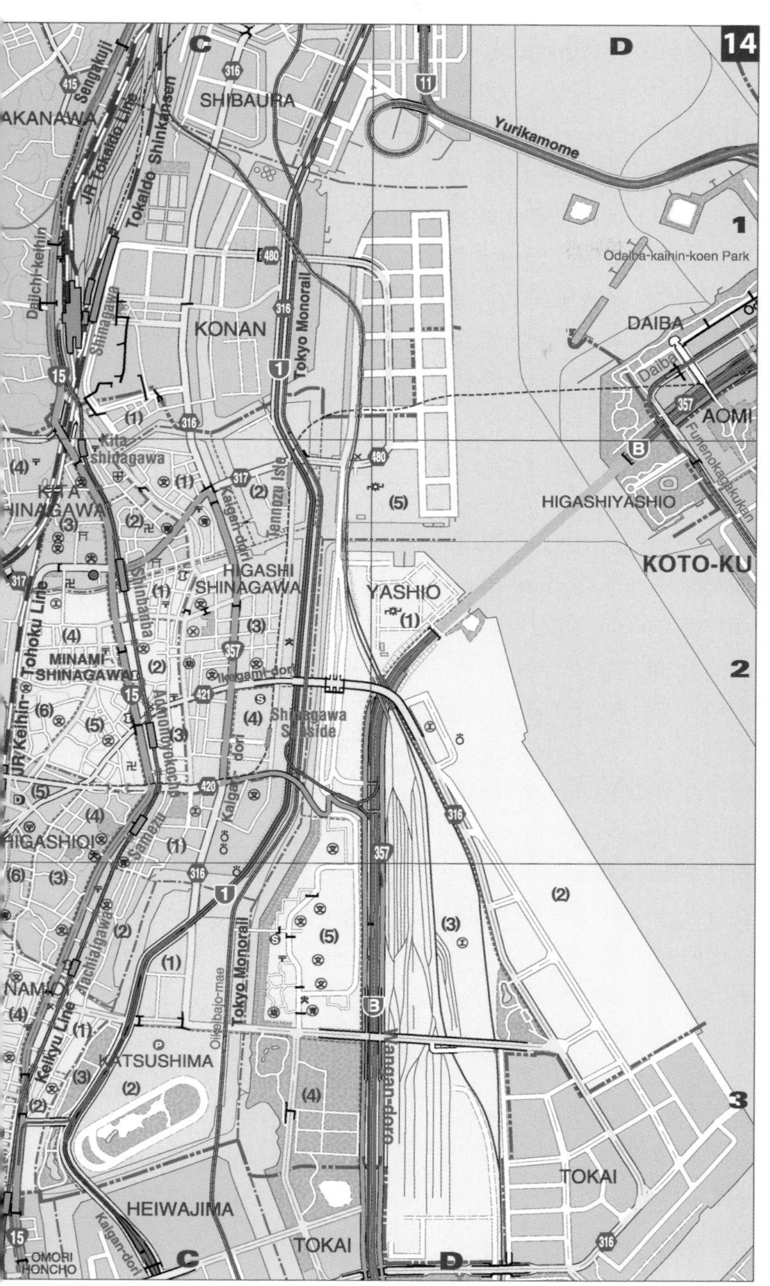

14
C
D
SHIBAURA
Yurikamome
Sengakuji
JR Tokaido Line
Tokaido Shinkansen
TAKANAWA
Odaiba-kaihin-koen Park
DAIBA
Daiba
AOMI
Funenokagakukan
KONAN
Tokyo Monorail
Shinagawa
Daiichi-keihin
Kita Shinagawa
KITA SHINAGAWA
Tennozu Isle
Kaigan-dori
HIGASHIYASHIO
KOTO-KU
HIGASHI SHINAGAWA
YASHIO
Shinbanba
MINAMI SHINAGAWA
Tohoku Line
Ikegami-dori
Shinagawa Seaside
Aomonoyokocho
JR Keihin
HIGASHIOI
Samezu
Tachiaigawa
Oikeibajo-mae
Tokyo Monorail
Keikyu Line
NAMIOI
KATSUSHIMA
Wangan-doro
TOKAI
HEIWAJIMA
Kaigan-dori
TOKAI
OMORI HONCHO

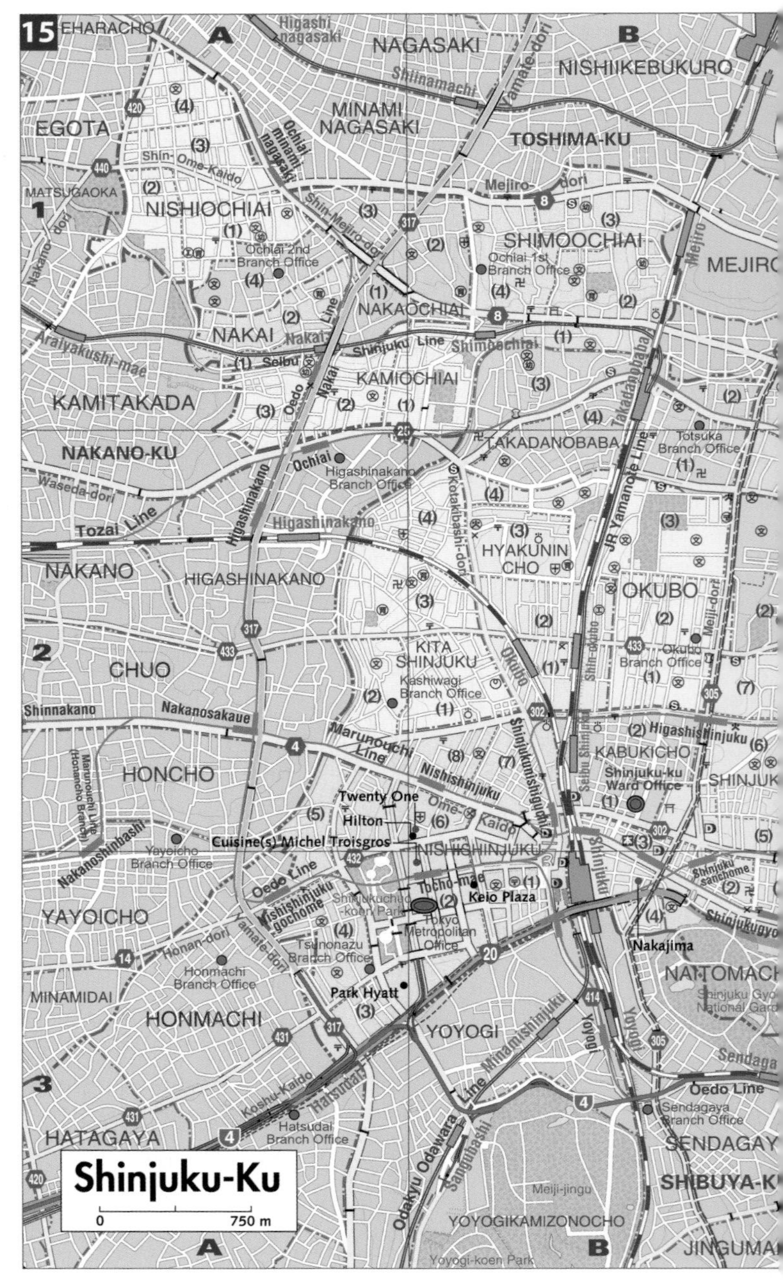
15
Shinjuku-Ku
0
750 m
NAGASAKI
MINAMI NAGASAKI
NISHIIKEBUKURO
TOSHIMA-KU
EGOTA
NISHIOCHIAI
SHIMOOCHIAI
MEJIRO
NAKAOCHIAI
NAKAI
KAMIOCHIAI
KAMITAKADA
NAKANO-KU
TAKADANOBABA
HYAKUNIN CHO
NAKANO
HIGASHINAKANO
OKUBO
CHUO
KITA SHINJUKU
KABUKICHO
HONCHO
NISHISHINJUKU
YAYOICHO
NAITOMACHI
MINAMIDAI
HONMACHI
YOYOGI
HATAGAYA
SENDAGAYA
SHIBUYA-KU
YOYOGIKAMIZONOCHO
JINGUMAE
Twenty One
Hilton
Cuisine(s) Michel Troisgros
Keio Plaza
Park Hyatt
Nakajima
Shinjuku-ku Ward Office
Tokyo Metropolitan Office
Ochiai 2nd Branch Office
Ochiai 1st Branch Office
Totsuka Branch Office
Higashinakano Branch Office
Okubo Branch Office
Kashiwagi Branch Office
Yayoicho Branch Office
Honmachi Branch Office
Tsunonazu Branch Office
Hatsudai Branch Office
Sendagaya Branch Office
Shinjuku Gyoen National Garden
Meiji-jingu
Yoyogi-koen Park
Shinjukuchuo-koen Park
Oedo Line
Tozai Line
Marunouchi Line
JR Yamanote Line
Odakyu Odawara Line
Seibu Shinjuku Line
Mejiro-dori
Waseda-dori
Yamate-dori
Ome-Kaido
Koshu-Kaido
Meiji-dori

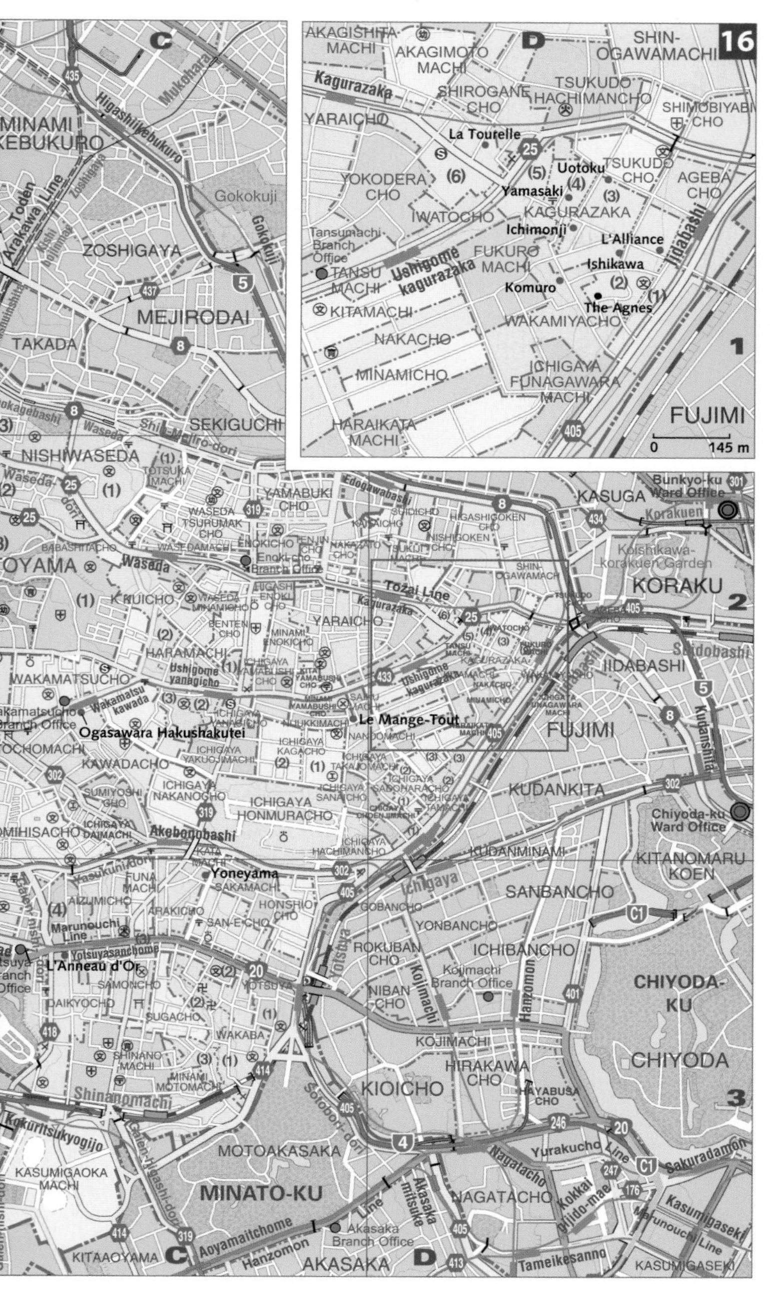
16
AKAGISHITA MACHI
AKAGIMOTO MACHI
SHIN-OGAWAMACHI
Kagurazaka
SHIROGANE CHO
TSUKUDO HACHIMANCHO
YARAICHO
La Tourelle
Uotoku
Yamasaki
KAGURAZAKA
Ichimonji
L'Alliance
Ishikawa
Komuro
The Agnes
YOKODERA CHO
IWATOCHO
FUKURO MACHI
TSUKUDO CHO
AGEBA CHO
Iidabashi
Tansumachi Branch Office
TANSU MACHI
Ushigome kagurazaka
KITAMACHI
NAKACHO
WAKAMIYACHO
MINAMICHO
ICHIGAYA FUNAGAWARA MACHI
HARAIKATA MACHI
FUJIMI
0 145 m
MINAMI IKEBUKURO
Higashiikebukuro
Mukohara
Gokokuji
ZOSHIGAYA
MEJIRODAI
TAKADA
SEKIGUCHI
NISHIWASEDA
Shin-Mejiro-dori
YAMABUKI CHO
Edogawabashi
KASUGA
Bunkyo-ku Ward Office
Korakuen
Koishikawa-korakuen Garden
KORAKU
TOYAMA
Wasedа
Tozai Line
Enoki-cho Branch Office
WAKAMATSUCHO
Ogasawara Hakushakutei
Le Mange-Tout
IIDABASHI
KAWADACHO
ICHIGAYA HONMURACHO
KUDANKITA
Chiyoda-ku Ward Office
Akebonobashi
KUDANMINAMI
KITANOMARU KOEN
Yoneyama
SANBANCHO
Marunouchi Line
L'Anneau d'Or
YONBANCHO
ICHIBANCHO
Kojimachi Branch Office
CHIYODA-KU
CHIYODA
YOTSUYA
KOJIMACHI
HIRAKAWA CHO
KIOICHO
Shinanomachi
MOTOAKASAKA
KASUMIGAOKA MACHI
MINATO-KU
NAGATACHO
Akasaka Branch Office
AKASAKA
KITAAOYAMA
Aoyamaitchome
KASUMIGASEKI
Sakuradamon
Yurakucho Line
Tameikesanno
Hanzomon

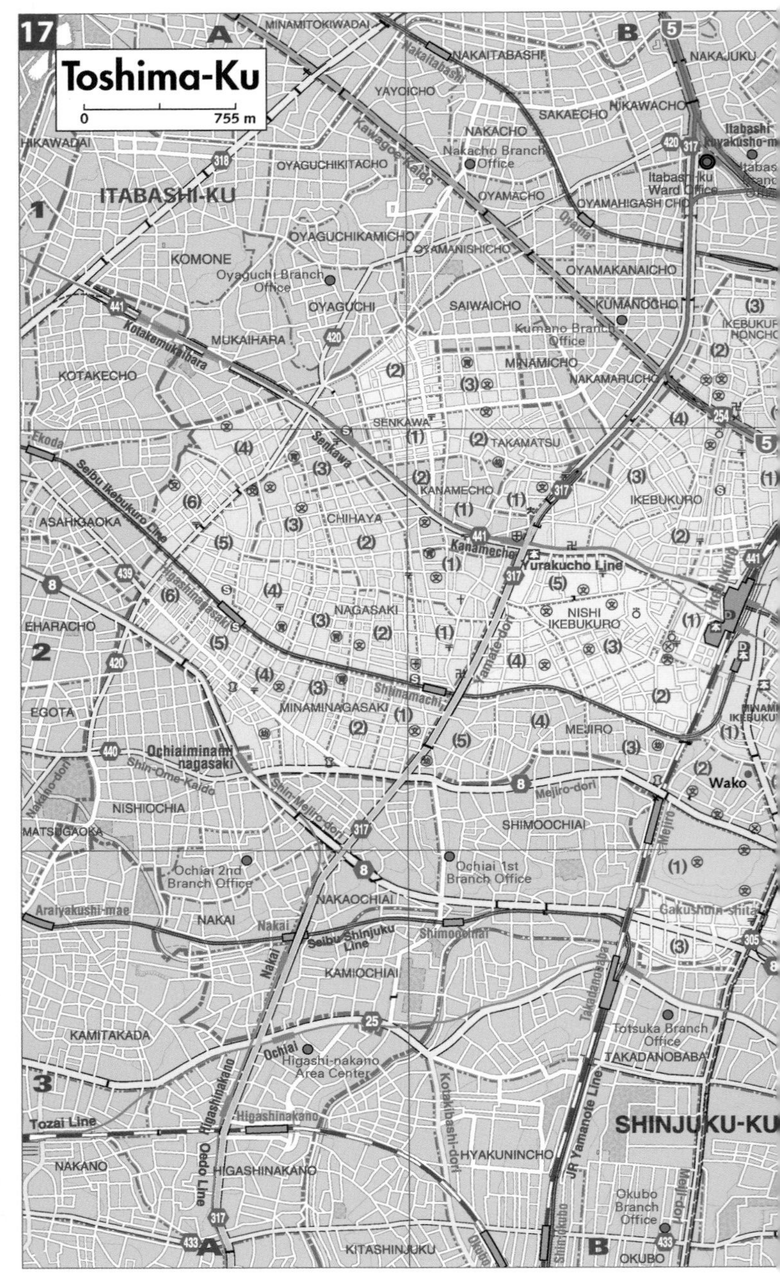
17
Toshima-Ku
0
755 m
ITABASHI-KU
SHINJUKU-KU
MINAMITOKIWADAI
NAKAITABASHI
NAKAJUKU
YAYOICHO
SAKAECHO
HIKAWACHO
NAKACHO
Nakacho Branch Office
Itabashi-ku Ward Office
HIKAWADAI
OYAGUCHIKITACHO
OYAMACHO
OYAMAHIGASHICHO
OYAGUCHIKAMICHO
OYAMANISHICHO
KOMONE
OYAMAKANAICHO
Oyaguchi Branch Office
OYAGUCHI
SAIWAICHO
KUMANOCHO
Kumano Branch Office
MUKAIHARA
KOTAKECHO
MINAMICHO
NAKAMARUCHO
IKEBUKURO HONCHO
SENKAWA
TAKAMATSU
KANAMECHO
IKEBUKURO
ASAHIGAOKA
CHIHAYA
Kanamecho
Yurakucho Line
NISHI IKEBUKURO
NAGASAKI
EHARACHO
EGOTA
MINAMINAGASAKI
MEJIRO
MINAMI IKEBUKURO
Ochiaiminami nagasaki
Wako
NISHIOCHIAI
MATSUGAOKA
SHIMOOCHIAI
Ochiai 2nd Branch Office
Ochiai 1st Branch Office
NAKAOCHIAI
Araiyakushi-mae
NAKAI
Nakai
Seibu Shinjuku Line
Shimoochiai
Gakushuin-shita
KAMIOCHIAI
Totsuka Branch Office
KAMITAKADA
Ochiai
Higashi-nakano Area Center
TAKADANOBABA
Takadanobaba
Tozai Line
Higashinakano
NAKANO
HIGASHINAKANO
HYAKUNINCHO
Oedo Line
JR Yamanote Line
Okubo Branch Office
KITASHINJUKU
OKUBO
Kawagoe-Kaido
Kotakemukaihara
Seibu Ikebukuro Line
Higashinagasaki
Senkawa
Shiinamachi
Yamate-dori
Mejiro-dori
Shin-Ome-Kaido
Shin-Mejiro-dori
Nakano-dori
Kotakibashi-dori
Meiji-dori
Higashinakano
Mejiro
Ikebukuro
Ekoda
Okubo
Shin-Okubo
Itabashi
Oyama
Nakaitabashi
A
B
1
2
3

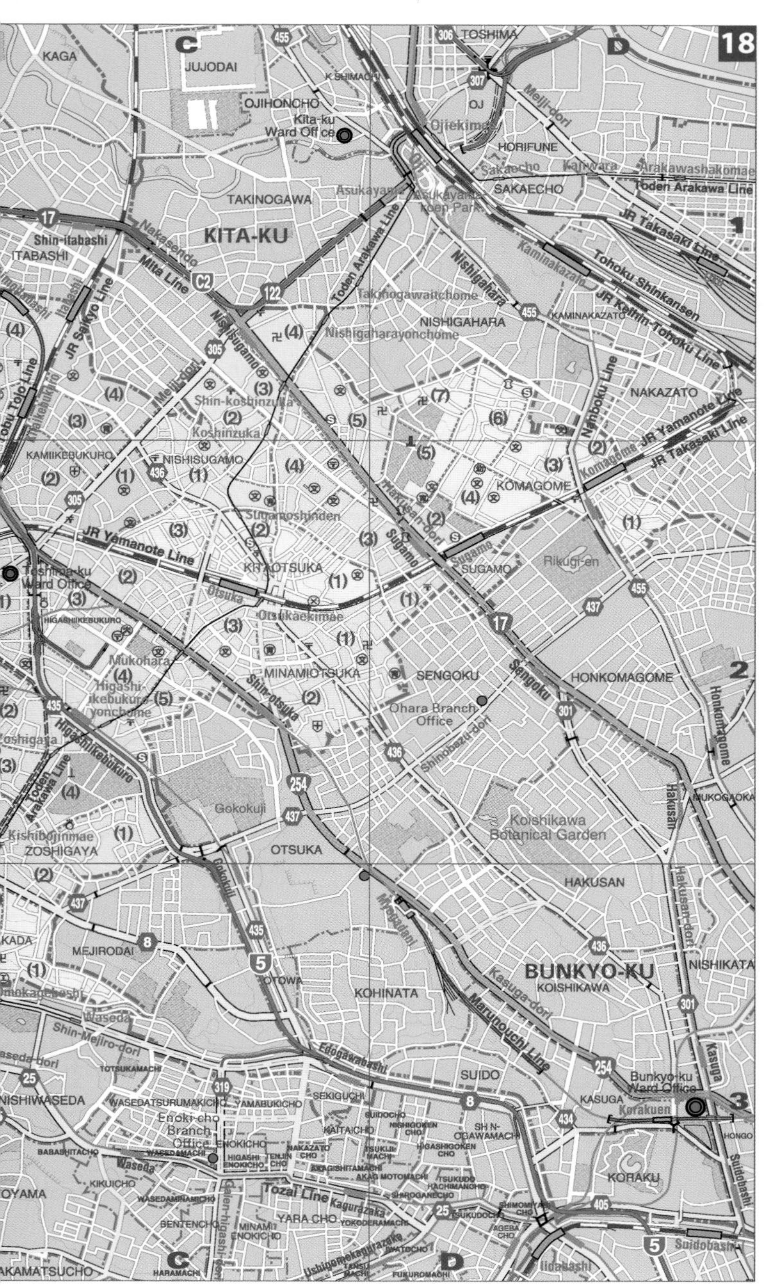
18
C
D
KAGA
JUJODAI
TOSHIMA
OJIHONCHO
Kita-ku
Ward Office
Ojiekimae
HORIFUNE
Sakaecho
SAKAECHO
Arakawashakomae
Toden Arakawa Line
TAKINOGAWA
Asukayama
Asukayama
Koen Park
KITA-KU
Shin-itabashi
ITABASHI
Nakasendo
Mita Line
JR Saikyo Line
Toden Arakawa Line
Takinogawaitchome
Nishigahara
NISHIGAHARA
KAMINAKAZATO
JR Takasaki Line
Tohoku Shinkansen
JR Keihin-Tohoku Line
Nishigaharayonchome
Nishisugamo
Meiji-dori
Shin-koshinzuka
Koshinzuka
NISHISUGAMO
KAMIIKEBUKURO
NAKAZATO
Namboku Line
JR Yamanote Line
Komagome
KOMAGOME
Sugamoshinden
JR Yamanote Line
KITAOTSUKA
Otsuka
Toshima-ku
Ward Office
HIGASHIIKEBUKURO
Otsukaekimae
Hakusan-dori
Sugamo
SUGAMO
Rikugi-en
MINAMIOTSUKA
SENGOKU
Sengoku
HONKOMAGOME
Mukohara
Higashi-
ikebukuro-
yonchome
Shin-otsuka
Ohara Branch
Office
Shinobazu-dori
Honkomagome
Higashiikebukuro
Toden Arakawa Line
Gokokuji
Koishikawa
Botanical Garden
MUKOGAOKA
Kishibojinmae
ZOSHIGAYA
OTSUKA
Hakusan
HAKUSAN
Hakusan-dori
Gokokuji
Myogadani
MEJIRODAI
OTOWA
KOHINATA
BUNKYO-KU
KOISHIKAWA
NISHIKATA
Kasuga-dori
Marunouchi Line
Waseda
Shin-Mejiro-dori
Waseda-dori
TOTSUKAMACHI
Edogawabashi
SUIDO
Bunkyo-ku
Ward Office
Kasuga
NISHIWASEDA
WASEDATSURUMAKICHO
YAMABUKICHO
SEKIGUCHI
KASUGA
Korakuen
HONGO
Enoki-cho
Branch
Office
ENOKICHO
SUIDOCHO
KAITAICHO
NISHIGOKEN CHO
SHIN-OGAWAMACHI
HIGASHIGOKEN CHO
BABASHITACHO
WASEDAMACHI
HIGASHI ENOKICHO
TENJIN CHO
NAKAZATO CHO
TSUKIJI MACHI
AKAGISHITAMACHI
AKAGI MOTOMACHI
KORAKU
Suidobashi
KIKUICHO
OYAMA
WASEDAMINAMICHO
Tozai Line
Kagurazaka
SHIMOMIYABI CHO
TSUKUDO HACHIMANCHO
TSUKUDOCHO
AGEBA CHO
BENTENCHO
MINAMI ENOKICHO
YARA CHO
YOKODERAMACHI
Gaien-higashi-dori
Ushigomekagurazaka
IWATOCHO
Suidobashi
Iidabashi
AKAMATSUCHO
HARAMACHI
FUKUROMACHI

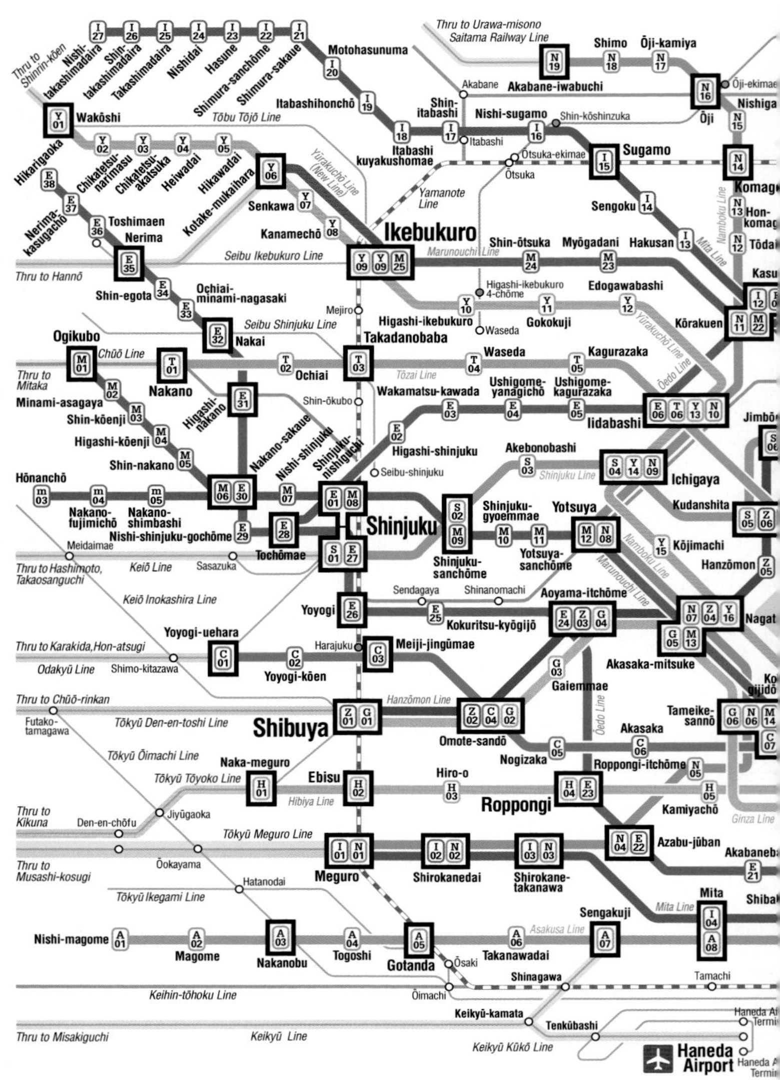

Thru to Shinrin-kōen
Nishi-takashimadaira
Shin-takashimadaira
Takashimadaira
Nishidai
Hasune
Shimura-sanchōme
Shimura-sakaue
Motohasunuma
Itabashihonchō
Tōbu Tōjō Line
Wakōshi
Hikarigaoka
Chikatetsu-narimasu
Chikatetsu-akatsuka
Heiwadai
Hikawadai
Kotake-mukaihara
Senkawa
Kanamechō
Ikebukuro
Nerima-kasugachō
Toshimaen
Nerima
Seibu Ikebukuro Line
Thru to Hannō
Shin-egota
Ochiai-minami-nagasaki
Nakai
Seibu Shinjuku Line
Mejiro
Takadanobaba
Thru to Urawa-misono Saitama Railway Line
Akabane
Akabane-iwabuchi
Shimo
Ōji-kamiya
Ōji
Ōji-ekimae
Nishigahara
Shin-itabashi
Nishi-sugamo
Shin-kōshinzuka
Itabashi
Itabashi kuyakushomae
Ōtsuka-ekimae
Ōtsuka
Sugamo
Komagome
Yamanote Line
Yūrakuchō Line (New Line)
Sengoku
Hon-komagome
Tōdai
Namboku Line
Mita Line
Shin-ōtsuka
Myōgadani
Hakusan
Marunouchi Line
Higashi-ikebukuro 4-chōme
Edogawabashi
Kasuga
Higashi-ikebukuro
Waseda
Gokokuji
Kōrakuen
Yūrakuchō Line
Ōedo Line
Ogikubo
Chūō Line
Thru to Mitaka
Nakano
Ochiai
Waseda
Kagurazaka
Tōzai Line
Minami-asagaya
Shin-kōenji
Higashi-kōenji
Shin-nakano
Higashi-nakano
Shin-ōkubo
Wakamatsu-kawada
Ushigome-yanagichō
Ushigome-kagurazaka
Iidabashi
Jimbōchō
Nakano-sakaue
Nishi-shinjuku
Shinjuku-nishiguchi
Higashi-shinjuku
Seibu-shinjuku
Akebonobashi
Shinjuku Line
Ichigaya
Hōnanchō
Nakano-fujimichō
Nakano-shimbashi
Nishi-shinjuku-gochōme
Shinjuku
Shinjuku-gyoemmae
Yotsuya
Kudanshita
Meidaimae
Thru to Hashimoto, Takaosanguchi
Keiō Line
Sasazuka
Tochōmae
Shinjuku-sanchōme
Yotsuya-sanchōme
Kōjimachi
Hanzōmon
Keiō Inokashira Line
Sendagaya
Shinanomachi
Aoyama-itchōme
Yoyogi
Kokuritsu-kyōgijō
Nagatachō
Yoyogi-uehara
Thru to Karakida, Hon-atsugi
Odakyū Line
Shimo-kitazawa
Harajuku
Meiji-jingūmae
Yoyogi-kōen
Akasaka-mitsuke
Gaiemmae
Kokkai-gijidō
Thru to Chūō-rinkan
Futako-tamagawa
Tōkyū Den-en-toshi Line
Hanzōmon Line
Shibuya
Omote-sandō
Tameike-sannō
Akasaka
Tōkyū Ōimachi Line
Naka-meguro
Nogizaka
Roppongi-itchōme
Tōkyū Tōyoko Line
Ebisu
Hiro-o
Hibiya Line
Roppongi
Kamiyachō
Ginza Line
Thru to Kikuna
Den-en-chōfu
Jiyūgaoka
Tōkyū Meguro Line
Ōokayama
Azabu-jūban
Akabanebashi
Thru to Musashi-kosugi
Hatanodai
Meguro
Shirokanedai
Shirokane-takanawa
Tōkyū Ikegami Line
Mita
Shiba-kōen
Sengakuji
Mita Line
Nishi-magome
Magome
Nakanobu
Togoshi
Gotanda
Takanawadai
Asakusa Line
Ōsaki
Shinagawa
Tamachi
Keihin-tōhoku Line
Ōimachi
Keikyū-kamata
Tenkūbashi
Thru to Misakiguchi
Keikyū Line
Keikyū Kūkō Line
Haneda Airport

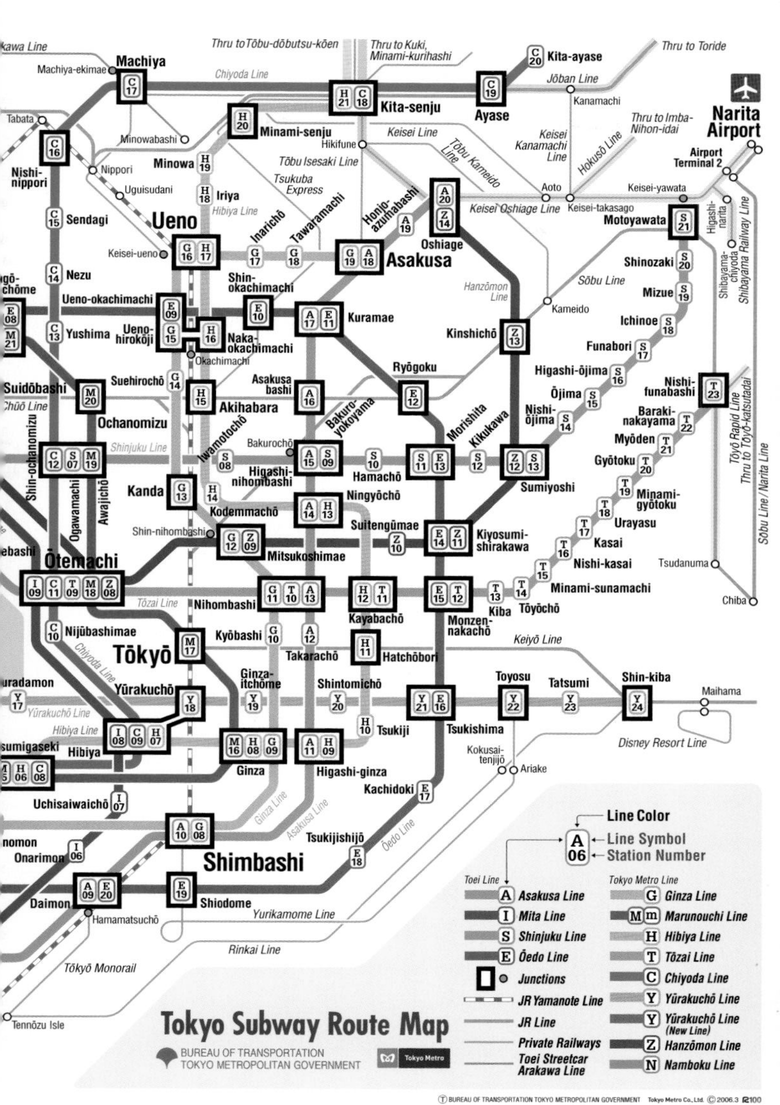
Tokyo Subway Route Map
BUREAU OF TRANSPORTATION
TOKYO METROPOLITAN GOVERNMENT
Tokyo Metro
Line Color
Line Symbol
Station Number
Toei Line
Asakusa Line
Mita Line
Shinjuku Line
Ōedo Line
Junctions
JR Yamanote Line
JR Line
Private Railways
Toei Streetcar Arakawa Line
Tokyo Metro Line
Ginza Line
Marunouchi Line
Hibiya Line
Tōzai Line
Chiyoda Line
Yūrakuchō Line
Yūrakuchō Line (New Line)
Hanzōmon Line
Namboku Line
Narita Airport
Machiya
Kita-senju
Ayase
Kita-ayase
Minami-senju
Ueno
Asakusa
Oshiage
Kuramae
Kinshichō
Ryōgoku
Akihabara
Ochanomizu
Ōtemachi
Tōkyō
Nihombashi
Ginza
Shimbashi
Shiodome
Daimon
Hibiya
Yūrakuchō
Tsukishima
Toyosu
Shin-kiba
Sumiyoshi
Kiyosumi-shirakawa
Monzen-nakachō
Kayabachō
Mitsukoshimae
Hatchōbori
Higashi-ginza
Tsukiji
Kachidoki
Tsukijishijō
Motoyawata
Nishi-funabashi
Tennōzu Isle
Tōkyō Monorail
Rinkai Line
Yurikamome Line
Disney Resort Line
Keiyō Line
Sōbu Line
Jōban Line
Thru to Toride
Thru to Tōbu-dōbutsu-kōen
Thru to Kuki, Minami-kurihashi
© BUREAU OF TRANSPORTATION TOKYO METROPOLITAN GOVERNMENT Tokyo Metro Co.,Ltd. ©2006.3

Notes

Notes